Graham M. S. Dann
A. V. Seaton
Editors

Slavery, Contested Heritage and Thanatourism

Slavery, Contested Heritage and Thanatourism has been co-published simultaneously as *International Journal of Hospitality & Tourism Administration,* Volume 2 Numbers 3/4 2001.

Pre-Publication
REVIEWS,
COMMENTARIES,
EVALUATIONS . . .

"**A**N ORIGINAL, GROUNDBREAKING, AND THOUGHT-PROVOKING TEXT . . . explores the interrelationship between two discrete and contrasting phenomena: the inglorious history of slavery and modern-day heritage tourism. POWERFUL AND INSIGHTFUL. . . . Essential reading for anyone with an interest in the heritage tourism debate and the appropriation of the past as a tourism attraction."

Richard Sharpley, PhD, Reader
Travel & Tourism Management
University of Northumbria
United Kingdom

The Haworth Hospitality Press
An Imprint of
The Haworth Press, Inc.
New York

Slavery, Contested Heritage and Thanatourism

Slavery, Contested Heritage and Thanatourism has been co-published simultaneously as *International Journal of Hospitality & Tourism Administration*, Volume 2, Numbers 3/4 2001.

The *International Journal of Hospitality & Tourism Administration* Monographic "Separates"

Slavery, Contested Heritage and Thanatourism, edited by Graham M. S. Dann and A. V. Seaton (Vol. 2, No. 3/4, 2001). *One of the fastest-growing segments of specialty tourism is* thanatourism, *which concentrates on violent death. One variant is tourism centered around plantation slavery. This volume on* "Slavery, Contested Heritage and Thanatourism" *raises a number of issues concerning the display of tourist attractions that are connected to historical events associated with violence, oppression, and disaster. It offers thoughtful research and astute advice for the management, interpretation, and visitation of slavery tourism sites that may lead to a substantial change in current ideas and practices.*

Tourism in South America, edited by Gui Santana (Vol. 1, No. 3/4, 2001). *Identifies and explores the major issues that influence and shape tourism in South America. Its informative discussions range from cultural tourism to substainable tourism to developing human resources. This valuable book, the first of its kind, examines current practices and suggests alternative models of development. Its varied points of view and original empirical research make* Tourism in South America *an essential reference tool.*

Global Alliances in Tourism and Hospitality Management, edited by John C. Crotts, Dimitrios Buhalis, and Roger March (Vol. 1, No. 1, 2000). *Provides you with the skills and strategies to build and create successful alliances in the hospitality and tourism fields. International in scope, this informative guide will help marketers, managers, and other professionals in the hospitality industry to lower company costs, raise profits, and gain strategic advantages in diversified markets.*

Slavery, Contested Heritage and Thanatourism

Graham M. S. Dann
A. V. Seaton
Editors

Slavery, Contested Heritage and Thanatourism has been co-published simultaneously as *International Journal of Hospitality & Tourism Administration,* Volume 2, Numbers 3/4 2001.

The Haworth Hospitality Press
An Imprint of
The Haworth Press, Inc.
New York • London • Oxford

Published by

The Haworth Hospitality Press®, 10 Alice Street, Binghamton, NY 13904-1580 USA

The Haworth Hospitality Press® is an imprint of the Haworth Press, Inc., 10 Alice Street, Binghamton, NY 13904-1580 USA.

Slavery, Contested Heritage and Thanatourism has been co-published simultaneously as *International Journal of Hospitality & Tourism Administration,* Volume 2, Numbers 3/4 2001.

The development, preparation, and publication of this work has been undertaken with great care. However, the publisher, employees, editors, and agents of The Haworth Press and all imprints of The Haworth Press, Inc., including The Haworth Medical Press® and The Pharmaceutical Products Press®, are not responsible for any errors contained herein or for consequences that may ensue from use of materials or information contained in this work. Opinions expressed by the author(s) are not necessarily those of The Haworth Press, Inc.

Cover design by Thomas J. Mayshock Jr.

Library of Congress Cataloging-in-Publication Data

Slavery, contested heritage and thanatourism / Graham M. S. Dann, A. V. Seaton, editors.
    p. cm.
    ". . . has been co-published simultaneously as International journal of hospitality & tourism administration, volume 2, numbers 3/4 2001."
    Includes bibliographical references and index.
    ISBN 0-7890-1386-X (alk. paper)–ISBN 0-7890-1387-8 (alk. paper)
    1. Slavery–History. 2. Slave trade–History. 3. Tourism–Social aspects. 4. Heritage tourism.
I. Dann, Graham. II. Seaton, A. V. III. International journal of hospitality & tourism administration. Vol. 2, no. 3/4 2001.

HT871 .S54 2001
3006.3′ 62′09–dc21   2001039875

Indexing, Abstracting & Website/Internet Coverage

This section provides you with a list of major indexing & abstracting services. That is to say, each service began covering this periodical during the year noted in the right column. Most Websites which are listed below have indicated that they will either post, disseminate, compile, archive, cite or alert their own Website users with research-based content from this work. (This list is as current as the copyright date of this publication.)

Abstracting, Website/Indexing Coverage .... Year When Coverage Began

- *Asian-Pacific Economic Literature*
  <www.blackwellpublishers.co.uk> **1997**

- *Australian Business Index, The* **1997**

- *BUBL Information Service, An Internet-based Information*
  Service for the UK higher education community
  <URL: http://bubl.ac.uk/> **1998**

- *CIRET (Centre International de Recherches et d'Etudes*
  Touristiques) <www.ciret-tourism.com> **2000**

- *CNPIEC Reference Guide: Chinese National Directory*
  of Foreign Periodicals **1997**

- *FINDEX <www.publist.com>* **1999**

- *FRANCIS, INISIST-CNRS <www.inist.fr>* **1998**

- *LEISURE, RECREATION, AND TOURISM ABSTRACTS*
  (c/o CAB Intl CAB ACCESS) <www.cabi.org> **1999**

(continued)

Special Bibliographic Notes related to special journal issues
(separates) and indexing/abstracting:

- indexing/abstracting services in this list will also cover material in any "separate" that is co-published simultaneously with Haworth's special thematic journal issue or DocuSerial. Indexing/abstracting usually covers material at the article/chapter level.

- monographic co-editions are intended for either non-subscribers or libraries which intend to purchase a second copy for their circulating collections.

- monographic co-editions are reported to all jobbers/wholesalers/approval plans. The source journal is listed as the "series" to assist the prevention of duplicate purchasing in the same manner utilized for books-in-series.

- to facilitate user/access services all indexing/abstracting services are encouraged to utilize the co-indexing entry note indicated at the bottom of the first page of each article/chapter/contribution.

- this is intended to assist a library user of any reference tool (whether print, electronic, online, or CD-ROM) to locate the monographic version if the library has purchased this version but not a subscription to the source journal.

- individual articles/chapters in any Haworth publication are also available through the Haworth Document Delivery Service (HDDS).

Slavery, Contested Heritage and Thanatourism

CONTENTS

ABOUT THE EDITORS

Graham M. S. Dann, PhD, obtained his doctorate at the University of Surrey, UK, in 1975. For the next 21 years he taught sociology and engaged in tourism research at the University of the West Indies in Barbados, before taking up his present position as Professor of Tourism at the University of Luton, UK. As well as being a founding member of both the International Academy for the Study of Tourism and the Research Committee on International Tourism of the International Sociological Association, he is on the editorial board of four leading tourism academic journals. He has published 6 books and more than 80 refereed articles, most of which are in the areas of tourism motivation, promotion and sociolinguistics, and, more recently, thanatourism.

A. V. Seaton, PhD, earned a first-class honors degree in the Social Sciences, a Masters in Literature from Oxford University and a PhD in Tourism Marketing from Strathclyde University. For more than 20 years he has taught and researched in the fields of marketing, cultural studies and tourism at five British universities. Between 1992 and 1998 he was Reader in Tourism at the University of Strathclyde and in 1993 founded the Scottish Tourism Research Unit which acted as advisor to governments on cultural tourism and thanatourism. In November 1998, he left Strathclyde to become Whitbread Professor of Tourism Behaviour at the University of Luton. Dr. Seaton has written or edited 5 books and published more than 70 articles and papers on tourism, and he is on the editorial board of 3 international tourism journals. He has lectured, researched, and been visiting fellow or professor in America, Australia, Scandinavia and many other countries in Europe. He is a Fellow of the Royal Society of Arts.

Slavery, Contested Heritage and Thanatourism

Graham M. S. Dann
A. V. Seaton

SUMMARY. This article introduces a collection of eight revised papers that focus on the connection between slavery and tourism. After tracing the history of the former from its origins to the present day, and after providing some examples of related attractions, it confronts a number of dilemmas associated with their juxtaposition. A brief overview of the contributions to the volume is supplied, along with some epistemological and methodological concerns that they raise. Slavery tourism is finally contextualized within a framework of thanatourism, dark tourism and dissonant heritage, a field which in turn poses several questions for further research into this new and exciting phenomenon. *[Article copies available for a fee from The Haworth Document Delivery Service: 1-800-342-9678. E-mail address: <getinfo@haworthpressinc. com> Website: <http://www.HaworthPress.com> © 2001 by The Haworth Press, Inc. All rights reserved.]*

KEYWORDS. Slavery tourism, history of slavery, slavery as tourist attractions, thanatourism, dark tourism, dissonant heritage

INTRODUCTION

This volume brings together two phenomena which at first glance are seemingly quite antithetical–slavery and tourism. It attempts to

Graham M. S. Dann and A. V. Seaton are affiliated with the International Tourism Research Institute, Luton Business School, Hitchin Rd, Luton, Beds LU2 8LE, UK.

[Haworth co-indexing entry note]: "Slavery, Contested Heritage and Thanatourism." Dann, Graham M. S., and A. V. Seaton. Co-published simultaneously in *International Journal of Hospitality & Tourism Administration* (The Haworth Hospitality Press, an imprint of The Haworth Press, Inc.) Vol. 2, No. 3/4, 2001, pp. 1-29; and: *Slavery, Contested Heritage and Thanatourism* (ed: Graham M. S. Dann and A. V. Seaton) The Haworth Hospitality Press, an imprint of The Haworth Press, Inc., 2001, pp. 1-29. Single or multiple copies of this article are available for a fee from The Haworth Document Delivery Service [1-800-342-9678, 9:00 a.m. - 5:00 p.m. (EST). E-mail address: getinfo@haworthpressinc.com].

show that, whatever the notoriety of the former, increasingly it is bestowing marked benefits on the latter. By including a number of papers from a conference imaginatively entitled *Plantations of the Mind*, held at the College of Charleston from April 6 to 9, 2000, this collection of select articles focuses predominantly on the British and American variants of slavery in the New World and those instances where its remnants have been put to use by the tourism industry today.

SLAVERY IN THE ANCIENT WORLD

The institution of slavery has far longer temporal antecedents than tourism. It harks back at least 10,000 years to the region of Mesopotamia, the "cradle of civilization" lying between the rivers Tigris and Euphrates, roughly equivalent to modern Iraq (Meltzer, 1993a: 9). In that predominantly hunting society, enemies were killed simply because the winners had insufficient meat and fish to sustain the losers. Subsequently, when animals became domesticated and the cultivation of crops began to yield a surplus, captives were fed and, in turn, worked their victor's land. Still later, enforced labor became a form of punishment, a pledge against debt or just a type of security (Meltzer, 1993a: 1-2).

Around 3000 BC there is evidence of the Sumerians settling in the southern half of the Mesopotamian plain, requiring slaves to install their irrigation systems and of using those taken in battle for that purpose. By 2000 BC, the Amorites from Syria had assumed control of what by then had become known as the kingdom of Babylon, complete with their own set of laws named after their monarch–the *Code of Hammurabi* (Meltzer, 1993a: 9-16). Although this hierarchical society of nobles, priests, free persons and slaves, with most of its servile class constituted by prisoners of war and debtors, could be described as rigidly authoritarian, it was nevertheless sufficiently liberal to permit manumission and to prescribe fines for killing or injuring a slave (Petrovich and Curtin, 1967: 25-26). However, the situation deteriorated with the conquest of Babylon by the Persians in 538 BC when slaves were typically branded and tagged like animals (Meltzer, 1993a: 22).

Ancient Egypt largely thrived without slavery on account of a vibrant peasant class, the main exception being the children of Israel who, circa 18th century BC, offered service in exchange for their lives

(Meltzer, 1993a: 3). The Chinese Chou Dynasty (1000-256 BC) was similarly pragmatic, only utilizing slave labor in the main for the production of salt and mining operations (Petrovich and Curtin, 1967: 613).

Greek society, by contrast, required slaves for labor-intensive farming (mainly grapes and olives (Petrovich and Curtin, 1967: 43)) and domestic purposes (ranging from such occupations as maids, teachers, nurses, civil servants, and even bankers (Meltzer, 1993a: 76)). By the 5th century BC, almost half of the Greek population were slaves with no democratic rights and there was a thriving slave market in the *agora* of Athens. Plato, who argued in his *Republic* that Barbarians were born to serfdom, died leaving five house slaves in his will. Aristotle, who maintained in his *Politics* that some were servile by nature, since they depended on the rationality of their master's will, left fourteen slaves in his testament. Aesop, being a slave himself, was somewhat less fortunate. Generally, the Greek variant of slavery was relatively benign (Meltzer, 1993a: 65-96). Certainly, no color bar operated, public slaves such as policemen could arrest free persons, the granting of liberty was a frequent occurrence and, with the exception of the helots (people from the Peloponnese conquered by the Spartans and forced into slavery), there were few revolts.

Ancient Rome, on the other hand (Meltzer, 1993a: 100-118; Petrovich and Curtin, 1967: 82-90), which had overthrown the Etruscans who themselves had slaves as part of the family unit, tended to draw most of its slaves from wars (against Germanic and Gallic tribes), where they were either sold on the very field of battle or later in the Forum. Piracy was another source of labor on Roman rulers' plantations, so that by 69 BC when Delos (dealing in up to 10,000 slaves a day) was sacked, Rome had become the center of the slave trade. Even though plebeian slaves were generally well treated under the Empire and were either given high positions by patricians on their estates, or else filled such roles as educators, librarians and craftsmen, rebellions were classified as wars and insurgents shown no mercy. Probably the worst case occurred during the aptly named Third Servile War (73-71 BC). Known also as the Spartacus rebellion, and put down by Pompey, it witnessed the crucifixion of some 6,000 slaves.

Practically every society, regardless of color and racial background, treated slavery as an economic fact of life (Meltzer, 1993a: 6). Slave trading and auctions were frequent in Ephesus, Byzantium and Chios

(Meltzer, 1993a: 110), and even on the other side of the globe, and well prior to European entry to the New World, the Aztecs employed slaves and used them for human sacrifice to their god Huitizilopochtli (Meltzer, 1993b: 61).

SLAVERY IN THE NEW WORLD

Long before 1441, when the first Portuguese ship under the command of Antam Goncalvez captured 12 natives from the Atlantic coast of Africa and brought them back as gifts for Prince Henry the Navigator (1394-1460), and prior to a 1445 papal bull authorizing Portugal to reduce to servitude the heathen peoples (Meltzer, 1993b: 1), overseas plantations had been firmly established in Palestine by Europeans during the Crusades. Once they were expelled from the Holy Land, the Crusaders lost no time in setting up sugar plantations first in Cyprus and Sicily, and later in southern Spain and Portugal. Their lands were worked either by prisoners-of-war or by those slaves purchased in Black Sea ports (Petrovich and Curtin, 1967: 386). These operations were subsequently transferred to Madeira (1420), Cabo Verde (1460) and São Tomé (1490) (Meltzer, 1993b: 2). As for the Africans themselves, they had 'practised slavery since prehistoric times . . . both benign and family based' (Meltzer, 1993b: 17). However, it was the presence of Europeans which led to inter-tribal wars of up to 500 miles into the interior, the taking of captives for slaves, and their subsequent on-selling to African middlemen on the coast. European guns were used by the Ashanti and others to capture slaves. The latter were subsequently confined in inland barracoons before being force marched in coffles to the sea and waiting ships (Meltzer, 1993b: 29).

Although the primary focus of this collection of articles is predominantly Anglo-American, it should not be forgotten that the arrival of the Portuguese and Spanish in Africa predated that segment of the slave trade by over a century. In response to Iberian demand, in 1461 raids by Berber chieftains were producing slaves and gold in exchange for silk and silver, with 10 to 15 men changing hands for one horse. By the time the first coastal fort was constructed by the Portuguese at Elmina in 1481, they had already discovered a flourishing slave trade among the Arabs and their Swahili agents for export to Arabia, India and Persia (see article by Essah in this volume).

Most of the Portuguese slaves were taken to Brazil. By 1540 sugar production was well under way and, some fifty years later, over 60 mills were in operation, along with acreage devoted to the cultivation of coffee, cotton and cacao. From just 30 plantations in 1576 the total had risen to 121 by 1625. By the turn of the 17th century, gold and subsequently diamond mines had become well established, all of them worked by slaves (Meltzer, 1993b: 75-79).

In 1492, and under the Spanish flag, Columbus set foot in Hispaniola and captured 1,500 Tainos Indians for slaves, most of whom died (Meltzer, 1993b: 2-6). Those who managed to escape were slaughtered on recapture. Since the remaining survivors who stayed behind were too sickly to dig for gold or labor on the sugar plantations, and many caught smallpox and measles from their captors, in 1518 the first cargo of Africans was brought in under Bartolomé de las Casas (Meltzer, 1993b: 10).

In Cuba the story was similar. Also discovered by Columbus in 1492, and taken by Diego de Velasquez in 1511, the Indians who initially worked the mines were soon replaced by Africans, the latter being found suitable for the cultivation of coffee and sugar (Meltzer, 1993b: 89). The same pattern occurred in Haiti (another of Columbus's 1492 discoveries). By 1506 sugar production was well under way and, by the time it was ceded to France in 1695, cacao, indigo and coffee were additionally being harvested (Meltzer, 1993b: 105-106).

By 1540, and with Charles V's agreement, as many as 10,000 Africans a year were being transported to the New World. Some 60 years later, the total had risen to 900,000. Even though many carried malaria and yellow fever, their constitutions were certainly stronger than those of the native Indians they replaced. Moreover, it was from these bases that expeditions were launched by the Spaniards into such American bases as Florida and Louisiana.

However, in 1564, the Spanish-Portuguese monopoly came under threat for the first time when Sir John Hawkins, an English sea captain, began transporting slaves from Sierra Leone to Venezuela. In spite of his subsequent defeat by the Spanish off the Mexican coast, he had at least challenged the status quo and opened the way for his compatriots to follow (Meltzer, 1993b: 39-40). By the 1620s they and the French were operating successfully in the Caribbean. In the 1630s and 1640s the Dutch West India Company had captured the Brazilian sugar lands of Pernambuco from the Portuguese as well as their main slaving posts on the African coast (Petrovich and Curtin, 1967: 401-402). For their part, the Dutch supplied the French and English with slaves and knowledge of sugar production, information which was put to good use in such early colonies as Barbados (settled in 1627) and Jamaica (taken from the Spanish between 1655 and 1660). By 1665, trading posts in Africa had been set up by both the English and the French and the latter had established the plantation society of Saint Dominique on Hispaniola. Some seven years later, under King Charles II, the Royal African Company was launched, and Britannia thereafter became the world's greatest slave trader (Meltzer, 1993b: 43), operating under the infamous system known as the Middle Passage (see articles by Seaton and Beech in this volume).

This trilateral process witnessed ships leaving from the principal ports of England bound for the west coast of Africa. There, guns (for rounding up more slaves) were exchanged for human cargo, the latter in turn being conveyed to the Caribbean and America. During the second leg of the journey, and in spite of being ironically supplied with rum and tobacco (the fruit of other slave labor), thousands of captives died or were thrown overboard alive. On arrival in the West Indies, survivors were auctioned off to planters in exchange for plantation fare, and the ships made their way back to such ports as Bristol and Liverpool bearing produce for the popular coffee houses: coffee, cocoa, tea, tobacco and sugar–exotic crops deemed to make life more palatable (Walvin, 1992: 5).

Barbados, a tiny 166 square mile island in the West Indies was one of the first territories to be settled by the British (see article by Dann and Potter in this volume) and to make use of the Middle Passage. After clearing acres of forest, the colonizers lost no time in establishing plantations. By 1650, 300 were in production. Less than twenty years later there were 900, along with a total of 400 working windmills. By 1680, there were 200 planters each with more than 60 slaves and another 200 each with between 20 and 60 slaves. Jamaica's economy witnessed similarly rapid expansion with 146 plantations in 1671 and 690 in 1684 (Walvin, 1992: 69-70).

In spite of a Spanish attempt to introduce slave labor to St Augustine, Florida in 1565, most colonial attention was focused on the Eastern seaboard. By 1626, the Dutch were landing slaves on Manhattan Island which, in 1664, was taken over by the English as their colony of New York. Subsequently, slavery was declared a legal institution, and many leading American families of the time availed themselves of its services, principally for domestic purposes. Before this enactment took place, however, the English had already established their first colony in Jamestown and, by 1660, slavery was on the statute books of Virginia and Maryland (Meltzer, 1993b: 127-132). Here the main crop was tobacco, and soon plantations and their Great Houses were springing up along the James River from Richmond to Chesapeake Bay (Walvin, 1992: 85). In 1638, the first slaves from the Caribbean were brought to Boston, and within six years a New England triangular trade was operating: food to the West Indies–rum to Africa–slaves to the West Indies–cocoa, sugar, rum and molasses to New England. Indeed, over a century later, slaves were still being priced in terms of volumes of rum, a man being equivalent to 115 gallons and a woman 95 gallons (Meltzer, 1993b: 139-145).

Meanwhile, North and South Carolina (not actually separated until 1730) were respectively settled by the English as early as 1585 and 1670, and soon after plantation slavery cultivating the alternative crops of indigo, cotton and rice was introduced. Boone Hall, just outside Charleston, for example, was a working estate producing indigo and cotton from 1681, and it was later joined by the Ashley River plantations of Drayton Hall, Magnolia and Middleton Place (Hudson and Ballard, 1989: 22, 240-241, 248). In such a manner, the English turned from the North to the Carolinas, the Southern states being looked upon as a source of food and livestock for their West Indian operations (Logan and Muse, 1989). In this endeavor, they were helped by the two-way traffic of planters such as the Draytons who, finding Barbados too cramped, looked to America for their fortunes.

Nearby Georgia was similarly regarded. Its principal crops were rice (e.g., Hofwyl-Broadfield Plantation from 1807) and cotton (e.g., Callaway Plantation from 1785), the latter being given a significant boost by the invention of Eli Whitney's cotton gin in 1793, but nevertheless subject to the incursions of the boll weevil (Logan and Muse, 1989: 271, 341, 345).

Spreading further afield, Tennessee in 1770 and Kentucky in 1775 were later settled, although they did not introduce plantation slavery until the turn of the nineteenth century. By 1818, for instance, Oaklands Plantation, near Murfreesboro, Tennessee, had devoted 1,500 acres to cotton production with 100 slaves providing the labor.

Louisiana soon followed, Destrehan in 1787 probably being the oldest plantation house in the Mississippi valley, and with plantations such as Saint Louis, Oaklawn, Mintmere, Nottoway and Parlange producing sugar, the last mentioned as early as 1750, and Chretien Point, Melrose and Magnolia Mound collectively harvesting cotton, indigo, rice, soy beans and pecans. Indeed, many planters from the Carolinas, Virginia and Georgia turned to Louisiana as an alternative to their own exhausted soil, and even Napoleon looked upon that state as a supplier of foodstuff to the sugar estates of Saint Dominique (Logan and Muse, 1989: 10-17, 58-88).

In Mississippi, the story was similar, with plantations such as Natchez, Rosswood and Aberdeen concentrating on cotton and indigo, and Holly Springs focusing on tobacco, hay, wheat, corn and livestock (Logan and Muse, 1989: 122-123, 140, 170, 173-175).

When comparing plantation slavery in the West Indies with that of America (Kolchin, 1993), it is important to recognize that the different conditions undergone were definitely predicated on the nature of the crop being produced. Sugar, for example, although sweet to the taste, was very much derived from a bitter work experience, both in temporal terms of hours and days and according to the type of work system employed, in this case the gang system complete with its cruel overseers. Tobacco cultivation, by contrast, could be allocated by task and thus, though more intense, resulted in much less labor time. In the Caribbean, too, plantations tended to be crowded, factory-style operations covering vast crop areas, frequently with absentee owners, whereas in America they were much smaller and scattered, and overseen in a more caring, if not in a more paternalistic manner. The health of the slaves often varied considerably under the two regimes. In places such as Barbados and Jamaica up to one third of all slaves died within the first three years (Walvin, 1992: 64), and those who did manage to survive experienced the rigors of the tropics, including the prevalence of related diseases. This situation, together with a much higher male sex ratio resulted in poorer birth rates and hence the need to import increasing numbers of replacements from Africa. In Barbados, for instance, between 1764 and 1771, 35,000 Africans were imported. Yet the slave population only grew by 5,000 persons over the same period (Walvin, 1992: 76). In temperate Virginia and elsewhere, on the other hand, the health of slaves was much better, helped no doubt by superi-

or nutritional intake, and inter-slave breeding was consequently far more prolific.

Then again, the severity of the West Indian system, along with its regime of harsh punishments, witnessed far more rebellions and escapes, with even worse punishments in store for those rounded up, than did the situation obtaining in the Southern and Eastern United States.

Finally, many of the leading members of American society were slave owners, thereby bringing a sense of "normalcy" to the scenario. In fact, by 1860, three quarters of the legislators in the Deep South were in this position, and it should not be forgotten that eight of the first twelve presidents of the United States were also slave owners. Indeed, Davis (1966: 3) relatedly notes that Americans are frequently embarrassed when they are reminded that the Declaration of Independence was crafted by a slaveholder and that black slavery was a legal institution in all thirteen colonies at the beginning of the Revolution. In the West Indies, by contrast, the planters constituted far from an élite class. While not exactly riffraff either, many constituted a motley crew of fortune hunters, soldiers and opportunistic businessmen, who customarily sought solace for their lonely lives in drink and promiscuous sex with their laborers (Walvin, 1992:74).

If there were one thing in common between the two systems it was probably the reluctance of both to treat slaves as human beings. Unlike the predominantly Catholic practice of the Portuguese and Spaniards extending the sacraments to those under their charge, the Protestant dominated plantocracy of the West Indies and American states feared that the literacy and awareness which religious instruction could bring might lead to the complete overthrow of their authority.

Nevertheless, and in spite of the outlined stark differences, slaves in the British colonies were freed in 1834, some twenty-one years before their American counterparts. Moreover, in the West Indies, and even allowing for a further four years before full emancipation, it did not take the trauma of secession, the separation of a country into a north/south divide, a civil war and considerable loss of life as experienced in the United States, in order to rid themselves of a pernicious system, one that continued for some time afterwards in parts of the deep south.

SLAVERY TODAY

There are some who maintain that, even with the post-bellum peri-od of Reconstruction, the implementation of civil rights and the exten-sion of the franchise, the central issue of land redistribution had not been solved (Kolchin, 1993). Gang labor, for instance, still persisted in the sugar fields of Louisiana well after emancipation, and the subse-quent emergence of Jim Crow practices, including those of the Ku Klux Klan, ensured that bitter racial divisions existed until the present era. Dependency theorists also maintain that populations of the Carib-bean continue to be locked into a neo-colonial system of haves and have nots predicated on color.

Indeed, by widening the geographical spectrum, and in Meltzer's (1993a: iii) words, 'Never has slavery disappeared . . . Millions of men, women and children, according to the United Nations' estimates are still held in slavery in many countries.' As evidence of this reality, Meltzer (1993b: 279) cites the 1956 UN Convention on the Abolition of Slavery which indicates that the phenomenon comprises chattel slavery, serfdom, debt bondage, exploitation of children and servile forms of marriage, the living contradiction of which is quite blatant among dozens of nations, including several that have signed the con-vention. As examples of the flagrant practice of slavery today, Meltzer (1993b: 280-300) instances wide stretches of the Sahara and into the Arabian peninsula, slave breeding in Arabia and Yemen, slave markets in Southwest Arabia, Haitian forced labor on the sugar plantations of the Dominican Republic, slave pearl divers in the Persian Gulf, the Mozambique slave trade to South Africa either as forced labor or as sex chattels, unpaid domestic servants in Ghana, the enslavement of southern Christians by northern Muslims in the Sudan, forced labor and rape in Myanmar (along with the beating to death or selling of escapees into Thai brothels), the exploitation of children and bonded labor in India, Bangladesh, Nepal, Pakistan and Sri Lanka, refugees from Afghanistan being forced into the Pakistani bonded labor market of paper picking and brick making, children working in mines and factories in Hong Kong, Malaysia, Singapore, Japan, Sarawak, Sri Lanka, Peru and Bolivia, rural peasants in Brazil being rounded up and forced at gunpoint to undertake forest clearance, charcoal production and mining in the Amazon, and Kenyans being similarly obliged to work the sawmills in Tanzania. To this extensive list Meltzer (1993b:

274-275) adds enforced labor in Hitler's Krupp works (which used up to 100,000 slaves in 100 factories in order to manufacture guns, tanks and ammunition), the whole question of Russian serfdom (Kolchin, 1993), the slavery and extermination of up to six million Jews under the Nazis (British Broadcasting Corporation, 2000b), the existing traffic in children from Benin and Togo to Gabon (Independent Television, 2000), and the fact that even today two million women are sold into sex slavery annually, including 2,000 to the United States alone (British Broadcasting Corporation, 2000a). Thus, even though 'Europeans brought 8 million black men and women out of Africa to the New World between the sixteenth and nineteenth centuries' (Solow, 1993: 1), the contemporary situation does not appear to be any better. Indeed, slavery seems to be as alive and well today as ever it was in the past.

SLAVERY AS TOURIST ATTRACTIONS

Tourism, although just as ubiquitous as slavery, has a far shorter temporal record. In fact, many argue that, in spite of its possible patrician prototypes in Ancient Greece and Rome (Nash, 1979), contemporary mass tourism can only trace its principal origins to as recently as the first Industrial Revolution. Even so, the greatest difference between the two phenomena appears to reside in their respective contrasting emphases on enforced labor and the pursuit of pleasure, an antithesis so marked as to render problematic the scenario of one working to the benefit of the other. Yet, however unlikely this collaboration, we maintain that slavery's pain can and does contribute to tourism's gain through one particular variant of the latter which will soon be discussed.

It thus comes as no surprise to discover that several American plantations, complete with slave quarters of yesteryear, have become tourism heritage sites of today. In North Carolina, for example, there is Somerset Place, the 1830s home of rice planter Josiah Collins, who had eighty slaves dig canals the length and breadth of 100,000 acres of swamp land in order to produce his crop. Now, thanks to archaeological and other historical records, its slave buildings are said to constitute 'one of the country's most important sites for the interpretation of the slaves' experience' (Hudson and Ballard, 1989: 36).

In its turn, South Carolina's Middleton Place (Hudson and Ballard, 1989: 242-246), whose gardens took one hundred slaves ten years to landscape, can offer a stable yard with craftsmen performing such plantation tasks as blacksmithing, woodworking and weaving, and even a living descendant of a slave family able to reminisce about former times. Meanwhile, Drayton Hall (Hudson and Ballard, 1989: 240-241) becomes promoted as the only existing antebellum plantation house not to be torched by General Sherman's Union troops.

Although most plantations in North and South Carolina do not have extant slave quarters, as we have seen, there are quite a few that do. Elsewhere in the south a similar situation obtains. Tennessee's 1858 Smith Trahern Mansion, for example, still has the original dwellings of slaves who worked for tobacco grower Christopher Smith (Hudson and Ballard, 1989: 330). Kentucky has Waveland (near Lexington) with its nineteenth century brick slave quarters and examples of the occupants' craftsmanship (Hudson and Ballard, 1989: 384). Over in Mississippi, there is Waverly Plantation, one of the largest in the pre-Civil War period, which has managed to retain a brick kiln, lumber mill, cotton gin and livestock pens (Logan and Muse, 1989: 167). North Florida, too, has Kingsley Plantation (near Jacksonville). Once a leading producer of sea island cotton, it still has twenty-four slave cabins preserved intact (Logan and Muse, 1989: 382), while the Yulee Sugar Mills ruins (of 1851) are able to display the original boiler, chimney, cane crushing rollers and cooling vats (Logan and Muse, 1989: 397).

The same sort of symbiotic pattern of past slavery and present tourism can be found wherever in the world the former was practiced. In Cidade Velha, for instance, on the Cabo Verde island of Santiago, once the center of the 15th and 16th centuries Portuguese trade, where evangelization of slaves took place prior to their shipment to the New World, there are remnants of the rituals in the Cathedral, Convent of São Francisco, Fortaleza de São Filipe and the Pelourinho (Cabo Verde Airlines, n.d.: 15).

In Tanzania, where 16th century Portuguese settlements were overtaken by the Omanis in the 17th century, the port city of Bagamoyo ('Here I throw down my heart') still features the old prison for slaves before they were taken out to the waiting dhows, as well as a somber collection of shackles, chains and whips (Tanzania Tourist Board, n.d.: 23).

In Zanzibar's Cape Stone Town, the 1879 Cathedral of the Church of Christ was built on the site of an open slave market. There is also the nearby Tippu Tip House, home of the notorious slave and ivory trader, Hamad bin Muhammad el-Marjab, as well as a former slave pit in Kelele Square and Changuu (or Prison) Island used by the Arabs for awkward slaves (Tanzania Tourist Board, n.d.: 27-30).

Meanwhile, in Ghana, Cape Coast Castle (2000), where thousands of slaves were held prior to shipment to the West Indies (see article by Essah in this volume, as also Bruner (1996)), today even has its own website, complete with pictures of the fortress and featuring "a dark male slave dungeon."

In the Caribbean itself, the link between tourism and slavery is far more pronounced. In Jamaica, for instance, Great House tours are on offer, along with a visit to a maroon village. As the brochure explains, 'Some 18th century sugar plantation owners were, effectively, fabulously rich, autocratic squires and their legacy to Jamaica has been their mansions, now called the Great Houses. One of the most interesting is Rose Hall in Montego Bay. It's said the owner, known locally as the White Witch, murdered several of her husbands (the reports vary between three and six). After her death in 1831, the house fell into ruin. It has now been restored and is open to the public' (Discover Jamaica, n.d.: 21).

Meanwhile, on Barbuda, where nearly all the residents are descendants of slaves brought to the island by the Codringtons, visitors can view the complex owned by that family from 1680 to 1870. As the text states, 'You can see the outline of the main house, slave quarters, offices and cistern of what was one High Land House' (The Antiguan, 1998: 9).

In St Lucia, too, one can 'learn about St Lucia's plantations, past and present, on a tour of one of its largest, the Marquis Plantation' (St Lucia Tourist Board, n.d.: 10).

THE DILEMMAS OF SLAVERY TOURISM

Due to the sheer ubiquity and phenomenal increase in slavery tourism sites, there is no gainsaying that heritage of this ilk is becoming increasingly popular. Colonial Williamsburg, for instance, with its 138 original 18th or early 19th century buildings, and 27 million visitors from 1932 to 1984, is easily Virginia's top tourist attraction. Indeed, its "historic atmosphere" is said to be particularly appealing to wealthy retired persons who are educationally motivated and prepared to spend above average time at sites of battles, colonial settlements, historic homes and places associated with famous Presidents, as well as being prepared to pay for nearby high standard accommodation (Zeppel and Hall, 1992). No doubt also, this type of tourist is responding to Rockerfeller's intentions for restoring Williamsburg in order to evoke patriotism, high purpose and devotion to the common good (Lowenthal, 1993: 32-36).

On the other hand, there is a very real danger that the neat and painted buildings on display, far brighter than the abodes they purportedly represent (shabbiness cannot bring history to life; relics must be in their prime), may simply be justified on the grounds that the colonists would have had such colors if they could have afforded them (Lowenthal, 1993: 145, 329), and lead to the conclusion that most restored houses in the United States 'look as if they'd had the same decorator . . . they are all Williamsburged' (Lowenthal, 1993: 351). A similar observation can be extended to the bands of clean and youthful interpreters at the site. According to Lowenthal, (1993: 13):

> To protect Williamsburg visitors from a deranged fondness for the past, the costumed guides should be toothless, and ready to admit that 'if we were really colonial people, most of us would be dead on account of the short life span.'

As for the related portrayal of slavery, Lowenthal (1993: 341) notes:

> In the sanitized American past not even slaves are wretched: porch columns and chimneys raise the restored slave quarters to the standard of overseers' dwellings . . . The touristic past jettisons seedy reality for spurious romance,

and again:

> Popular modern depictions of Washington and Jefferson, for example, are utterly at variance with their lives as eighteenth-century slave holding planters. (Lowenthal, 1993: 343)

Richter (1989: 187) sums up the situation well when she relates it to MacCannell's (1989) "staged authenticity" and Boorstin's (1987) "pseudo event." As she says:

In most cases, tourists like to believe that they are being told the truth about a destination or are getting a taste of what the place is or was all about. Few may be well enough informed to distinguish the accurate from the inaccurate, which leads to the selling of 'staged authenticity.'

One thus arrives at a point where there is a distortion of the past for touristic purposes, what Fjellman (1992) so appropriately calls "distory." In specific reference to plantation tourism and the Charleston conference dedicated to that theme, Widdup (2000: 13) observes:

Amid the bright pink and purple azaleas and the rolling green lawns of Lowcountry plantations lies a gray area. Interpretations of these attractive historic sites aim to educate visitors by sharing stories of the legendary Old South. But their tales seem to have some black holes–both literally and figuratively.

She continues:

Visitors hear about wealthy owners, antique furnishings, and fine art, but missing is the underlying tale of those who helped build the plantations, the story of slaves who were fundamental in keeping these properties productive and beautiful. (Widdup, 2000: 13)

Subsequently, Widdup (2000: 13) adds that plantations:

Often a blend of fact and fiction . . . have become contested terrain where both black and white Southerners confront a painful past and the continuing impact of that past on the present.

There is thus a general failure to acknowledge the contribution of Afro-Americans and a significant omission of the roles they played. Black history is short-changed whenever references to slavery are absent or, when they occur, slave quarters are referred to as servant quarters or carriage houses (Widdup, 2000: 14).

It is this incompleteness and the injection of euphemism and distory into the black holes of heritage that is so disturbing. Even worthwhile attempts by interpreters at some sites to restore the balance (e.g., the Black Focus Program of South Carolina's Drayton Hall) are usually only made upon special demand and do not form part of the general tour as, arguably, they should. One notable exception seems to be the incorporation of the slave girl, Sally Hemings, into the discourse of Monticello, home of former President Thomas Jefferson. However, it is doubtful whether this salacious titbit would have featured in the guide's account were it not for the widely publicized results of recent DNA testing revealing that Jefferson and Hemings were lovers and that their illicit union produced at least one child (Widdup, 2000: 13-14).

Although at a few other sites personnel are given a freer hand, tailoring their narratives to suit their clientele and responding to questions posed by participants, many of the issues raised are simply polite requests for technical information about such mundane matters as household skills, crops and beverages (Lowenthal, 1993: 298), rather than what slavery was really about in another era.

Furthermore, there is an additional dilemma that, by providing the whole truth about Afro-American history to an overwhelmingly white audience, the presumed ensuing alienation among the latter could result in lower attendance figures. With the bottom line of tourism apparently being profit and that of history seemingly being truth, a delicate course has to be steered through the troubled waters of the authenticity they both purport to share. In this regard, at Middleton Place, a few miles outside Charleston, a tour guide, in response to a recent query in our presence, admitted that only one per cent of the visitors was black, a disproportionately low figure given its high representation among the population of the area. However, and even if such a lack of interest were attributable to psychological discomfort, there is some evidence to suggest that a similar unease may also be present among white tourists at this and other plantation sites (see article by Butler in this volume).

Possibly the greatest paradox and problem of all, though, is that tourism, particularly in those former colonies which have experienced the plantation system, is seen not as its polar opposite but as its natural successor.

CONTRIBUTIONS TO AN UNDERSTANDING OF SLAVERY TOURISM

As previously noted, this volume derives from a symposium devoted to an examination of the implications of the Afro-Caribbean slave trade of yesteryear for the heritage industry of today. It provides a selection of articles from scholars working in different disciplines who focus on the historical dimensions of slavery, their consequences for tourism and their relationship to broader heritage issues.

The papers that follow do not represent any single justified theoretical viewpoint since this hybrid field is too new and controversial to impose such premature closure. Indeed, as co-editors we have not always agreed on some issues, and this introduction may be seen as evolving from such creative tensions. Nevertheless, and in spite of these differences, our main aim has been to pick out and provide contributions that, it is believed, open up an area within heritage tourism that is novel, contentious and clearly due to expand in the future. The primary emphasis in this choice has been on case studies that demonstrate the variety and number of sites that, in the wake of the colossal scale and ruthless industrialization of slavery, now pose problems or opportunities for heritage development.

Notwithstanding their speculative nature, there are four common threads to these papers. One obvious and important structuring feature is their geographic orientation since they focus on slavery and its legacies in a number of countries implicated in the Afro-Caribbean slave trade, namely, Ghana, Barbados, Britain and the United States. Second, there is a shared recurrent historical contextualization based on the gradual emergence of the Middle Passage and the triangular pattern of human and other cargo. Third, there is an underpinning ideology (that will shortly be discussed), and fourth a certain methodological homogeneity (about which further comment is also offered later).

In order of appearance and in historical order, the main idiosyncratic features of the articles are as follows:

Essah provides an historical account of slavery along the west coast of Africa in the wake of Portuguese "exploration." She concentrates particularly on the forts built to support imperial occupation that were also the traffic and trading centers for slavery, but which today constitute heritage tourism sites and arenas of commemorative festival for the black diaspora.

Dann and Potter supply a socio-historical overview of the evolution of Barbados from its early colonial days to the present. They subsequently examine a range of contemporary tourism issues and explore how they ignore or negotiate the subject of mainly black slavery within the framework of hedonistic appeals to predominantly white tourists. The link between the two sections of their paper is that, by converting the past into postmodern spectacle, the selective presentation of heritage for purposes of visitor entertainment trivializes and compromises the very object of portrayal.

The articles of Beech and Seaton have a natural complementarity since they both focus on Britain, albeit in different ways. The former offers a useful summary of the main slavery sites in the UK and concludes with a particularly interesting comment on the way that, in the past, slavery has been marginalized within maritime museums and exhibits, thus positioning them within a white discourse of spatial mobility that effectively excludes black participation. Seaton, while admittedly covering some of the same ground as Beech, nevertheless includes a much more detailed examination of the development of the Slave Exhibition in Liverpool based on an extended interview with its curator. His essay principally concentrates on differences between the speed and extent of slavery heritage in the US and UK, along with reasons for them. It concludes with a model of heritage development based on the work of Tunbridge and Ashworth (1996), as a force field that constitutes a site of action, interaction and negotiation among four main participatory groups.

Goings undertakes a post-Barthian analysis of the role of tourism souvenirs in representing black people as racially inferior in ways that have continued to contribute to their subordination even after their alleged legacy of "freedom" derived from the Civil War. Dividing the collectible industry into two time periods, pre- and post-1930, he shows how racist images have been institutionally supported and dispersed, not just by the tourism industry, but by advertisers, authors, newspaper columnists and broadcasters, all of whom have acted in concert to naturalize notions of Afro-American inferiority. His paper contrasts the images of happy laughing blacks circulating across the tourism circuit with the reality of lynchings and violence in the South, the very area from which such commoditized memorabilia originate.

Butler is more empirical in his approach when he initially documents the extent to which plantation tourism engages with, or ignores slavery heritage narratives in New Orleans and South Carolina. His study later extends to an analysis of brochures and publicity materials which promote more than a hundred attractions in over a dozen southern states. A particular strength of his investigation is a proposed typology of plantations that allows distinctions to be made in accounting for differences in their emphasis of slavery. His contribution (in common with those of Dann and Potter and Roushanzamir and Kreshel), offers a number of interesting observations on the changing connotations of the word "plantation." It also identifies several essential areas for future research, particularly as regards the motivations and audience reactions to both black and white slavery heritage.

Roushanzamir and Kreshel adopt a cultural studies approach in drawing on methodologies and perspectives derived from Said, Barthes, Jameson and Baudrillard for their case study of heritage development at one plantation site in Louisiana visited by Butler. In particular, their article focuses on constructions of gender and "Creole-ness," thereby highlighting the necessity of including the asymmetries of sex and race in a discussion of slavery heritage.

Finally, Eskew supplies an outline of the transformation of Civil Rights locations to tourism attractions. His article offers several useful insights into the political machinations behind such developments, especially in those states noted for being at the forefront of racist policies and opposition to civil liberties in the 1960s and 70s.

EPISTEMOLOGICAL CONSIDERATIONS

To what extent should these contributions be regarded as a first collection of their kind and how are the ideas they contain related to or derived from the conference where they were originally presented? In order to answer these questions it is necessary to provide some background.

In engaging in the conference, most of the participants shared a profound consensus that slavery was one of the worst crimes perpetrated against humanity, and that the fate inflicted on millions of black Africans constituted a holocaust. These assumptions underpinned the presentations and produced an overall skepticism about the packaging of slavery as heritage tourism and a concomitant suspicion that it might end up as commodification, cosmeticization or suppression of historical truth in the interests of attracting predominantly white visitors. The majority of the papers thus rested on a politically left-of-center "domination" critique which suggested that the determination of slavery heritage was mainly by powerful business institutions, their commercial agenda and the mainly white audiences they targeted.

However, perhaps the most important effect of the symposium was, through the variety of empirical case studies presented and the discussions that followed, to complicate this initial worldview and to high-light the contradictions and complexities of the issues involved in transforming heritage into tourism attractions. If this more critical stance is adopted, the articles, when read as a totality, would seem to indicate that the "domination" model's preferred conceptions do not fit all the evidence. A number of sites (particularly those in the UK, but also several in South Carolina) are not private enterprise develop-ments, and profit is not their central purpose. Indeed, many of those that do operate on some commercial basis attract less than 20,000 to 30,000 visitors a year, hardly a major financial success by any reckon-ing. Others which have developed with black participation (again in the UK, but also elsewhere) cannot be said to be catering exclusively to white consumption.

Further critique of the "domination" model shows that it fails to confront a number of central dilemmas and paradoxes that only be-come apparent from closer examination of specific sites. In Charles-ton, for example, there is the realization that, like it or not, plantation houses continue to exist, due partly to historical accident and partly to their being declared national monuments in the 1930s. In other words, at that time something *had* to be done about these properties. One solution would be simply to reverse the preservation order and to let them fall into disrepair and ruin, or actively demolish them as tainted sites, in the way that the home of mass murderer Frederick West was pulled down in Gloucester, UK. However, this strategy might provoke accusations of cover-up. The "domination" perspective is thus caught in a double bind: If slavery heritage is not memorialized, it can be read as suppression; if it is commemorated, such heritage may be construed as unethical or compromised truth.

The question as to whether or not slavery should be remembered was initially seen, within the "domination" framework, as an issue of black versus white, with the latter wishing to manipulate narratives of slavery for ideological and commercial reasons, and with the former keen to foreground it. In subsequent discussion among delegates, a number of alternative perspectives were posed against this interpreta-tion. One view was that, since slavery was a thing of a past, dwelling on it was dysfunctional in a pluralistic society for both racial groups. Though there was dissent with this position, it nevertheless served to bring into focus the implicit *psychiatric social model* that lies behind the often unchallenged assumption that community healing occurs by keeping alive dissonant issues, rather than by "letting them rest," or "sweeping them under the carpet."

An even more unexpected view, posed in discussion against the conventional wisdom that slavery should be commemorated and narrated, was the idea that many black people might oppose slavery heritage development, having no desire to be permanently situated within historical discourses that construct their identity within a self-definition whose main feature is servitude. Seen in this light, slavery could represent a twofold historical disablement–a source of traumatic suffering in the past and a psychological liability in the present. Indeed, accentuating slave origins might not clear out Augean stables that thwarted black attempts to achieve equality, but frustrate them still further by manacling them to a legacy that has not yet been transcended. At no slavery heritage site in Britain or America has such development been started by a groundswell of popular black demand; it has always been initiated by white or black intellectuals. Some evidence for black majority disinterest in, or opposition to, slavery heritage attractions is the fact that attendance, even at those sites that represent slavery overtly and have been assembled with the participation of black communities (e.g., the slavery exhibition in Liverpool), is negligible. This lack of enthusiasm contrasts strikingly with Jewish support for Holocaust heritage sites and museums in the US and Europe. For Jews, the Holocaust is regarded as a temporary caesura in the history of a successful nation that has withstood and triumphed over persecution. There is thus no parallel problem with the construction and visitation of Holocaust sites; indeed, they have nearly all been driven by Jewish initiative. The same cannot be said of the enslavement of Afro-Caribbean people, an event that lasted nearly five centuries, and one which, even after it was abolished, left blacks with most of their original culture obliterated and in a state of chronic misery from which they have still not recovered.

A final issue, not fully recognized by the "domination" model, is the question of how, if some kind of slavery heritage is to be undertaken, is it to be achieved in ways that are economically viable and sustainable. Should it be developed by private ownership, public grant or private foundation, and would any of these possibilities depend upon some kind of income from visitor revenue? These economic considerations require that further qualifications be made to initial critiques of the commodification hypothesis underpinning the "domination" model. Indeed, and as one political scientist has observed in relation to tourism in the former slave colonies of the West Indies, what has here necessarily been described in shorthand as a "domination" perspective may be even more complex than suggested. In fact, it may comprise not just elements of "commoditization," but also those of "trickle down," "mass seduction" and "black servility" theories, none of which has gone beyond the realms of speculation, far less been systematically tested (Erisman, 1983: 359-360).

METHODOLOGICAL ISSUES

It is this last point which inevitably opens up a general discussion on the relationship between theory and method in tourism research (Dann et al., 1988) and a more specific debate over the extent to which this current collection of articles on slavery tourism addresses methodological questions. Table 1 provides an outline of the situation.

From Table 1 it is clear that all of the papers are, in a sense, *overviews* of issues relating to slavery heritage development, derived from five main sources of data: literature searches; content analysis of brochures and other promotional material; discourse analysis of guides' narratives; unobtrusive observation of site settings, festivals and related entertainment; and interviews with key informants. They collectively provide an array of contextual material (particularly on current international developments in slavery heritage), along with a number of critical hypotheses and preliminary attempts to model the slavery heritage process.

However, the special strengths of these various contributions also, paradoxically, constitute a weakness. Based, as many are, on a supply-side perspective, the emphasis has typically been on investigations of the many ways that a number of tourism attractions have been promoted and presented. In this regard, there are several useful content analyses of publicity material that have been placed in historical context in order to gauge its accuracy and suitability for different audiences.

Yet, missing from most of these inquiries is the all-important demand-side of the equation. Few of the articles, for example, explore the manner in which targets of these messages, actual and potential tourists, interpret and redefine the communications they have received. Nor, for that matter, are there many complementary analyses

TABLE 1. Methods and Topics of the Articles on Slavery Heritage

Author	Methodologies	Subject Summary
Essah	Literature search	History of slave forts in Ghana
Dann and Potter	Literature search, observation and content analysis of promotional materials	History and historiography of Barbados. Analysis of its heritage tourism
Beech	Literature search and personal observation	Overview of slavery museum development in the UK
Seaton	Literature search, key informant interview and direct observation	History of English slavery. Account of differences in slavery heritage in US and UK
Goings	Historical appraisal based on artefacts, observational analysis of artefacts	An evolutionary history of black collectibles as racists ideology in relation to political change in US since the late 19th century
Butler	Content analysis of over 100 promotional materials, personal and telephone interviews with key informants	Study of occurrence and level of focus on slavery at plantation sites
Roushanzamir and Kreshel	Content/structural analysis of brochures, discourse of tourist narratives by guides	Cultural studies view of suppression/distortion of slavery at New Orleans creole heritage sites
Eskew	Content analysis of state tourism brochures and documentation and literature search (including newspapers) on recent political history	The political dimensions behind the development of Civil Rights as heritage sites in US

of the extent to which custodians, curators and guides produce verbal texts of their own, discourses that may variously converge or differ from those whose attractions they purport to represent. In other words, and with the possible exception of the paper by Roushanzamir and Kreshel, there are no studies here that can be described as "constructivist" in nature, ones that treat culture, not as simply given, but emergent, in the fashion of work conducted by Bruner (1994) or Katriel (1994), for instance, at a number of heritage sites.

More significantly, however, there are no examples in this collection of the reactions of those depicted in the exhibits (or more realistically their descendants) to the ways in which they have been portrayed. There is thus a certain "voicelessness" to the accounts, a parallel to which may be found in those studies of tourism destinations which tend to overlook the opinions of members of the local community, the perceived benefits they derive and the disadvantages they experience.

Hence, there is an overall absence of data on the actors' perspectives within the slavery heritage force field. There is, for example, no ethnography that engages with black views on slavery heritage or why their attendance is so low at such sites. Lacking, too, are any data on why other audiences who do patronize plantation and slavery heritage attractions to a far greater extent. In short, the research represents structure rather than agency perspectives, without first hand evidence of the relationships involved in the marketing, reproduction and enactment of slavery heritage. The agendas for further research are therefore clear. If this volume will not settle any conceptual, ideological and methodological issues, what it does do is provide a worthwhile set of case studies, open up the emergent field, provoke ideas and encourage others to continue where these preliminary accounts end.

SLAVERY HERITAGE AS THANATOURISM, DARK TOURISM AND DISSONANT HERITAGE

Although, as previously noted, the Afro-Caribbean slave trade constituted a uniquely repugnant and calamitous series of events in historical and human terms, it nevertheless requires understanding if it is to be interpreted more from the head than from the heart. From an academic standpoint, slavery tourism may be considered as forming a sub-set of, sharing characteristics with, and raising similar problems to a wider tourism heritage field that has already begun to attract attention, one which has been variously labelled "thanatourism" (Dann, 1998; Seaton, 1996), "dark tourism" (Foley and Lennon, 1996; Lennon and Foley, 2000) and "dissonant heritage" (Tunbridge and Ashworth, 1996). As several authors point out in their contributions to this volume, this broader domain comprises heritage staged around attractions and sites associated with death, acts of violence, scenes of disaster and crimes against humanity.

Even so, the three designations[1] are not quite synonymous and reflect different emphases. Seaton and Dann's work, for instance, focuses predominantly on historical and contemporary typological dimensions of what they call "thanatourism," "milking the macabre" or "the dark side of tourism" (Dann, 1994), a kind of tourism unrecognized by scholars until the mid 1990s. They have provided an initial inventory through a taxonomy of its diverse forms, and have indicated the extent to which it pervades tourism in general. In this regard, Seaton (1996) has identified five broad categories, while Dann (1998) has discovered sixteen variants. More recently, Dann (forthcoming) has begun to explore the motivational components of such tourism by linking it to his previous studies of "the tourist as child" (Dann, 1989, 1996).

Lennon and Foley's research is less concerned with the types of dark tourism and more with its ethical and ontological aspects, as exemplified in the developments of infamous atrocity and murder sites of the twentieth century, particularly those related to the Holocaust and Nazi war crimes, the Civil Rights movement and the Kennedy assassination (Lennon and Foley, 2000). Their work initially conceptualized the phenomenon of dark tourism within a postmodernist framework (Foley and Lennon, 1996), rather than as a traditional form with a distinctive historical pedigree (Seaton, 1996, in preparation).

Ashworth and Tunbridge, as urban planners, adopt a third approach which focuses primarily on neither the typological or ethical dimensions of what they call "dissonant heritage," but rather on the competing spatial implications and dilemmas associated with reconciling the interests of, and potential conflicts between rival groups with a separate stake in the development of controversial sites. They see dissonant heritage as posing to an extreme degree the problems of ownership, control and representation inherent in all heritage development. Ashworth and Hartmann (forthcoming) hope to extend this analysis to the investigation of specific issues involved in a diverse range of memorials and sites internationally.

All three approaches may be regarded as complementary and as offering a cumulative framework within which to locate and deal with the particular questions raised by slavery heritage. Among the problematics identified in them are: Should such sites be memorialized? If so, what ethical issues have to be confronted and resolved? How should history be presented as a heritage subject? Who should control the forms of heritage development at dissonant sites? Whose past should be privileged? How, in pluralistic societies with a diverse ethnic mix, is it possible to narrate histories that include all constituent variants equitably?

Above all, thanatourism poses a fundamental question about the relationship between heritage and history, since criticisms of heritage made by scholars in the past have tended to imply that the former can, and should be a transparent translation of the latter. According to them, the task is simply that of converting the unproblematic facts of history into an "authentic" heritage presentation.

However, and to our way of thinking, such a view fails to engage with three crucial difficulties. First, history is not a final, completed and given reality that can be unproblematically mined and reprocessed into definitive heritage. It is an evolving construction, determined by the value-laden choices of the historian and, as such, is likely to change through the revelation of new information and alternative perspectives. Thus, if heritage is always a selection from history, and history itself is a construction, then it is possible to envisage heritage as a selection from a selection.

Second, whereas heritage has to operate within constraints, history is not so obliged. The ideal of history (however impossible to attain) is the disinterested and comprehensive recovery of the past outside of any restrictions of audience or time, and its documentation occurs in a manner whose worth is ultimately determined by its internal coherence and research quality guaranteed by peer assessment. Heritage differs in several ways from this situation. Most importantly, it has to take into account the sensitivities of the present. Unlike historians, whose main and only task should be the analysis of the past, the heritage promoter must consider how the past "plays" in the present. Once history is moulded to heritage and committed to being represented as public spectacle, questions about its effects on potential target groups and stakeholders are impossible to avoid. History, since it is primarily recorded in books aimed at specialists, rarely has this overt impact. As the "force field" model in Seaton's article in this volume suggests, heritage may have to accommodate and reconcile the concerns and intentions of at least four distinct contemporary groups (owners/controllers, subjects, audiences and communities), all of whom historians can and should ignore in their quest for truths that are not distorted by sectional vested interest. Moreover, whereas history is primarily based on the single medium of print, heritage is required to find ways of narrating a story via several alternative channels of communication whose "theatrical" choice precipitates a new range of problems that can be happily overlooked by the historian.

Finally, while history ultimately aims for a comprehensive recounting of the "world of the past," heritage is always only a discourse about a comparatively small slice of that past–one which relates to given communities in particular places and at specific times. The temporal dimension in heritage is itself another problematic that can be discounted by historians who take *all times* as their legitimate province. In heritage development, the choice of an era has to be considered against the backdrop of the present. What periods should be selected as subjects of heritage narrative? This issue is especially salient to dissonant heritage decisions because, during their history, most countries have committed atrocities and acts of repression or, conversely, have been victims of them. How far back in the past must they have occurred in order to be memorialized or discarded in heritage terms?

At the end of this introductory article, it is thus relatively easy to be found in a situation where there are "more questions than answers." Consequently, there is an ongoing need for further research to provide ways of integrating what at the moment constitutes a somewhat eclectic area of academic study. Seen in this light, it is hoped that, by its focus on slavery tourism, a sub-field that has never been satisfactorily contextualized within the burgeoning field of "thanatourism," "dark tourism" and "dissonant heritage," this volume will help to encourage work that responds to the challenges raised on this occasion as well as those which inevitably lie ahead.

NOTE

1. Here, for reasons of simplicity, expressions have been identified which represent three different ways of treating the phenomenon. This stance should not be seen as failing to recognize that other terms (such as those referred to by Dann and Potter in this collection) have been employed. Rather, these alternative expressions should be considered as identifying with one of the foregoing positions.

REFERENCES

Ashworth, G. and Hartmann, R. (Eds.). (forthcoming). *Horror and human tragedy revisited: The management of sites of atrocities for tourism.* New York: Cognizant Communication Corporation.

Boorstin, D. (1987). *The image. A guide to pseudo events in America*, 25th anniversary edition. New York: Atheneum.

British Broadcasting Corporation (2000a). *BBC World Service News*, 0500 GMT, 23 February.

British Broadcasting Corporation (2000b). *BBC TV Channel 1 News*, 1800 GMT, 9 March.

Bruner, E. (1994). Abraham Lincoln as authentic reproduction: A critique of postmodernism. *American Anthropologist*, 96 (2): 397-415.

Bruner, E. (1996). Tourism in Ghana: The representation of slavery and the return of the black diaspora. *American Anthropologist*, 98 (2): 290-304.

Cabo Verde Airlines (n.d.). Brochure. Cidade da Praia, Santiago: Cabo Verde Airlines.

Dann, G. (1994). Tourism: The nostalgia industry of the future. In Theobald, W. (Ed.). *Global tourism: The next decade* (pp. 55-67). Oxford: Butterworth-Heinemann.

Dann, G. (1989). The tourist as child: Some reflections. *Cahiers du Tourisme*, serie C, no. 135.

Dann, G. (1996). *The language of tourism. A sociolinguistic perspective*. Wallingford: CAB International.

Dann, G. (1998). The dark side of tourism. *Etudes et Rapports*, serie L, Vol. 14.

Dann, G. (forthcoming). Children of the dark. In Ashworth, G. and Hartmann, R. (Eds.). *Horror and human tragedy revisited: The management of sites of atrocities for tourism*. New York: Cognizant Communication Corporation.

Dann, G., Nash, D. and Pearce P. (1988). Methodology in tourism research. *Annals of Tourism Research*, 15: 1-28.

Davis, D. (1966). *The problem of slavery in western culture*. Oxford: Oxford University Press.

Discover Jamaica (n.d.). Brochure. London: Mediamark Publishing.

Erisman, H. (1983). Tourism and cultural dependency in the West Indies. *Annals of Tourism Research*, 10: 337-361.

Fjellman, S. (1992). *Vinyl leaves. Walt Disney World and America*. Boulder, CO: Westview Press.

Foley, M. and Lennon, J. (1996). Heart of darkness. *International Journal of Heritage Studies*, 2 (4): 195-197.

Hudson, P. and Ballard, S. (1989). *The Smithsonian guide to historic America. The Carolinas and the Appalachian states*. New York: Stewart, Tabori and Chang.

Independent Television (2000). *Channel 4 News*. 1900 GMT, 21 February.

Kolchin, P. (1993). *American slavery 1619-1877*. Harmondsworth: Penguin.

Lennon, J. and Foley, M. (2000). *Dark tourism. The attraction of death and disaster* London: Continuum.

Logan, W. and Muse, V. (1989). *The Smithsonian guide to historic America. The Deep South*. New York: Stewart, Tabori and Chang.

Lowenthal, D. (1993). *The past is a foreign country*. Cambridge: Cambridge University Press.

Katriel, T. (1994). Remaking place: Cultural production in an Israeli pioneer settlement museum. *History and Memory*, 5 (2): 104-135.

MacCannell, D. (1989). *The tourist. A new theory of the leisure class*, 2nd edition. New York: Schocken Books.

Meltzer, M. (1993a). *Slavery. A world history. Vol. 1: From the rise of western civilization to the Renaissance*. New York: Da Capo Press.

Meltzer, M. (1993b). *Slavery. A world history. Vol. 2: From the Renaissance to today.* New York: Da Capo Press.

Nash. D. (1979). Tourism in pre-industrial societies. *Cahiers du Tourisme*, serie C, no. 51.

Petrovich, M. and Curtin, P. (1967). *The human achievement.* Morristown, NJ: Silver Burdett Co.

Richter, L. (1989). *The politics of tourism in Asia.* Honolulu: University of Hawaii Press.

Seaton, A. (1996). Guided by the dark: From thanatopsis to thanatourism. *International Journal of Heritage Studies,* 2 (4): 234-244.

Seaton, A. (in preparation). *From ampullae to Althorpe: Death and tourism in history.* London: London Books.

St Lucia Tourist Board (n.d.). *St Lucia: Simply beautiful* (brochure). London: St Lucia Tourist Board.

Solow, B. (1993). Introduction. In B. Solow (Ed.). *Slavery and the rise of the Atlantic system* (pp. 1-20). Cambridge: Cambridge University Press.

Tanzania Tourist Board (n.d.). *Tanzania. The land of Kilimanjaro and Zanzibar* (brochure). Dar Es Salaam: Tanzania Tourist Board.

The Antiguan (1998). *Guide to Antigua and Barbuda.* St John's, Antigua: FT Caribbean.

Tunbridge, J. and Ashworth, G. (1996). *Dissonant heritage: The management of the past as a resource in conflict.* Chichester: Wiley.

Walvin, J. (1992). *Black ivory. A history of British slavery.* London: Harper Collins.

Widdup, E. (2000). Pulling the cotton over our eyes. *Charleston City Paper,* 3 (32), 5 April, 13-15.

Zeppel, H. and Hall, C. M. (1992). Arts and heritage tourism. In Weiler, B. and Hall, C. M. (Eds.). *Special interest tourism* (pp. 47-68). London: Belhaven Press.

Slavery, Heritage
and Tourism in Ghana

Patience Essah

SUMMARY. This paper examines the past and present of the approximately 80 slave trade-related structures erected by Europeans on the shores of the Gold Coast (now Ghana). Built between the sixteenth and nineteenth centuries, these monuments bear testimony to a shameful commerce in human beings, one that served to inextricably link the fate of peoples of three continents: Africa, the Americas and Europe. The meaning of these monuments remains powerful, bringing to Ghana and the slave forts a stream of tourists, primarily from Europe and the Americas, on a pilgrimage to view the virtual history of buyers, sellers and victims of the Atlantic Slave Trade. *[Article copies available for a fee from The Haworth Document Delivery Service: 1-800-342-9678. E-mail address: <getinfo@haworthpressinc.com> Website: <http://www.HaworthPress.com> © 2001 by The Haworth Press, Inc. All rights reserved.]*

KEYWORDS. Gold Coast, slave forts, Atlantic Slave Trade, Elmina Castle, Panafest, Ghana heritage tourism

INTRODUCTION

On the Atlantic coast of Ghana, a stretch of coastline of approximately 300 miles, European trading companies from Portugal, France,

Patience Essah is affiliated with Auburn University, 310 Thatch Hall, Auburn, AL 36849, USA.

[Haworth co-indexing entry note]: "Slavery, Heritage and Tourism in Ghana." Essah, Patience. Co-published simultaneously in *International Journal of Hospitality & Tourism Administration* (The Haworth Hospitality Press, an imprint of The Haworth Press, Inc.) Vol. 2, No. 3/4, 2001, pp. 31-49; and: *Slavery, Contested Heritage and Thanatourism* (ed: Graham M. S. Dann and A. V. Seaton), The Haworth Hospitality Press, an imprint of The Haworth Press, Inc., 2001, pp. 31-49. Single or multiple copies of this article are available for a fee from The Haworth Document Delivery Service [1-800-342-9678, 9:00 a.m. - 5:00 p.m. (EST). E-mail address: getinfo@haworthpressinc.com].

England, the Netherlands, Denmark, Sweden and the German state of Brandenburg built approximately eighty castles, forts, lodges and other trade-related structures. Scholars estimate that these edifices account for approximately two-thirds of all the trade posts built by European traders in Africa (Anquandah, 1999: 20).

Although European companies set up trade posts in many parts of Africa, nowhere did this construction reach such a level of intensity as it did in that section of West Africa called the Gold Coast, now Ghana. Such a heavy concentration of forts and castles in the Gold Coast begs many questions: Why were so many fortifications built there? Why did the rulers and people of the Gold Coast allow the European trading companies to establish so many forts and castles on their land? What impact did these lodges, forts and castles have on the history of the Gold Coast? What role do these forts and castles continue to play in the politics, economy and society of contemporary Ghana? The following account attempts to address some of these issues.

EARLY HISTORY: PORTUGUESE INITIATIVES

The construction of trade forts and castles in Africa began in the fifteenth century during Europe's "Age of Exploration." Led by Portugal, Europeans began exploring the coast of Africa in search of gold and for a sea route to Asia. While striving to fulfill this quest, Portuguese navigators in 1471 arrived on the shores of the Gold Coast where, in an area near the mouth of the River Pra, they made contact with an indigenous people wearing gold ornaments and using gold. From this encounter evolved a trade system involving the exchange of European merchandize for the precious metal. Believing they had discovered the source of Africa's gold, the Portuguese named the area *A Mina de Ouro* [the Gold Mine], from which evolved the name "Gold Coast." To promote this trade in gold, John II of Portugal in 1482 commissioned the construction of a fortress in the Gold Coast. Under the leadership of Diego d'Azambuja, twelve ships carrying building materials and 600 men (one hundred artisans and five hundred soldiers) left Portugal for the Gold Coast. In a relatively short period of time, they built the castle that was named *São Jorge da Mina* [St George of the Mine], or Elmina Castle as it is popularly known today (Daaku, 1970: 1-20; van Dantzig, 1980: 1-10).

Elmina Castle was the first and only European trading post built in the Gold Coast in the fifteenth century. Nevertheless, it marked the beginning of a construction boom in castles, forts, lodges, lighthouses and other trade-related structures that continued through the nineteenth century. Although a small number of trade posts were built during the sixteenth century, the most dramatic rise in the construction of trade posts in the Gold Coast coincided with the peak of the Atlantic slave trade in the seventeenth and eighteenth centuries. To accommodate the heightened interest and profits in the Atlantic slave trade, the European trading companies undertook modifications and enlargements of the earlier trade structures, changes that increased the space for holding slaves and improved the defense capability of the fortifications (Carmichael, 1993: 84; van Dantzig, 1980).

Trading companies representing seven major European nations built an assortment of trade castles, forts and lodges along the shore of the Gold Coast. These structures differed in size and degree of protection, ranging from well-fortified castles and forts to under-defended or unprotected forts and lodges. The least protected of these trade edifices were the lodges and, not surprisingly, only a few have survived the test of time. The archaeologist Kwesi J. Anquandah defines a lodge as a "miniature fort," or an "indefensible trading post." Typically built to serve as temporary trading posts and to house company agents, the lodges tended to be small in size and poorly constructed from such materials as wood, mud and stone. The majority of trade structures in the Gold Coast were forts. As testimony to how well constructed most were, many still stand and are in use today. More elaborate than the lodges, the forts were designed with defense and security in mind. Often built in brick and stone, a typical fort had the capacity to mount up to 50 cannons, had room to comfortably house the European traders, staff and garrison, and included an underground prison for holding slaves and other articles of trade. Three trade posts built in the Gold Coast–Elmina, Cape Coast and Christiansborg–rose to the level of castles. Anquandah defines a castle as a structure spanning 'a wider area than a fort, was larger in size and had more complex network of buildings.' Each of the three Gold Coast castles had the capacity to mount up to 100 cannons and sufficient room to accommodate the European traders, garrison and staff, while the subterranean dungeons could hold up to 1,000 slaves at a time (Anquandah, 1999: 10-11).

CHALLENGES FROM OTHER EUROPEAN POWERS

Following the construction of Elmina Castle, Portugal in the sixteenth century built five additional forts and lodges in the Gold Coast, among which were Fort *São Antonio* at Axim and Fort *São Sebastião* at Shama, both located at the mouths of rivers leading to the heart of the gold bearing areas of the Gold Coast (van Dantzig, 1980: 5-8). From the mid sixteenth century, Portugal's tenure on the Gold Coast faced serious challenges from other European traders. The French and English arrived there in the 1550s, the Dutch in 1595, while the 1640s witnessed the arrival of the Swedes and the Danes, followed by Germans from the state of Brandenburg in 1683 (Carmichael, 1993: 77; van Dantzig, 1980: 1-38). All these European companies erected fortified posts in the Gold Coast but, unlike Portugal's, theirs were not state-owned. Instead, they belonged to private companies that enjoyed the protection and support of their respective home governments.

The first sustained threat to Portugal's monopoly of the Gold Coast trade came from Dutch traders during the early part of the seventeenth century. The Dutch challenged Portugal's hegemony in the Gold Coast trade for both economic and political reasons. In part, profits from the Gold Coast trade guided the behavior of the Dutch traders. Additionally, however, their actions reflected their support for a Dutch nation fighting for its independence from Spain. In the aftermath of the merger of the Spanish and Portuguese crowns under Philip II and, particularly after 1592, when Philip II closed off trading in Spanish possessions to Dutch nationals, Dutch traders extended their battle against Spain to include Portuguese possessions. Simply put, Dutch traders came to regard Portuguese forts in the Gold Coast and elsewhere as fair game (Daaku, 1970: 11-12; Feinberg, 1989).

In 1613, the Dutch built their first fort in the Gold Coast at Mori, later expanding and renaming it Fort Nassau. In all, the Dutch proceeded to build approximately thirty additional lodges, forts and other trade structures, the last of which were constructed in the eighteenth century. But even as the Dutch established other trade fortifications in the Gold Coast, they relentlessly pursued the Portuguese. In 1625, the Dutch attacked the Portuguese castle at Elmina and failed to take it. They later returned in 1637, this time successfully wresting it from Portuguese control. The Dutch followed with attacks on other Portuguese forts and, by 1642, had taken over all remaining Portuguese posts on the coast, thereby totally excluding the Portuguese from the Gold Coast trade (Feinberg, 1989: 26; van Dantzig, 1980: 13-14).

No sooner had the Dutch eliminated the Portuguese than they found themselves in a similar situation, for other European companies soon entered the fray over trade in the Gold Coast, with the English posing the most serious threat. Closely following on the heels of the Dutch, the English in 1618 built their first trade post at Kormantin. This structure began as a lodge but, by the 1640s, expanded to become a defensive fort including dungeons for holding slaves. Over time, the name Kormantin was corrupted to "Cormantee," the generic term used to describe Gold Coast slaves imported by the English to the West Indies. The building of other English forts soon followed and, by the nineteenth century, the English had constructed another fifteen lodges, forts and castles in the Gold Coast (Feinberg, 1989: 40; van Dantzig, 1980: 21-23).

Castles, forts, and lodges built by the Danes, Swedes, French and Brandenburgers also dotted the shores of the Gold Coast. However, because these trading companies were less powerful than the English and the Dutch, their trade posts were fewer in number, their defences were usually not as strong, and the sites of their fortifications tended to be located in less favorable trade positions on the coast. The participation of these smaller companies in the Gold Coast trade did not endure. The precipitous decline in profits following the abolition of the Atlantic Slave Trade hastened their departure from the Gold Coast. In their hurry to leave the area, some forts and lodges were simply abandoned, while the well-constructed trade posts were sold to either the Dutch or the English. Two of the three castles in the Gold Coast began as possessions of the Danes and the Swedes, but both companies failed to exercise effective control over their castles and thus lost ownership to others. Cape Coast Castle started out as the Swedish Fort Carolusburg, but the Swedes lost control over the fort several times: first, to the Danes, next to the Chief of Fetu, then to the Dutch, and finally to the English who tendered it to the government of Ghana on its achieving independence. The Danes fared no better at maintaining control over Christiansborg Castle. In 1679, it fell into the hands of mutineers who sold it to the Portuguese. In 1683, the Portuguese sold it back to the Danes, who ten years later lost it to the chief of Akwamu. The Akwamu kept it for a year before selling it back to the Danes who, in 1850, offered it to the English.

The forts and castles served a variety of purposes ranging from company headquarters, residence for agents, staff and servants, a stronghold for storing trade goods, and a defensive bulwark against enemy attacks. Even so, all shared the common goal of helping to facilitate trade involving the exchange of European goods for gold, ivory and slaves in the Gold Coast.

No law obliged European companies to construct forts and castles in order to participate in the Gold Coast trade. Nevertheless, building these fortified posts certainly eased the path to increased trade. In light of the fierce competition and trade wars that broke out among the European companies operating in the Gold Coast, ownership of fortified trade posts seemed essential. Pieter de Marees, a Dutch national who visited there in 1602, wrote a vivid account of the region and of the practices and concerns of the European trading companies in his *Description and Historical Account of the Gold Kingdom of Guinea* (1602). Commenting on some of the problems that the early Dutch merchants encountered in the Gold Coast, he observed:

> Not having (like the Portuguese) any stronghold on the Coast, where we might take goods and merchandise ashore to be stored in Warehouses till the time was ripe to sell them, and being on very inimical terms with the Portuguese, our people were not allowed and did not dare to go ashore anywhere on the Coast. Instead, they were obliged to stay out at Sea on their Ships and anchor off the Towns, waiting for the traders to come in their Canoes and trade with them. (de Marees, 1987: 45)

When de Marees visited the Gold Coast in 1602, the Dutch West Indian Trading Company still faced difficulties in carving out a niche in the profitable Gold Coast trade, since it had no trade forts in the area and the nature of the coastline inhibited ships from anchoring close to the shore. To trade with the Dutch, local traders had to board canoes that ferried them to and from the Dutch ships lying in wait on the ocean. Continuing his description of the interior traders and their experience with trading on the high sea, de Marees revealed: 'the Peasants who come from the Interior cannot stand the sea; and when they come aboard they can neither stand nor walk, but lie down like Dogs, vomit and are very sea-sick' (de Marees, 1987: 46). Clearly, this inconvenient way of conducting business demanded change, particularly since the key local traders, those with the gold and slaves that

Europeans craved, lived in the interior of the Gold Coast and thus remained unfamiliar with trading by sea. Building trade forts on land eliminated such problems while boosting the company's involvement and profits.

THE FORTS AND SLAVE TRADING

Much thought went into the selection of a site for a fortification, as it had to afford the company the most advantageous access to the major slave and gold trading routes. It was no accident that companies often located their trade posts at strategic positions, near the rivers and waterways leading to the gold bearing regions and gold markets of the Gold Coast. Of equal interest to the companies were locations that provided direct links to existing trade routes to the interior (Perbi, 1997: xiii, 59-116). The Portuguese, for example, chose the Elmina site for their castle because of these very considerations, a fact that did not escape the notice of the perceptive de Marees:

> This Castle d'Mina is renowned throughout the world, not only on account of its strength, but also of its age: indeed, it is more famous on account of the latter than for its strength. It is situated in a place which is very suitable both for trade and for a Castle to defend the Country; for not only was it built in the most convenient area of the whole Country, in the middle of the most famous places from which the Peasants of the Interior come with their Gold in order to trade with the foreigners: it is also situated in the best part of the whole Coast for obtaining provisions, such as Livestock, Fruits and other edible wares for the needs of the Inhabitants of the Castle. (de Marees, 1987: 218)

Defence was an equally important consideration in the selection making process. The chosen site had to be defensible so as to ensure the safety of persons and offer protection for the valuable trade items. Security concerns became even more acute as profits in gold and slaves soared. Whereas forts and castles provided protection against rival European companies, they also served to prevent slave captives held in the dungeons from escaping or resorting to mutiny. Again, de Marees' description of Elmina castle reveals the defense position taken by the European traders:

It is also well situated on account of the natural defences of the place, for it is built on a Rock, on one side of which the Sea breaks, and moreover, it has many fine Flank-defences, two on the seaward-side, which are strongest, and two others on the Landward-side, which are not built as strongly as the two front ones on the Seaward-side. It is mostly built of stones which they have cut out of the cliffs, and most of the Castle stands on a Cliff, being so well made that Cliff is by no means inconvenient to them, but rather reinforces their defences. . . . All around they have also dug a moat. (de Marees, 1987: 218)

As the slave trade superseded the trade in gold, a new danger emerged, one that lay in the very depths of the forts and castles, and one that created the very real possibility of an additional hazard, for now the dungeons no longer simply stored inanimate trade items like gold and ivory, but increasingly served to enclose slaves. Given the potentially explosive nature of the slave captives, the trading companies began building new and better-defended forts and castles that were fitted with prisons. At the same time, they also authorized that extensive structural changes be made to the older forts and castles in order to strengthen their defences. Jean Barbot, a French national who visited the Gold Coast in 1682 has left a first hand account of the defensive modifications carried on at Cape Coast Castle:

The lodgings and apartments within the castle are very large and well-built of brick, having three fronts which with the platform on the south almost make a quadrangle answering to the inside of the walls and form a very handsome place of arms, well-paved; under which is a spacious mansion or place to keep the slaves in, cut out of the rocky ground, arched and divided into several rooms so that it will conveniently contain a thousand blacks let down at an opening made for the purpose. The keeping of the slaves underground is good security to the garrison against any insurrection. (in Anquandah, 1999: 49)

A century later, another visitor, the Englishman John Atkins, reached Cape Coast Castle in 1781. In his account, he mentions that 'in the Area of this Quadrangle, are large Vaults, with an iron Grate at the Surface to let in Light and Air on those poor Wretches, the Slaves, who are chained and confined there till a Demand comes. They are all marked with a burning Iron upon the right Breast, D.Y. Duke of York' (Atkins, 1970: 98).

Given the high value of gold and slaves, defence of the forts and castles remained of utmost importance throughout the period of the European Gold Coast trade. Defence against the local population interfering in such a matter was clearly a serious concern, but it paled in comparison to the dangers posed by rival European traders. On occasion, usually in instances where the Europeans violated a taboo or a local tradition, the local states were known to attack the forts and the traders. However, prior to the nineteenth century such incursions rarely occurred, for the Gold Coast people remained keenly aware that wars inhibited trade. The major defence concern lay in the high incidence of attacks originating from rival European companies. Often, an outbreak of war in Europe or in the American colonies seemed an open invitation for European trading companies in the Gold Coast to attack and seize property belonging to another. The Anglo-Dutch Wars, the Seven Years War, wars between Denmark and Sweden and those between the Dutch and the French were also fought on Gold Coast soil with seizure of forts and castles as the prize for the victors. This situation explains why most forts and castles mounted their best and biggest cannons facing toward the sea, the very direction that an attack from a rival European company would originate (van Dantzig, 1980: 28-62). Regarding the defence of Elmina Castle, de Marees adds: 'the Castle is also well provided with heavy ordnance . . . and large Metal stone pieces, and of these the best and heaviest pieces lie mostly on the seaward-side' (de Marees, 1987: 221).

While Elmina Castle followed the rule of placing its heavier artillery facing toward the ocean, it belatedly discovered a flaw in this plan; that is to say, it had a vulnerable spot inland from which rival European companies could mount an attack against the castle. The Dutch did just that in 1637. Capitalizing on this weakness, the Dutch managed to decisively defeat the Portuguese in Elmina. The existence of this frailty explains the uniqueness of Fort *Coenraadsburg* in the town of Elmina, a structure built not for trade or residence, but solely to provide defence for Elmina Castle. Following their failure to take the latter in 1625, the Dutch resumed their attack in 1637, this time successfully bombarding it from an elevation overlooking the castle, St. *Jago* Hill. Recognizing the security risk that St. *Jago* Hill posed to Elmina Castle, the Dutch in 1665 bolstered the castle's defence by constructing Fort *Coenraadsburg* on St. *Jago* Hill. At first glance, the architecture of Fort *Coenraadsburg* looks bizarre. As the historian Albert van Dantzig points out: 'The fort, seen from the sea, seems to have been built back to front; it stands behind the [Elmina] Castle and its strongest and biggest bastions do not face the sea but the hills inland: it was from inland that an attack might be expected' (van Dantzig, 1980: 16). The expected inland attack, in this instance, was not one by the local states, but by a rival European company that wished to assault the Dutch position at Elmina.

THE FORTS AFTER ABOLITION

From the late eighteenth century onward, the forts and castles served a different purpose. Protection against rival companies no longer remained the central issue, since the fierce competition among the European traders had by then abated. In the wake of the abolition of the Atlantic slave trade and slavery, five of the European companies in the Gold Coast sold off or abandoned their forts, leaving only Dutch and English traders still operating by the mid nineteenth century. Rather than fight over the dwindling spoils, the English and the Dutch tried cooperation, agreeing in 1868 to an exchange of forts that placed the Dutch in possession of all the forts from Elmina westward while the English took control over the trade posts from Cape Coast eastward. But even this arrangement failed to save the day for the Dutch. Unable to secure any meaningful profits from "legitimate trade," in 1872 they sold their forts to the English. Thus, by that year, only the latter remained in the Gold Coast (van Dantzig, 1980: 71-74).

Three additional forts were built in the Gold Coast during the last decade of the nineteenth century. Constructed by the English at Kumasi in 1896 and in Wa and Bole in 1897, these three forts were designed not for the pursuit of trade but to facilitate Britain's imperialistic quest. Unlike earlier structures, these last three forts were located hundreds of miles inland for the sole purpose of extending colonial rule into the Asante and northern regions of the Gold Coast. To further aid the cause of the British Empire in the Gold Coast, changes were made to the bastions of the earlier forts, this time around, by placing the best and most powerful cannons toward land in preparation for warding off attacks from those internal states resisting European colonial rule (van Dantzig, 1980: 77-80).

THE FORTS AND PEOPLES OF THE GOLD COAST

Certainly European trading companies built these fortifications in order to promote their interests, but why did the states and peoples of the Gold Coast permit these companies to erect such structures? Like the Europeans, trade remained a primary motive for the rulers and peoples of the Gold Coast. It afforded them an opportunity to exchange gold, slaves and ivory for European manufactured goods. Gold Coast rulers were not forced to cede the lands on which the European companies built these forts. Indeed, prior to the nineteenth century, the companies were in no position to dictate to any of the major states and kingdoms in the Gold Coast. Rather, the people of the Gold Coast held an even hand in this trade relationship, a position they maintained until European imperialism overwhelmed them in the mid nineteenth century. Sustained European penetration into the interior of the Gold Coast did not occur until that time. In part, this situation was because local states refused to permit such action, while the Europeans lack of immunity to several diseases prevalent in West Africa, especially malaria, limited them to the relative safety of their forts on the coast. Additionally, European traders in the Gold Coast remained few in number, often lacked the military strength to take on the local population, and they shared the view that trade was better conducted in a peaceful atmosphere.

By allowing forts and castles to be built in their states, Gold Coast rulers and their people could reap many economic benefits. First, they encouraged different European companies to locate forts in their states, thereby creating the opportunity for playing off one European trading company against another and thus also improving the odds in their favor. Secondly, states that enjoyed direct access to European trading companies could readily purchase the guns and ammunition that proved so crucial in enabling a state to effectively defend itself against hostile states, or perversely, using the guns for slave raiding activities. Many in the coastal states benefited by playing the role of middlemen: purchasing goods from the European traders, selling such goods to the people in the interior in exchange for gold and slaves, which they in turn sold to the European traders in the forts at a profit. Also, benefits accrued to the state through payment of annual rents and gifts by the European trading companies who leased the land on which they built their forts. European traders who sought to circumvent such practices often fell foul of the local rulers and people, resulting in attacks on their agents and forts. While some Gold Coast rulers and individuals who participated in the Atlantic Slave Trade benefited economically, the same could not be said for the majority of the Gold Coast population, nor could such profits be justified in the face of the suffering endured by the thousands who passed through the doors of these trade forts and castles on their way to slavery in the Americas.

Although the histories of the forts and castles in the Gold Coast, from Elmina Castle in 1482 to the last forts built in 1897 at Wa and Bole in the northern region of Ghana, are all fascinating and merit individual attention, out of all these structures, the history of Christiansborg Castle stands out. It has, perhaps, the most colorful history of all the forts and castles in the Gold Coast; it is the one that the people of Ghana call "Castle." Today, Christiansborg Castle, this former slave trading post, serves as the seat of the government of Ghana. Its origins date back to 1661 when the Danish Guinea Company received permission from the local chief to construct a fort at Osu, Accra. The Danes named it Christiansborg Castle in remembrance of their monarch, Christian IV. Holding on to the castle proved no easy task for them. In 1679, their own employee, a Greek by the name of Pieter Bolt, led a mutiny against his employers, killed the Danish commander, and sold the castle to the former Portuguese governor of *São Tomé* Island. Portuguese tenure (1679-1683) brought changes to the castle, including its new name of St. Francis Xavier, the construction of a Catholic chapel within the premises and other significant modifications. In 1683, Portugal sold it back to the Danes who promptly changed its name back to the original and turned it into the headquarters of the Danish Trading Company. Ten years later, in 1693, the Danes again lost control over the castle, this time to the chief of the Akwamu. The Akwamu gained entry into the castle by posing as traders and through this ruse overpowered the unsuspecting Danish traders. For a year, the Akwamu flew their own flag over the castle and conducted trade with all and sundry. In 1694, the Akwamu sold the castle back to the Danes for a steep fee. Akwamu, however, kept the keys to the castle, and to this day displays it as a state trophy (Anquandah, 1999: 24-29; Norregard, 1966: 42-45, 55-62; van Dantzig, 1980: 31-32). In the aftermath of the abolition of the Atlantic slave trade, Danish attempts to find a profitable slice in the market for "legitimate trade" proved unsuccessful, and thus in 1850, they sold Christiansborg Castle and four other forts in the Gold Coast to the British for the sum of £10,000 (van Dantzig, 1980: 72).

The English acquisition of Christiansborg Castle occurred at the very time that European imperialism in Africa was on the rise and the "Castle" played a key role, serving as headquarters for the British colonial government in the Gold Coast from 1876-90. In 1902, following extensive rebuilding and remodeling, the British colonial office resumed using the castle as the seat of government, a position that the castle still holds today (Anquandah, 1999: 24-29; Boahen, 1975: 59; Carmichael, 1993: 87). The castle has since been remodeled several times. It now houses not only the head of state of Ghana, but is also used to house visiting heads of state and dignitaries.

THE FORTS AND CASTLES OF TODAY: HERITAGE AND TOURISM

These forts and castles have had an impact and continue to influence the history of Ghana. But scholars disagree on the nature and degree of this impact. In his book, *Trade Castles and Forts of West Africa* (1963), A. W. Lawrence writes:

> It was along the Gold Coast that the forts had been concentrated most densely and it was not fortuitous that this was the first native African territory to become an independent state on a modern pattern; the only generations of literate Africans that had learnt to hold their own in the white man's world. In all history, there is nothing comparable with the effects produced by the forts of West Africa, nowhere else have small and transitory communities of traders so changed the life of the alien peoples who surrounded them and indirectly of a vast region beyond. (in Anquandah, 1999: 18)

Without doubt, Lawrence exaggerates the impact of these fortifications on the people of the Gold Coast. To conclude that Ghana led sub-Saharan Africa in the struggle for independence because of the impact of these forts is highly questionable. Indeed, it is quite easy to argue the reverse by suggesting that, but for the presence of these forts, forts that provided a base for the invading British army, Britain would have found it particularly difficult, or perhaps even impossible, to impose colonial rule in the Gold Coast. Equally strange is the reference to the people of Ghana as aliens surrounding the European traders in their forts, since it is difficult to see how they could have become foreigners in their own country. Yet, there is no denying that these forts and castles have left an indelible mark on the economic, social and political life of Ghana.

The political impact of the trade forts and castles is still clearly visible in Ghana: The seat of the government of Ghana is housed in the former slave fortification of Christiansborg Castle, one of the symbols on Ghana's coat of arms is an image of a castle and the Ghanaian term for government, *aban*, is the *akan* word for fortification, an unambiguous reference to the forts and castles found along Ghana's coast (Anquandah, 1999: 18). The beginning of a western style education and system of justice as well as Christian missionary activities in the Gold Coast can all be traced to the forts and castles. Today, some of these trade structures contain government offices such as post offices, customs houses, prisons and schools, while others have been turned into inns that primarily serve visiting tourists (Anquandah, 1999: 124-129).

Some of the uses to which the forts and castles were put in the post Atlantic Slave trade era give new meaning to the word "ironic." For four years, Elmina Castle, the castle that launched the age of fortification building in the Gold Coast, served as a prison for holding the Asantehene, Prempeh I, before the British exiled him and his entourage to the Seychelles (Boahen, 1975: 73-77; van Dantzig, 1980: 15-16, 78-79). Prempeh I was imprisoned because he refused to give in to British imperialism, choosing instead to defend the right of the Asante to remain free. And yet for well over a century, the Asante rode roughshod over the freedom of others, selling thousands into the Atlantic Slave Trade system. No less ironic was the use of these forts and castles during the age of imperialism as military posts for organizing wars of conquest against states that dared oppose colonial rule, especially the Asante. From 1811-1901 the Asante fought nine wars against the British and their Gold Coast states allies (Boahen, 1966: 78-81; 1975: 73-77). Among the troops sent by the British to fight the Asante were soldiers from the British West Indies. It is highly possible that the ancestors of these troops passed through the gate of one of these Gold Coast forts and castles en route to slavery in the Caribbean.

It is most ironic that centuries later, descendants of slaves sold into the West Indies would be employed by a major participant in the Atlantic slave trade–the British–to help impose British colonial rule on Gold Coast states that may very well have had a hand in the enslavement of these West Indian soldiers (Edgerton, 1995: 103-133).

Today, the legacy of the forts and castles continues to live on in Ghana. These monuments to the inglorious past of slavery and the slave trade serve as a top drawing card for the nation's tourism industry and help 'bring socio-economic benefits, including generating foreign exchange earnings, income employment, government revenues and a multiplier effect on [Ghana's] economy' (Ghana, 1998). Beginning in 1985, the Ghana Government started developing and promoting tourism as a 'major contributor to the expansion of the nation's economy' (Ghana, 1995; cf. Bruner, 1996). To this end, the government began working toward preparing the nation's tourism landscape, hoping its programs for restoring, preserving and promoting the culture, history and natural resources of Ghana would help attract an increasing number of tourists. Armed with funding and/or assistance from such diverse organizations as the United Nations Development Program, World Tourism Organization, USAID and the private sector, the Government of Ghana began implementation of its "Five-Year Integrated National Tourism Development Program." Five tourism-related areas were targeted for special development: the promotion and linking of Ghana's culture, history, ecology, recreation and business to the tourism industry (Ghana, 1995). To meet this goal, the government in 1993 created a Ministry of Tourism with primary responsibility for formulating policies for the enhancement of tourism, and charged the Ghana Tourism Board, an agency created in 1973, with serving in an advisory role to the Ministry of Tourism. The contribution of the private sector to the tourism industry was seen as crucial, and agencies such as the Ghana Tourist Development Company received encouragement from the government to promote tourism-related investments. Moreover, to further support the private sector's contribution to tourism and the economy in general, the government continues to offer tourism-related enterprises with such incentives as tax rebates (Ghana, 1998).

Judging from official reports, the government seems pleased with its performance in increasing the growth of the tourism industry, a case in point being the number of tourists visiting Ghana where the authorities set out to boost the reported figure of 145,000 for 1991 to 270,000 arrivals by 1995. Reporting on the state of tourism in 1995, the government claimed success in meeting its goals. The report identified tourism as 'the fastest-growing sector of the Ghanaian economy in the past five years,' and ranked it 'third as a priority after gold and cocoa.' Additionally, the report claimed that tourism 'has achieved growth rates of 16 to 30 percent per annum in terms of the number of tourists as well as foreign exchange revenue,' and praised the industry for contributing over 5 percent of the 1995 Gross Domestic Product, a total of US$370 million to the Ghanaian economy' (Ghana, 1995; Library of Congress, 1994).

To attract visitors and the much-needed foreign exchange earnings that they contribute to the treasury, Ghana has promoted its tourist attractions far and wide. Through the use of traditional advertising methods such as travel brochures, newspapers, conferences, etc., and increasingly, through the medium of the World Wide Web, Ghana has sought to target tourists on a global scale, albeit with heavy emphasis on Europe and the Americas. For example, advertisements for the 1994 Pan-African Historical Theatre Festival (PANAFEST) were run in both Ghanaian newspapers and in such international journals as *West Africa* and *Newsweek*, while programs to launch the festival were held in Accra, New York, London and Johannesburg (Dake, 1998). From Europe, Ghana attracts tourists interested in viewing those monuments that testify to the imprint left by European traders and colonial powers, while from the Americas, and especially among Africans of the diaspora, come those tourists making the emotional journey in search of a past deeply rooted in Africa (Bruner, 1996).

The history of PANAFEST provides a vehicle for assessing Ghana's attempts to link its past history of slavery and the slave trade to the development of the nation's tourism industry. With the support of the Organization of African Unity (OAU), Ghana hosted PANAFEST in 1992, 1994, 1997 and 1999. The stated goals of PANAFEST include the advancement of development in Ghana, promotion of "the ideals of Pan-Africanism," and the enhancement of the interests of 'Africans and peoples of Africa[n] descent as well as all persons committed to the well-being of Africans on the continent and in the diaspora' (Panafest, 1997).

It comes as no surprise that the greater part of PANAFEST events have been held in the venues of Cape Coast and Elmina, the sites of the most historic and best preserved forts and castles in Ghana. A look at the programs for PANAFEST events testifies to Ghana's continuing interest in drawing tourists from all over the world, especially among Africans of the diaspora, to the nation's monuments to slavery and the slave trade. The report on the 1994 PANAFEST, for example, reveals the prominent role played by Cape Coast and Elmina castles and their programs titled "reverential events." In Cape Coast, the paramount chief of the Oguaa Traditional Area, Nana Kodwo Mbrah V, 'welcome[d] the brothers and sisters from Africa and its diaspora home to Cape Coast,' while a torchlight procession through the city streets ended in 'the Cape Coast Slave dungeons in the evening of 9th December to mark the holocaust of the Slave Trade.' Elmina's events geared toward welcoming 'the African kith and kin back to their roots' included a performance of 'traditional rites of reunion, a non-denominational church service, a wreath laying ceremony in the Elmina Castle and a regatta' (Dake, 1998). By 1999, Ghana's courting of the African American or African diaspora tourist had entered a higher stage when the PANAFEST held in that year was advertised as "PANAFEST '99 & Emancipation Day." The program was replete with events earmarked to cleanse and emancipate Ghanaians, Africans and Diaspora Africans from the evils of the institution of slavery. From the opening ceremony at Elmina, signals went out to those looking for a soul-searching experience: Elmina hosted a "Remembrance Day-Traditional Get-Together" and, at Cape Coast Castle, the film *A Call From Home* was shown. The subsequent days saw the launching of several events marking Emancipation Day: a declaration of emancipation at midnight in the slave dungeons in Cape Coast Castle, followed by a Caribbean Day a North and South America Day and an Africans in Europe Day (Panafest, 1999).

The number of tourists visiting Ghana's forts and castles continues to grow. For example, in 1993, Elmina Castle recorded 17,091 visitors, the overwhelming majority, 67 percent of whom were Ghanaians, with European and North American tourists accounting for 12.5 percent and 12.3 percent respectively (Bruner, 1996). The number of local visitors to Elmina and the other slave fortifications is particularly noteworthy, a marked departure from the past when Ghana's educational system made little or no effort to educate its own people about the history of these fortifications. From this writer's own experience, and as a person born in Ghana, it must be admitted that one's first exposure to the history of these fortifications was as an "Upper Sixth" student preparing for "A" Levels. Oddly, this initial introduction and visit to the slave forts and castles came by way of a history teacher, a missionary from Scotland. Missing from that early education was the history of these forts and castles and of the roles played by European and Ghanaian traders. Instead, the official curriculum of those days stressed the history of the abolition of the slave trade and especially of Britain's "humanitarian" role in the abolition movement. Decades later, when the author was a visiting professor at the University of Ghana in 1998-99, there was an opportunity to ask Ghanaian students about their knowledge of these fortifications and a resulting pleasant surprise at the number of those who knew about the history of these slave forts and castles and had actually visited them.

CONCLUSION

The restoration and preservation of these buildings lie at the heart of the government's plan to attract an increasing number of tourists and the potential wealth they can contribute to Ghana. But the effort to save these symbols of slavery has not been free of controversy. Debates over what should be restored, the nature of the restoration and exactly which group or nation's history should be at the heart of the preservation effort continue to bedevil the restoration and preservation program. For others, the real issue lies in the question of funding, for they fear that major financial sponsors would exert an undue influence over the outcome of the preservation and thus, distort the history of the slave forts and castles (Bruner, 1996). Although there are no easy answers, at least Ghana seems to be searching its way through this maze of conflicting beliefs and emotions by attempting to accommodate the different positions.

REFERENCES

Addo, E. (1997) *Kwame Nkrumah: A case study of religion and politics in Ghana.* Lanham (MD): University Press of America.
Anquandah, K. (1999) *Castles and forts of Ghana.* Atalante: Ghana Museums and Monuments Board.
Atkins, J. (1970) *A voyage to Guinea, Brazil and the West Indies.* London: Cass.

Boahen, A. (1966) *Topics in West African history.* London: Longman.

Boahen, A. (1975) *Ghana: Evolution and change in the nineteenth and twentieth centuries.* London: Longman.

Bruner, E. (1996) Tourism in Ghana: The representation of slavery and the return of the black diaspora. *American Anthropologist* 98 (2): 290-304.

Carmichael, J. (1993) *African Eldorado.* London: Duckworth.

Daaku, K. (1970) *Trade and politics on the Gold Coast, 1600-1720.* London: Oxford University Press.

Dake, A. (1998) *Report on the second Pan-African historical theatre festival (PA-NAFEST '94),* http://www.panafest.net/dake.html.

De Marees, P. (1987) (1602) *Description and historical account of the gold kingdom of Guinea,* trans. A. van Dantzig and A. Jones. London: Oxford University Press.

Edgerton, R. (1995) *The fall of the Asante Empire.* New York: Free Press.

Feinberg, H. (1989) Africans and Europeans in West Africa: Elminians and Dutchmen on the Gold Coast during the eighteenth century. *Transactions of the American Philosophical Society* 79 (7): 1-186.

Ghana (1995) *Republic of Ghana: Ghana tourism,* http://www.ghana.com/republic/tourism.

Ghana (1998) *Ghana embassy–Tokyo: Ghana resorts and excursions,* http://www.ghanaembassy.or.jp/ghal3.html, 27 November.

Library of Congress (1994) *Federal research division: Ghanian information,* http://lcweb2.locgov/cgi-bin/query/r? *frd/astudy@field* (DOCID + gh0101), November.

Norregard, G. (1966) *Danish settlements in West Africa, 1658-1850,* trans. S. Mammen. Boston: Boston University Press.

Panafest (1997) http://www.africaonline.com.gh/panafest/, 3 June.

Panafest (1999) http://www.panafest.com/program.html.

Perbi, A. (1997) *A history of indigenous slavery in Ghana from the fifteenth to the nineteenth centuries.* PhD dissertation, University of Ghana, Legon.

van Dantzig, A. (1980) *Forts and castles of Ghana.* Accra: Sedco Publishing.

Supplanting the Planters:
Hawking Heritage in Barbados

Graham M. S. Dann
Robert B. Potter

SUMMARY. After briefly examining the plantation-as-hotel model, this contribution focuses the remainder of its attention on the conversion of plantation slavery into entertainment on the Caribbean island of Barbados. First, and by way of contextualization, it is shown that an extensive and well-documented history of plantation life exists, one that is drawn from early accounts of travelers, missionaries and others, as well as later expert commentaries offered by indigenous and extra-regional scholars. Second, it is argued that the tourism industry has largely ignored or been highly selective in borrowing from this rich source of material in its attempt to supply the sort of a-historical diversion which it believes its clientele enjoys. Examples provided include the Open House Programme of the Barbados National Trust, the annual Crop Over Festival and Plantation Spectacular dinner shows. Finally, a few suggestions are advanced in order to try and understand the success of this type of tourism. They include references to postmodernity, nostalgia, dark tourism and varieties of promotion. *[Article copies available for a fee from The Haworth Document Delivery Service: 1-800-342-9678. E-mail address: <getinfo@haworthpressinc.com> Website: <http://www.HaworthPress. com> © 2001 by The Haworth Press, Inc. All rights reserved.]*

Graham M. S. Dann is affiliated with the International Tourism Research Institute, University of Luton, Putteridge Bury, Hitchin Road, Luton.

Robert B. Potter is affiliated with Royal Holloway, University of London, Egham Hill, Surrey.

[Haworth co-indexing entry note]: "Supplanting the Planters: Hawking Heritage in Barbados." Dann, Graham M. S., and Robert B. Potter. Co-published simultaneously in *International Journal of Hospitality & Tourism Administration* (The Haworth Hospitality Press, an imprint of The Haworth Press, Inc.) Vol. 2, No. 3/4, 2001, pp. 51-84; and: *Slavery, Contested Heritage and Thanatourism* (ed: Graham M. S. Dann and A. V. Seaton), The Haworth Hospitality Press, an imprint of The Haworth Press, Inc., 2001, pp. 51-84. Single or multiple copies of this article are available for a fee from The Haworth Document Delivery Service [1-800-342-9678, 9:00 a.m. - 5:00 p.m. (EST). E-mail address: getinfo@haworthpressinc.com].

51

KEYWORDS. Plantations as hotels, plantation slavery as entertainment, history of slavery in Barbados, Open House Programme, Crop Over Festival, Plantation Spectaculars, postmodernity, nostalgia, dark tourism, tourism promotion

INTRODUCTION

You can't live in the past, but it's a glorious place to visit.

–Cunard, 1999

The Plantation as Hotel

The expression "plantation tourism." if not something of an oxymoron, at first conjures up images of five-star accommodation in former Great Houses for contemporary rich tourists wishing to savor the power and the glory of their colonial forbears. It can also represent an ego-enhancing experience for the less affluent, as Buck (1978: 111) observes:

> To live for a short time surrounded by gracious deferring servants may have powerful appeal among those seeking to escape from "egalitarian affirmative action norms" as well as those middle-class, do-it-yourself capitalists who are ready to pay for a week or two of being treated as visiting potentates. Sleeping in a castle or chateau surrounded by a covey of fawning attendants are (sic), for more than we may appreciate, a dream realized.

In the Caribbean, where such pleasures can be taken by visitors from the Metropole with anonymity and impunity, Nevis is one territory which follows the plantation-as-hotel model, with such dedicated places as The Old Manor Estate and the Nisbet Plantation Club (*Condé Nast Traveler*, 1998: 54). According to one travel writer, Nevis has "an island history as colorful as any in the British West Indies: dozens of old sugar plantations, some turned into inns, some just crumbling ruins" (Schnayerson, 1998: 100). One of these up-market hostelries–the Montpelier Plantation Inn–was purchased "for a pittance in the mid 60s" by "an impeccably polite Etonian" who now hosts gastronomic evenings for a mainly British clientele (Schnayerson, 1998: 100, 104). Other plantation inns, such as the Hermitage, are also foreign owned.

Nearby is a seven hundred strong expatriate community "who keep up an active social life as any nineteenth century British colonialist's" (Schnayerson, 1998: 105) and, just to make sure that control from abroad is retained over the interpretation of the remainder of the island's heritage, 'Peace Corps workers head up Nevis' Historic and Conservation Society.' No small wonder that Schnayerson (1998: 103) subsequently admits, 'the whole scene when I half closed my eyes might have been from the colonial era.'

A similar pattern is repeated in other Caribbean destinations. The whole of Mustique, for instance, was bought for a paltry £45,000 in 1957 by Colin Tennant, later Lord Glenconner (Miller, 1992) and, ever since, has been exclusively patronized by the rich and famous, not to speak of royalty from the mother country. Then there is the 488-acre all-inclusive resort occupying the former Jalousie Plantation of St Lucia, for which the same Lord Glenconner paid £200,000 when he grew tired of Mustique. Situated between the Pitons, its opening in 1992 aroused considerable opposition from many of that island's prominent inhabitants (not least from Nobel laureate Sir Derek Walcott) who, understandably, regarded the twin peaks of their homeland as constituting a natural symbol of nationhood (Davies, 1993; Potter and Dann, 1994). Other examples of this genre are the eighteenth century Richmond Great House, the last remaining relic of this type in Tobago (*Condé Nast Traveler*, 1999), as well as Rawlins Plantation and Ottleys Plantation in St Kitts (*Condé Nast Traveler*, 1998: 54), and the Sugar Mill Hotel in Tortola (*Condé Nast Traveler*, 1998: 56). Meanwhile, over in Barbados, one of the best-known plantation houses is currently in the process of being transformed into tourist accommodation. Built in 1832, and regarded by many to be one of the finest examples of a sugar plantation great house, Villa Nova was at one time owned by Sir Anthony Eden, a former British Prime Minister. Both Queen Elizabeth II and Sir Winston Churchill stayed there as guests. Currently, a Swiss-based corporation is converting the property into what is described as the Caribbean's foremost five-star country resort hotel, consisting of 17 junior and 11 spacious one-bed suites (Ins and Outs of Barbados, 1999: 58-59).

Over two decades ago, Hills and Lundgren (1977: 262) summed up the situation as follows:

In many of the Caribbean islands, old plantations complete with
the great house and slave compounds are being resurrected as
tourist attractions. The tourist is invited in magazine advertisements and TV commercials to live in the past and to experience
the features of a "slave"-based past. What an affront to the
sensitivities of free people trying desperately to outlive the past.

Other commentators were equally quick to criticize this form of tourism, one founded on the perceived similarities between tourism and
slavery. Harrigan (1974) and Perez (1974, 1975), for instance, noted
the clear parallels between the Great House as the hotel, massa as the
overseas manager, house-keepers and concubines as maids, field workers
as beach attendants and gardeners, visiting colonials as white guests
from the Metropole. Indeed, Finney and Watson (1977), albeit in a
different geographical context, even went as far as to describe tourism
as "a new kind of sugar," while relatedly Turner and Ash (1975)
alluded to a "new form of colonialism"; Nash (1989) referred to it as
a "form of imperialism," and Bruner and Kirshenblatt-Gimblett
(1994: 467) spoke of tourism's "recidivism, atavism and anachro-
nism." Black Power leader Evan Hyde was more succinct when he
simply stated that 'tourism is whorism' (Time, 1970: 24 in Erisman,
1983: 339), a description echoed by political scientist Neville Linton
(Washington Post, 1972 in Matthews, 1977: 29). Harrigan (1974: 20)
sums up these views well when he observes:

> This new "industry" could be organized along traditional lines.
> Like sugar, it was based on expatriate capital and locally labor
> intensive; it had a structure of local demands based on foreign
> needs; it perpetuated absentee landlordism under a new guise in
> which the outside shareholder replaced the colonial planter; it
> required the usual expatriate management, a new kind of house-
> slave and substantial numbers of field-slaves.

Matthews (1977: 23) shares the same sentiments, while reflecting the
view of radical Trinidadian activist Lloyd Best (1968) when he notes:

> Metropolitan tourism institutions in developing nations are a new
> version of the colonial plantation. The management-worker rela-
> tions are similar, and the host society remains an outpost of produc-
> tion, the profits from which get calculated in metropolitan banks.

Plantation Slavery as Spectacle

However, there is another, and perhaps more important variant of plantation tourism which is growing in popularity. Instead of being based on an ego-enhancing, passive sojourn amid the sumptuous trappings of yesteryear (Buck, 1978), it focuses rather on the tourist's wandering gaze (Urry, 1990) upon the plantocratic past.

In the Caribbean, the conversion of plantation life into a spectacle is evident in a number of ostentatious displays. Carnival in Trinidad and Tobago, Junkanoo in the Bahamas and Crop Over in Barbados are well known examples of Caribbean extravaganzas related to plantation slavery. Today, however, they and their counterparts elsewhere in the region have been "watered down" (Hills and Lundgren, 1977: 259) by financial interests to a common denominator that "locals" barely recognize as West Indian in origin, in order to cater to the presumed tastes of capricious tourists. Nassau's Crystal Palace Resort and Casino, for instance, stages a Las Vegas-style review featuring such borrowed melodies as *Island in the Sun* with male dancers on roller skates and a topless woman reclining on a large banana (in spite of the latter's symbolism of trade conflict and declining revenue) (Pattullo, 1996: 178). In Haiti, visitors can take in contrived voodoo shows, complete with intermissions, where spirit possession is guaranteed and synchronized according to the schedule of the tour bus (Goldberg, 1983), while Cuba's *Tropicana* spectacular, which was once patronized by the likes of Frank Sinatra, Ava Gardner, Carmen Miranda and Nat King Cole, not to speak of Lucky Luciano and Al Capone (Suderman, 1991; Sylvain, 1993), now caters to a mass market of recreational tourists. Meanwhile, in the Lesser Antilles, Heritage Quay offers "A Night of Antiguan Culture" with "steel band, limbo dancers, gambling, children performing, late night shopping" as well as Dows Hill Interpretation Centre and, of course, English Harbour itself (Pattullo, 1996: 182, 190). Not to be left out of the action, Jamaica, over the Internet (Insiders' Jamaica, 1999), promotes such "insiders'" attractions as trips round Rose Hall Great House (where the White Witch, Annie Palmer, met a violent death at the hands of her slave lovers (Dann, 1998a; Gray, 1991; Macdonald, 1991)) and forays into the "Land of Look Behind" with opportunities to meet the "Colonel," chief of the maroons (the latter being strangely identified as descendants of escaped Spanish slaves). If that is not enough, there is always the Seville Great House (providing a microcosm of Jamaican history at one location) and Heritage Park in St Anne's Bay (site of Columbus's shipwreck and birthplace of Marcus Garvey), as well as Jamaica's Heritage Trail, comprising The Emancipation Trail, The Gingerbread House Trail and The Plantation Trail (Pattullo, 1996: 189-190).

According to Pattullo (1996: 181), the Caribbean, without the widespread benefit of castles, ancient buildings, art galleries and museums, has been unable to put its culture on display in quite the same way as, say, Venice or Prague. It is therefore only within the last three decades that it has appreciated the commercial potential of its heritage, however ignominious that might be, and to acknowledge with Morley (1972) (in Lowenthal, 1993: 4) that 'there's no business like old business' (Dann, 1998a). At the same time, it has been quick to realize that it cannot portray its history as it really happened, since the presentation of centuries of overt racism, slavery, cruelty, bloodshed and exploitation, with all the corresponding guilt that it could evoke in the descendants of the perpetrators, is hardly a recipe for touristic success. There has consequently been a selective rendition of the past based on collective amnesia, one which, like nostalgia itself, calls forth a "feel good" sentiment in the subject. However, the very real danger of just supplying visitors with what they supposedly want, is that it can result in a loss of identity for the provider, and indigenous culture becomes reduced to the strains of *Yellow Bird*–a flattened caricature of reality (Pattullo, 1996: 179). Relatedly, and in the words of Barbadian Professor Elliott Parris (1983 in Pattullo, 1996: 182):

> If we ignore our history and the cultural legacy that it left us, we run the risk of developing tourism as an industry which puts the dollar first and our people last. We are saying to ourselves, perhaps unconsciously we are the field labourers on the modern plantation of the tourist industry.

Although some reference will be made to other West Indian islands for purposes of comparison, it is the aim of this paper to focus on some of the ways that one Caribbean destination–Barbados–has ignored this warning in attempting to exploit its plantocratic past by supplying similarly derived entertainment for its visitors. The choice of this island is based on several premises: the shared experience of having lived and/or worked and conducted research there, a familiarity with its history (Potter and Dann, 1987), the realization that it is the only Caribbean country to have suffered unbroken colonial rule under a single power, the concomitant appreciation that its plantations (unlike many other West Indian territories with a tradition of absentee land-lords) were presided over by owners in residence, and the subsequent pattern of tenantry existence after emancipation (due to a lack of viable alternatives).

The argument is developed in three stages. First, it will be shown that there is an extensive literature on Barbadian plantation life, a significant part of which is based on the observations of early overseas travelers who, in many ways, constitute the prototype of the contemporary visitor.

Second, it will be demonstrated that the local tourism industry has largely overlooked, or at least selectively drawn from this rich source of historical information, preferring instead to provide that sort of a-historical entertainment which it believes that its clientele enjoys. In this connection, examples will be provided from the Open House programme of the Barbados National Trust, the annual Crop Over Festival and biweekly Plantation Spectacular dinner shows.

Third, it will be maintained that the success of this type of heritage tourism is predicated on four principal considerations: a postmodern ethos that characterizes the home environment of most of Barbados' visitors, the nostalgia pervading their motivation, the related appeal of dark tourism attractions and the effective ways in which they are promoted.

In this manner, it is believed that, while the plantocratic system of colonial proprietors, managers, overseers and laborers has been supplanted, its replacement by a tourism that dwells on the re-presentation of such a past can be thought of as a new manifestation of cultural dependency, if not mental servitude.

ACCOUNTS OF PLANTATION SLAVERY IN BARBADOS

Not long after Barbados was established as a settlement in 1627, the English planters, with the help of Irish and Scottish indentured servants, directed their energies towards the cultivation of cotton, indigo and tobacco (Innes, 1970). When these crops ceased to be economically viable, they turned their undivided attention to sugar production and, with the latter, a change from agricultural small holdings to larger plantations worked by far more profitable slave labor from Africa, via the notorious Middle Passage (Harlow, 1926 (1969); Hoyos, 1976). This system prevailed for almost two hundred years until emancipation in 1834. Indeed, some would maintain that remnants of that state of affairs continued well beyond that year, even to the present day, due to a persistent pattern of mono-crop agriculture, the ownership of tenantry house spots by plantations and the corporatization of the economy by plantation interests in the form of the "Big Six" companies (Karch, 1979).

One of Barbados' earliest visitors from the "mother country" was Richard Ligon (1970) who stayed on the island from 1647 to 1650. Certainly, his *A True and Exact History of the Island* written from the debtors' prison at Newgate was, in 1657, the first published account of the territory, one that provided details of plantation life, including the contrast between the gastronomic delights of the planters and the subsistence rations of the slaves.

Soon after, a series of missionaries arrived. Initially, there was the three month visit of the French Catholic priest Fr Antoine Biet in 1654, whose *Voyage* compared the lifestyle of the rich with that of the slaves whom they mistreated (Handler, 1967). The next year, Quakers Mary Fisher and Anne Austin arrived, followed in 1671 by none other than the founder of the Society of Friends, George Fox (Durham, 1972). In 1700, Père Labat (1931 (1970)) came to Barbados and, even though he only stayed ten days, that short period was sufficient to record in his *Memoirs*, impressions of the cruel treatment meted out to both black and white slaves. Other early missionaries included the Quaker Thomas Chalkley, whose natural sympathy with the plight of the slaves was highlighted in his gruesome journal account of a mastiff devouring the carcass of a negro during his three month visit in 1718 (Cadbury, 1943) and co-religionist John Smith of Burlington, New Jersey in 1742 (Cadbury, 1942). In 1765, two Moravians, Andrew Rittmansberger and John Wood, initiated a mission to the slaves, since preaching to them was then prohibited by both the plantocracy and the established Anglican Church (Maynard, 1968). This observation was further reinforced by the Wesleyan Thomas Coke (1808-1811 (1971)) in the company of a colleague who, in 1788, noted in his three volume *History of the West Indies* that infraction of this practice resulted in automatic corporal punishment.

In the nineteenth century, Quakers Joseph Sturge and Thomas Harvey (1837 (1838)), who visited the island just after emancipation, were able to write up their account of "the condition of the negro population." To their impressions of religion, education and life in the fields were added those of companions Lloyd and Scoble who went to Bridgetown jail and witnessed stone breaking, the infamous treadmill and the flogging of those men and women who could not keep up with their punishment. Some time between 1840 and 1841, three more Quakers, George Truman, John Jackson and Thomas Longstreth (1844 (1972)) came to Barbados and stayed with two Moravian missionaries who were able to tell them about their battle against slavery, as also about the post-emancipation situation, where tenants who were unwilling to accept the low wages and high rental charges imposed by the planters were threatened with eviction (which in practice meant a life of starvation since there was nowhere else for them to grow their subsistence crops).

Among secular sources of the pre-emancipation period, there was an early account by John Atkins (1735 (1970)), a surgeon in the Royal Navy whose ship stopped at Barbados in August 1722 to take on provisions. Here the high life of the plantocracy was described along with its accompanying predilection for drinking and gaming and the course language of its womenfolk. Later, Richard Wyvill, an army officer who spent three days on the island in 1796 and sixteen months from 1806 to 1807, described the appalling living conditions of the black slaves when contrasted with the luxurious lifestyles of whites and free mulattos (Handler, 1975). Also in 1796, there was the visit of Dr George Pinckard (1806), a physician attached to General Abercromby's military expedition, who recorded his impressions of fighting slaves, negro music and funerals, rum production and plantation life in a series of letters about the West Indies. Another Royal Navy surgeon, Dr John Waller, provided contrasting descriptions of Barbadian plantation houses and slave huts in a book published in 1820. The good doctor was firmly of the belief that the white population was unnecessarily indolent and that the morals of its males left much to be desired. Some five years later, Henry Coleridge (1825 (1970)) arrived with his distinguished relative, William Coleridge (about to become the first Anglican bishop of the island). According to the former, the local whites were thoroughly unsophisticated and foul-mouthed. For his part, the prelate sought to ameliorate the condition of the slaves who, up until that point, had been excluded by his church from receiving the sacraments (Caldecott, 1898 (1970)). As Campbell (1982) has it, the refusal of baptism to the slaves by the Church of England authorities was the main difference between themselves and Catholics, the Protestants arguing that since slaves were not human they could therefore not be in spiritual communion with their masters. Another comparison between whites and blacks was provided by John Davy (1854 (1971)), an inspector general of army hospitals who resided in Barbados from 1845 to 1848. His account provided a wealth of detail about the "redlegs," indentured servants and evicted criminals from Britain, who lived a virtual slave existence while awaiting their freedom. Their health, anatomy, education and behavior were contrasted with other whites and the members of the emancipated black population.

Other nineteenth century visitors included the novelist Anthony Trollope (1859 (1968)) who reached Barbados in 1858. He was not impressed. As a frequent patron of the Ice House, he reflected on the inane conversations he held with planters. What with their nasal twang, their claim to know all things about everything and their constant self-praise, they were altogether quite insufferable. The negroes, whom Trollope did not meet, while reckoned to be more intelligent than those of other islands, were nevertheless considered to be more indolent and quite humorless. James Froude (1888 (1969)), an Oxford historian, by contrast, was far more racist. Visiting in 1887, he was a firm believer in the benefits of colonial rule and the subordination of the negro to white interests, a treatise that soon provoked attack against "Froudacity" by the Trinidadian author J. Thomas (1889 (1969)). Not that Froude was alone in his anti-emancipation sentiments. Before him, James McQueen (1825 (1969)) had published a tract arguing for the maintenance of plantation slavery, which strangely cited the humanitarian Joshua Steele of Kendal Plantation (a unique case of an owner paying his slaves) as an economic reason in favor of its retention. On the other side, the abolitionist cause had been pleaded by William Dickson (1789 (1970a)); 1814 (1970b)) who, having minutely described slave life and its accompanying cruelty, also referred to Joshua Steele's kinder treatment of slaves as an argument for an extension of this practice to other plantations prior to emancipation. Even so, Dickson agreed with Steele that, until laws were enacted admitting the evidence of negroes against whites, and until their quality of life was improved, it made little sense to instruct them in the ways of Christianity.

Two traveler-writers of the latter part of the nineteenth century included William Sewell (1861 (1968)), an American who arrived by horse boat. After describing the negroes in terms of their indolence and moral turpitude, he nevertheless went on to argue that the post-emancipation system of sugar production was more commercially viable than the pre-emancipation situation. There was also William Paton (1887 (1969)), a fellow New Yorker, whose visit by steamship coincided with the collapse of the price of sugar. In spite of this reverse of fortune, the planters still managed to keep up their attendance at the Ice House, therein consuming vast quantities of pepperpot and rum swizzles.

By the twentieth century, travel accounts which referred to slavery understandably began to register a decline. Nevertheless, Frederick Treves (1913), a former surgeon to British royalty, managed to produce a 378 page book relating his journey through the West Indies. The Barbados section, in addition to supplying descriptions of the island's black majority population, also provided details of the prices paid for slaves, poor whites and the life of the plantocracy. The famous author Patrick Leigh Fermor (1950 (1955)), who visited the island in the late 1940s, played up the "Little England" image more than most with references to plantation houses, redlegs, parish churches and the role of exclusive clubs in perpetuating racism. Some of these clubs, while retaining their original names, have now become equally exclusive hotels. Others, such as the Bridgetown Club and the Yacht Club, continue to be the haunts of the white plantocracy, as Raymond Savage (1936), Harry Luke (1950) and Charles Graves (1965) all noted on their visits to the island.

If these travelers' tales, in spite of their careful eye for detail and cumulative provision of information about plantation life through the ages, are perforce a trifle impressionistic, and if their tourist gaze is predominantly white, male and heterosexual (Morgan and Pritchard, 1998), such deficiencies are more than compensated by an array of scholarly output by indigenous regional historians and other independent Caribbeanists covering the same period. If, for instance, the lives of black slaves become the subject of focus, there are a number of detailed works chronicling the Middle Passage and subsequent slave auctions (Craton, 1974; Pope Hennessy, 1967). There are also those which minutely examine their demographic characteristics, geographical distribution, living conditions, health, reproduction and mortality (e.g., Higman, 1984), missions to the slaves (Goveia, 1965), slave laws and the treatment of slaves (Craton, 1974; Drayton, 1983; Goveia, 1970), religion, music and dance (Abrahams and Szwed, 1983). Furthermore, there are accounts of uprisings, rebellions and black consciousness (Beckles, 1982, 1984; Belle, 1983; Craton, 1982), case studies of slave life on particular plantations (e.g., Codrington (Bennett, 1958; Butler, 1984), Newton (Handler, 1972; Handler and Lange, 1978)), the latter based on archaeological evidence. Additionally, there are studies of poor whites (Craton, 1974; Harlow, 1926 (1969)), along with their escapes, attacks on plantations and punishments (Beckles, 1981).

Lives of the planters are also well covered. Apart from the compilation of excerpts from actual diaries of the likes of General Robert Haynes of Clifton and Newcastle Plantations (Haynes et al., 1910) and accounts of their administration (Haynes, 1934), there are works derived from early poll tax and census returns which provide profiles of the planters and explore their difficulty in adapting to the novelties of tropical life (e.g., Dunn, 1972 (1973)), details of diet and recreational activities (Oldmixon, 1741 (1969)), the economic problems they encountered in the face of crippling stamp duties (Littleton, 1689) and their eventual loss of agricultural power due to a combination of wastefulness, conservatism, inter-colonial rivalries, protectionism, taxation and war (Ragatz, 1928).

Then there are studies of abolitionism which include an analysis of the Colthurst Journal and how this Irish magistrate, in spite of attempts to bribe him, was opposed to the ignorance and cruelty of the planters (Marshall, 1977), emancipation and apprenticeship (Burn, 1937; Levy, 1980; Marshall, 1971), freedmen and manumission (Handler, 1974; Handler and Sio, 1972).

Finally, there are more general works which seek to account for the existence and persistence of plantation slavery, notably those by Sheridan (1970 (1976)) and the former Prime Minister of Trinidad and Tobago, Dr Eric Williams (1942 (1969); 1964 (1983))), one scholar even suggesting that it was a unique hybrid phenomenon blending elements of African (bondsmen) and English (feudal) cultures (Puckrein, 1984).

If all these historical commentaries are combined with the accounts of travelers, there is a huge amount of detailed information which could be used by the tourism industry as a cumulative base from which to promote heritage tourism of the plantation variety. However, and in contrast to this untapped potential, it is argued here that most of this valuable material has been studiously ignored by both the authorities and their clientele, the former preferring to provide kitsch-stereotypes of reality which they believe cater to the tastes of the postmodern consumer. Although the planters have been supplanted, their place in the sun has been taken over by an even more culpably ignorant collection of entrepreneurs seeking only to maximize profit from a distortion of the past. Upon reflection, such a situation is not all that surprising, given that some of the local tourism managers of today are direct descendants of the plantocracy of yesteryear (Harrigan, 1974: 18)!

PLANTATIONS AS TOURIST ATTRACTIONS

From the preceding section, it should be quite evident that Barbados is the quintessential plantation society. As the plantopolis framework so clearly exemplifies, the plantation was the foundation stone of settlement patterns in the small island states of the Caribbean (Potter, 2000). However, with the development of tourism and the expansion of urban-oriented coastal zones, the plantation and all its works and pomps have been appropriated by the tourism industry for its own commercial ends. With such exploitation comes the postmodern prospect that historical events and icons are at best re-interpreted in ways that are highly beneficial to the tourism business and, at worst, systematically subverted in the name of enhancing the free market. In particular, this appropriation involves the peddling of forms of a-historicism in the name of tourism promotion.

Opening Up the Great Houses

The Sunbury Plantation House, located in the parish of St Philip in the south-east of Barbados, was built over 300 years ago. The Ford Map of Barbados of 1681 designates the property as "Chapmans," so named after one of the early planter families. In 1780, a hurricane damaged the roof of the main building and, four years after emancipation, in 1838, it was bought by Thomas Daniel, in whose family it remained until 1981.

At that juncture Sunbury House was sub-divided from the sugar estate and purchased by a white couple–Mr and Mrs Keith Melville– who returned the edifice to its former glory. Like many of their color, the Melvilles as descendants of planters were both keen horse lovers. As an offshoot of their hippophilia they began to assemble a collection of horse-drawn carriages. They happily lived in such a manner until 1985, when they returned to their second home. Their departure enabled all of the rooms to be opened to the public, just one year after Sunbury had been declared a Heritage House by the Barbados National Trust. In 1995, the house suffered a major fire, with reports at the time suggesting arson at the hands of disgruntled black indigenes, whose predecessors were, of course, slaves. Whatever the truth of the matter, the house was restored and reopened to the public in 1998.

Today, the promotional material for Sunbury (1999) depicts an elegantly dressed, parasol-bearing lady descending from a carriage, with a footman tending the horse to the front. Noticeably, all of the accompanying photographs relate to fixtures, fittings and room layouts. They are anchored by the following text:

> Sunbury Plantation House is over 300 years old, steeped in history, featuring mahogany antiques, old prints and a unique collection of horse drawn carriages. . . .

> Fascinating furnishings and memorabilia of life in bygone days are presented . . . The public rooms are furnished in Victorian style with traditional Barbadian style mahogany and other antiques.

In the *Ins and Outs of Barbados* (1999: 179), a guide to the attractions of Barbados, the marketing discourse suggests that:

> A leisurely stroll through Sunbury, in the company of an informative guide will give you a very vivid impression of the *gracious lifestyle* of a bygone era (emphasis added).

Meanwhile, earlier copy, dating from the 1990s had claimed that:

> Sunbury creates a vivid impression of life on a sugar plantation in the 18th and 19th centuries which visitors are very welcome to see. (Dann and Potter, 1994: 17).

Needless to say, the previously cited historical sources clearly demonstrate that partaking of the realities of plantation life for slaves in the 1700s constituted quite the opposite sort of experience to such gracious living and would have involved far more than being simply surrounded by mahogany furniture and antiques. It comprised the backbreaking work carried out by slaves and the savage punishments meted out to those considered to have transgressed the rules of the plantocracy. However, in the Sunbury pamphlet of today there are no references whatsoever to the realities of plantation life as endured by slaves or the hardships and horrors which they experienced in order to make such opulent living possible (Dann and Potter, 1994; Potter and Dann, 1994; 1996).

Essentially the same comments can be made in relation to another leading Barbadian plantation house, Francia, located in the inland parish of St George. This mansion, too, is promoted primarily in terms of its architectural interest, its spacious tropical gardens and terraced lawns. As regards the interior décor, emphasis is placed on the mahogany furniture, along with original prints and maps. Both Francia Plantation House and Sunbury are featured in the Barbados National Trust (1999) Heritage Passport which, for a single fee, permits the holder to enter, at a 50 per cent discounted price, fifteen so-called "Treasures of Barbados." The passport allows ingress to other historic buildings such as Codrington College (centerpiece to the former surrounding sugar estates), the Barbados Synagogue and St Nicholas Abbey (one of the oldest Great Houses), together with natural attractions such as Welchman Hall Gully, Harrison's Cave and the Andromeda Gardens. Collectively, these sites are referred to as "both man-made (sic) and God-given wonders." Even so, it is noticeable that at every given stage, the opportunity to educate visitors to Barbados as to the historical realities of slavery is largely missed or ignored.

These particular examples, although purporting to offer informed glimpses of the past, instead seem to be pandering to the diversion of tourists. In other words, the connoted realities which lie behind these denoted historic icons are being sanitized to suit the demands of recreational tourism. While there is a pretence to education, the entire visitor experience amounts to little more than passing entertainment. This ludic quality is common to many plantation houses throughout the Caribbean. Thus, tourists are invited to visit the Soufrière Estate (1999) in southern St Lucia, and thereby to:

> 'Step back into history'. . . at the 1765 built estate, now offering . . .
> therapeutic Diamond Mineral Baths, Botanic Gardens and Water-
> falls, plus restaurant.

However, as noted previously, some plantations display no inclination
whatsoever towards illuminating the past, but rather have been, or are
in the process of being, converted lock, stock and rum barrel to form
tourist complexes. This appraisal is true, for example, of the Plantation
House in Bequia (1999), one of the Vincentian Grenadines. The promotional literature for this property simply states that the Plantation
Great House is a place:

> Where one goes not to escape the realities of life, but rather to
> *return to them* (emphasis added).

Again, one can only insist that the social and economic realities involved in the plantation system for slaves are most certainly not those
to which holiday-makers would seek to return! In the process of eulo-
gizing, the opportunity to inform realistically is negated once more.

Plantation-Related Vernacular Architecture

However, the exploitation of social and architectural heritage does
not inevitably have to take place. The Morne Coubaril Estate in Soufrière (1999), St Lucia, for example, is a working family plantation
house which produces cocoa, coffee and flowers. At the same time, it
is open to visitors. For a small fee, they can learn how cocoa is
processed to make chocolate and gaze upon an 18th century sugar
mill. More importantly, though, and in the present context, they can
also walk through and observe a very realistic "street village" consisting of vernacular architecture, including slave houses and wattle and
daub dwellings. But, however authentic the representation of these
habitats, the experience is somewhat marred by the promotional copy
used as part of the leaflet to support the estate, which regrettably
reverts to the old clichéd stereotype in the following excerpt which
describes the:

> Original street used by mule carriage bringing you back to the
> authentic way of life on a plantation *in the good old days* (em-
> phasis added)

Similar positive comments can also be made about the recently designated Tyrol Cot Village in Barbados, which was opened to the public in 1994-95. This site, located on the edge of the capital Bridgetown, is based on a house which was built in 1854, and which later became the home of Sir Grantley Adams, the Prime Minister of Barbados. Tyrol Cot Village (1999) features a collection of Barbadian houses plus a rum shop. There is now a slave hut, and at least some reference is made to the hardships endured by slaves. For example, it is noted that there exists as part of the complex:

> A fully restored slave hut, so authentic a visit will make *the hair on the back of your head stand up* (emphasis added)

However, in nearly every other context in Barbados, the traditional wooden chattel (or moveable) house, which has its origins in the insecurity of land tenure inherent in the plantation system, is used as a tourist icon and promotional device.

Thus, there are now several Chattel House Shopping Villages, the best known of which is located in the St Lawrence Gap tourist strip (Chattel House Shopping Village, 1999). These villages comprise an array of traditional Bajan-style vernacular houses which act as the physical shells for tourist-oriented retail premises vending surf gear, T-shirts and all manner of souvenirs. Other locations find re-created chattel houses doubling as buffet dispensing units in hotel grounds and one-off retail outlets (Potter and Dann, 1996). In all these cases, the origin of the house form in plantation slavery is entirely ignored. Once again, an opportunity to educate tourists about the historical specificity of the region they are visiting is lost.

Plantation Dinner Shows

As noted elsewhere (Dann and Potter, 1994; Potter and Dann, 1996), it is but a short step from promoting plantation Great Houses to the staging of history via dramatic reproductions. The most popular of these performances–*1627 And All That*–is enacted in the courtyard of the Barbados Museum (1999) and includes a complimentary tour of the latter. Subsequently, there follows what is described in the *Ins and Outs of Barbados* (1999: 299) as a "folkloric show":

> Transported back in time . . . as the haunting sounds and sad, slow procession of the slaves trek into the fields . . . And just

> when you begin to feel *a little bit of sympathy for their hardship*, they break into the dance of emancipation, and shrieks of delight as the spellbinding eruption begins (emphasis added).

Through dance and drama, the extravaganza, which is put on by the Pinelands Community Creative Workshop, endeavors to chronicle the fusion of English and African cultures from the year of original colonization in 1627 to the present. Although the costumes are extremely flamboyant, it is noticeable that the hardships endured by the slaves in the field are at least openly mentioned, if not in any detail.

However, other tourist-related floorshows fall well short of the mark with respect to historical accuracy. Elsewhere (Dann and Potter, 1994), reference has been made to the *Barbados by Night* dinner show. This display is put on in the Plantation Restaurant and Garden Theatre, located close to the prime St Lawrence Gap tourist area. The event features an evening meal and "a show for everyone." In one of its early versions, the advertising hyperbole invited visitors to:

> See the cultures of the Caribbean as influenced by the Spanish, French and *African settlers*, plus fire-eating, flaming limbo and steelband (emphasis added).

In two published papers (Dann and Potter, 1994; Potter and Dann, 1996) and one newspaper article (Potter, 1995), it was pointed out that there had been a complete rewriting of history in this promotional material, whereby the greatest enforced movement of black slaves was reduced by sleight of type to the status of "settlers." The newspaper which carried the article had direct links with the floorshow. Interestingly, by late 1995, the copy had been changed. Just as association is not causation, one would not normally claim to have uniquely brought about such a modification were it not for the coincidental fact that a few years previously alterations had been made to the yellow pages of *The Barbados Telephone Directory* (produced by another local newspaper) in relation to instances of sexism and racism that had been exposed in an article (Dann and Potter, 1990). Thus, while mildly flattering, it is not surprising that, enacted as before under the title "Barbados Tropical Spectacular" (1994), the *Barbados by Night* (1999) advertisement now focuses on the cultural plurality of the Caribbean and its peoples:

> A potent blend of folklore, history, revelry and the splendour of
> festival celebrations of the Caribbean people. . . . Depicting the
> colourful Market Scenes, Celebrations and Carnivals that are part
> of the mixed cultures of the Caribbean people.

Although the present version is obviously a vast improvement in terms
of historical accuracy, the show still offers an essentially postmodern
pastiche of aspects of Caribbean contemporary culture, and the use of
words such as "potent," "revelry," "colourful" and "Celebrations"
has some odd connotations in the regional context. These kaleidoscopic
highlights of the show are further exemplified in the *Ins and Outs of
Barbados* (1999: 298):

> Extracted from this Caribbean melting-pot, the show delights the
> audience with vibrant scenes of the original Arawak Indian in-
> habitants, the Yoruba dancers of Africa, the gaiety of old Bridge-
> town Market, the Zombie Jamboree of the Bahamas, the seduc-
> tive Cuban "Festival Latino," "Jamaican Reggae Sunsplash,"
> the wild celebration of Carnival in Trinidad, and Barbados' own
> magnificent Crop Over Festival.

Barbados Crop Over Festival

The foregoing cultural pot pourri leads to the final event to be
discussed here, namely Barbados' annual Crop Over Festival. Historically, "Crop Over" derived from the days of plantation slavery where
the end of the sugar season was celebrated with a procession of decorated carts bringing in the last load of cane. A party in the mill yard
would then ensue. The associated ceremonial burning of an effigy of
Mr Harding symbolized both the cruelty of the overseers and the hard
times which lay ahead (Spencer, 1974). However, throughout, the
accent was very much on community.

Today, Crop Over has evolved into a huge exercise in commoditization spanning a three week period in July. The entire event is now
clearly targeted at tourists and coincides with a major off-peak period
in the calendar of visitor arrivals.

Apart from a diluted version of the delivery of the canes and a
sponsored "coronation" of the king and queen of the crop, all that
remains of the original is a parade of decorated carts. However, the
latter is now so heavily commercialized with carnivalesque floats

bearing the names of leading companies, that few would remember its traditional significance. Sponsored calypso competitions and the "jump up" of Kadooment have replaced the earlier and simpler celebrations. The advert used to publicize Crop Over in 1999 depicts a local recording artist, and stresses "music, culture, arts and crafts, cuisine and kadooment." It is jointly underwritten by the Barbados Tourism Authority and the Barbados National Cultural Foundation. Once more, references to the horrors of plantation life, subsistence rations and slave attire have been significantly omitted and, in their place, is a brightly costumed crowd of happily drunken revelers consuming vast quantities of Kentucky Fried Chicken, all washed down with equally large doses of rum and Coca Cola.

REASONS FOR THE SUCCESS
OF PLANTATION TOURISM

Elsewhere (Dann and Potter, 1994: 17) the expression "hawking heritage" was coined as one of five non-mutually exclusive varieties of Caribbean tourism, the others being "peddling paradise," "commoditizing culture," "playful placelessness" and "blurring boundaries." There it was described as the selective inclusion of certain historical representations as part of the need for ever-increasing diversification of the tourism product and their coterminous manipulation for commercial gain. It was also argued that the appeal of visiting Barbadian Great Houses, attendance at plantation spectaculars and participation at the annual Crop Over Festival was largely due to a playful hankering after a differentiated premodern world by tourists from a postmodern de-differentiated home environment.

On this occasion, however, and following MacCannell (1989), the additional suggestion is made that some tourists, initially at least, may also, while on holiday, be looking for greater meaning in their daily lives. This quest for absent order and missing structure is particularly evident in the hierarchical ranking of Third World populations along racial lines, one derived from the pre-existing division of the society of the Other into masters and slaves, especially when such differentiation is no longer politically, legally or morally permissible in a culture of touristic origin. Even so, this quest for aura (Urry, 1990) is only a partial rendition of a shared period of history, a contested version of the past (Allcock, 1994). For it to be effective there must be agreement over a common interpretation, which, in turn, is dependent on compliance from the subordinate members of the local society, driven as many areas are by considerations of financial well-being which, in the context of a developing country, may not always be readily available by other means. Since these destination people also may have acquired postmodern tastes through the processes of their own travel, the demonstration effects of alternative lifestyles by visitors in their midst, exposure to the metropolitan mass media, and so on, many hosts would experience little difficulty in staging the past for the popular entertainment of their guests. Other commentators have also noted such apparent host complicity–Greenwood's (1989) account of the contrived performances by Basque villagers of the sacred ceremony of the Alarde being the most often quoted example. However, additional cases can be found, for instance in tourists' attending celebrations surrounding the Day of the Dead in the Mexican town of Tzintzuntzan (Brandes, 1988 in Boissevain, 1996: 9) or participating in the Pentecostal pilgrimage to the Andalucian shrine of El Rocio (Crain, 1996). Where there is less host desire to open the past and present to the tourist gaze, a number of resistance strategies have been identified (Boissevain, 1996), ranging from parody, hiding and fencing to organizing alternative rituals, collective protest and communal aggression. Generally speaking, however, willingness to parade indigenous culture depends on the degree of economic dependence on tourism and the success of the local tourism authorities in persuading their people to take part.

Thus a situation currently obtains where some tourists, however serious their original intentions or however strong their thirst for authenticity, are provided instead with contrived experiences by those who are no longer primitives but have become ex-primitives (Mac-Cannell, 1992). These knowledge-hungry visitors are hence obliged to join the much larger throng of surrounding recreational tourists who are quite satisfied with the enjoyment of "as if" experiences provided by Caribbean natives. In the words of the emblem of such ludism–*Playboy magazine* (1976)–under the title of "The Best Kept Secret in the Caribbean. Thrills and Romance in the Leewards and Windwards":

Their up-for-grabs, blood on the bougainvillea (sic) past is everywhere a presence, different on every island, visible in ruins of dead forts and sugar mills and plantation houses again becoming rock heaps among the coco (sic) palms–and felt as subtle vibrations from the people who live there and have inherited it all, whose anything-goes genealogies usually include whatever you'd care to name but nearly always spin back to slave or planter of ferocious Carib. (in Matthews, 1977: 25)

Already reference has been made to the presence of nostalgia among tourists yearning for a past that they can no longer find in their own social settings. Unable to tolerate their present alienated condition, and ever fearful of the future, they seek solace in days gone by–a world where it was once possible to distinguish right from wrong and, correspondingly, pleasure from pain. However, since they perceive that their own societies can no longer apparently provide this missing moral dimension, such a need must be satisfied in countries where it is assumed that they still retain a natural system of justice. Thus, although the British, for example, can metaphorically travel back to their industrial past by really visiting the Wigan Pier Heritage Centre in Lancashire, Quarry Bank Mill in Cheshire, Black Country World near Dudley and Iron Bridge Gorge in Shropshire, and even though Americans can patronize Plimoth Plantation, San Antonio's Alamo, the Californian gold town of Bodie, Elvis' Graceland and, of course, Main Street in Disney World, many are still aware that these sites are more safely frozen in time, and hence less related to everyday life than, say, Auschwitz in Poland, the Inquisition Museum in Lima, the KGB Lubyanka headquarters in Moscow or a plantation house in Barbados. The latter, they may feel, are that much closer to reality. They are not just part of a dim collective memory. They could, it is believed, arise again, albeit in modified forms. Furthermore, whereas heritage attractions in their own home environments may call forth weak sentiments of long disappeared law and order, similar sites in developing countries can actually mirror existing conditions of authority and hierarchy after which they yearn. A Malaysian execution, for instance, as evoked by the *son et lumière* of a hanging in Kuala Lumpur's Pudu Prison, is surely a much more potent symbol of missing contemporary justice than a waxwork model of capital punishment in Madame Tussaud's. It is the former's closer association with mortality and the transitoriness of human existence which makes it somehow more relevant to life in a changing world.

This type of nostalgia, one based on death, especially violent death, has been variously termed "milking the macabre" (Dann, 1998a), "dark tourism" (Foley and Lennon, 1996a; 1996b; Lennon and Foley, 2000), the "dark side of tourism" (Dann, 1998b), "thanatourism" (Seaton, 1996; 1999), "tragedy tourism" and "*mea culpa*" tourism (Richter, 1999), a tourism that focuses on "black spots" and "sensation sights" (Rojek, 1997), is one that is becoming increasingly important today. The reasons for its appeal are many (Dann, 1998a) and range from touristic regression to a childlike state, the need for novelty, the return to a bloodlust "eye for an eye" morality, the reversal of justice by sympathizing with the underdog, the search for near-death adventure experiences, the need to accept blame for past wrongs or "historical self-flagellation" (Lowenthal, 1993: 346) and the ability to simulate deathlike phenomena. So too are there many forms of dark tourism which extend from visits to perilous places, including towns of terror (e.g., Tombstone, Arizona) and dangerous destinations (e.g., Algiers), to houses of horror comprising dungeons (e.g., Robben island) and hotels associated with the notorious (e.g., Hitler's Bavarian hideout), fields of mortality among which are battlegrounds (e.g., Waterloo), concentration camps (e.g., Dachau), cemeteries (e.g., Père Lachaise in Paris), tours of torment (e.g., Hollywood's Grave Line Tours) and themed thanatos, including morbid museums (e.g., the Japanese Death Railway Museum in Burma) and monuments to morality (e.g., Singapore's Haw Par Villa).

Plantation tourism would seem to fit most closely into the "houses of horror" category, although, admittedly, it also demonstrates some features found in others (e.g., towns, jails, prisoner of war camps and graveyards). More importantly, however, it is necessary to realize that the plantation was a total institution (Goffman, 1973) in which all roles were carried out, if not under the same roof, then at least within the same clearly identified territorial compound. Additionally, there were several sharp divisions between the overseers and the laborers, as there are between wardens and inmates in a prison, staff and pupils in a boarding school, abbot and monks in a monastery. There were also similar rules and regulations, similar chains of command, similar time-tables and a similar system of arbitrary punishments. This authoritarian microcosm of society was an autonomous unit operating within the wider social environment (Rojas, 1989), just as there are many enclave hotels today, cut off as they are from the surrounding population by driveways, fences and private beaches. The most significant difference, however, between visitor accommodation and a total institution, is that temporary tenants of the former are free to enter and exit the premises at will. Even so, it would come as no surprise that, if and when they do leave the carefully administered schedule of controlled leisure, that they gravitate towards a similarly ordered institution of days gone by. All they have to do is board a tour bus at the hotel entrance and travel with like-minded passengers of similar complexion to an Open (Great) House where they are presented with a complimentary drink on arrival, typically a "planter's punch."

Finally, it must be noted that the success of plantation tourism very much depends on the way that it is marketed. As Palmer (1994) shows, beginning with Orientalist travel accounts and their Occidentalist parallels in relation to the Caribbean, and continuing with guidebooks and brochures, the majority black populations of this part of the world are constantly revealed as living in a bygone era. In her words:

> Local people are portrayed as existing in the past, not the present, as though time for them has stood still. Thus, for the duration of the holiday, the local people become the servile blacks of the former colonies by virtue of the images "sold" through the brochures. (Palmer, 1994: 805)

For Palmer, the promotional literature depicts the colonial era and tourists, in the absence of any other source of information, respond favorably to such imagery (Palmer, 1994: 806). As instances of how such misrepresentation can be self-inflicted, she reproduces publicity emanating from the Bahamas Ministry of Tourism describing its very own people as follows:

> Warm hearted inhabitants who speak the colonial dialect of their Tory ancestors (Bahamas Ministry of Tourism, 1991)

> Our distinct British influenced personality (Bahamas Ministry of Tourism, 1992a)

[in the attempt to persuade visitors to]

> Escape the quaint 18th century tropic isle of colonial charm and casual elegance. (Bahamas Ministry of Tourism, 1992b)

In this article an analogous attempt has been made to demonstrate that in the case of Barbados the promotional hype surrounding plantation tourism has been similarly a-historical and stereotypical in nature (Potter and Dann, 1994). Rather than relying on the vast amount of scholarly analysis at their disposal, the tourism authorities, in league with overseas tour operators, have chosen instead to caricature both host and guest within the romantic feudal framework of the seventeenth century Great House. The visitors who are duped into assuming a position of benign superiority (often at total odds with their status at home) naturally warm to such a scenario, and the natives, portrayed as fun loving servants, play along with the subordinate roles to which they have been assigned. With all the tourist world a stage, the ludic nature of postmodernity becomes a self-fulfilling prophecy while reality is replaced with fantasy. As Matthews (1978: 82 (in Palmer, 1994: 805)) notes, 'the (tourist) fantasy includes also a commitment to total servility on the part of everyone except the tourist.'

Certainly such tourism can provide an alternative to the jaded formula of sun-sand-sea and sex and, by and large, since it is located inland and is non-intrusive, it can be described as environmentally friendly (Dann and Potter, 1997). But what of the discourse that proclaims such gossamer? Is that sustainable or indeed responsible (Dann, 1999)? This question surely constitutes an issue that all those engaged in the hawking of heritage most sooner, rather than later, confront.

CONCLUSION

In spite of its growing importance, strangely there is relatively very little written about plantation tourism from an academic standpoint. One of the few references can be found in Young's (1977) early paper on the Caribbean in which she describes this form of tourism as being the most luxurious to be found in those societies with the greatest disparities between rich and poor, the hotel symbolizing *par excellence* a haven of affluence in a sea of surrounding destitution.

There are also Matthews' (1978) useful insights which relate tourism to plantation economics within the paradigmatic framework of dependency, and Erisman's (1983: 357-359) discussion of black servility theory. According to the latter, the Caribbean's maintenance of a white (guest)/black (slave) tourism, predicated as it is on the persistence of racism in the Metropole, "represents a crucial ingredient for the emergence in modern dress of the old plantation culture" (Erisman, 1983: 358). In the words of Perez (1975: 19 (in Erisman, 1983:358)):

> In more ways than one, tourism revived the spectre of the past colonial systems of imperial Europe. Current travel to the West Indies preserves intact, if in immediately unrecognizable forms, the essential qualities of the colonial order. Monoculture, white-black superordinate-subordinate relations, and the organization of society around the gratification of metropolitan needs find immediate counterparts in the tourist culture.

Crick (1989), too, includes servility among his five S's of tourism, associated as it is with slavery of a colonial past, and English (1986) likens the development of tourism to that of slavery, racial discrimination and inequality. The related contributions of commentators such as Hills and Lundgren (1977), Perez (1974; 1975), Harrigan (1974) and Palmer (1994) have also been noted. Yet none of these works concentrates exclusively on plantation tourism and, where it is mentioned, the focus is generally on that sedentary variant described here as the plantation-as-hotel model.

By contrast, (and along with Pattullo (1996)) attention in this study has been directed toward the more peripatetic and ocularcentric version which comprises festivals, events and displays. In that regard, Barbados has been examined as a representative and generalizable case. There has also been an attempt to demonstrate that, far from the tourism authorities availing themselves of the accounts of travelers, missionaries and temporary residents, and while studiously avoiding the works of their own regional and internationally recognized scholars, they have preferred instead to cater to the presumed recreational needs of their clientele. Visitors, who may have been nostalgically looking for something deeper to fill a meaningful gap in their lives, are instead provided with superficial and contrived experiences by the industry. This postmodern task is made all the easier with the realization that playfulness and inauthenticity have long since been acknowledged as marketable commodities, and that there seems to be no shortage of locals willing to play their part in exchange for a far higher standard of living than those of their slave ancestors whom they portray. In the words of Matthews (1978: 81 (in Erisman (183: 355)):

Especially in sunspot destinations such as the Caribbean . . . the growth of tourism promotes a playground mentality in visitors and residents alike.

As for the promotion of this type of tourism, nothing could be easier. In one of the most recent advertisements from the Barbados Board of Tourism (1999), the potential visitor is simply asked:

When was the last time you celebrated absolutely nothing but the pure joy of being alive?

Underneath the life-is-for-living tautology is a full picture of a young black girl in period carnival costume (the ludic metaphor for showbiz slavery) and, below her, the word "REJOICE" stretched over the by-now-familiar end line:

Barbados: Just Beyond Your Imagination.

Certainly it requires a great deal of imagination to forget centuries of past exploitation, just as it does to overlook the present exploitation of such a history by the tourism industry. In this regard, Palmer (1994: 808) makes a salutary observation, one which provides a fitting conclusion to this study:

Colonialism was concerned with power, domination and control and with the superiority of one group over another through the perpetuation of inequality. These are all criticisms that at some time or another have been levelled at tourism.

REFERENCES

Abrahams, R. and Szwed, J. (Eds). (1983). *After Africa*. New Haven, Connecticut: Yale University Press.

Allcock, J. (1994). International tourism and the appropriation of history. In J. Jardel (Ed.), *Le tourisme international entre tradition et modernité* (pp. 219-228) Nice: Laboratoire d'Ethnologie, Université de Nice.

Atkins, J. (1970). *A voyage to Guinea, Brazil and the West Indies*. London: Cass.

Bahamas Ministry of Tourism (1991). *The family islands of the Bahamas: Travel and map guide*. Nassau: Ministry of Tourism.

Bahamas Ministry of Tourism (1992a). *Bahamian culture*. Paper presented during Bahamahost training course. Nassau: Ministry of Tourism.

Bahamas Ministry of Tourism (1992b). *Green Turtle Club and Marina: Abaco, Bahamas*. Nassau: Ministry of Tourism.

Barbados Board of Tourism (1999). Advertisement. *Condé Nast Traveler*, October: 32.

Barbados by Night (1999). Advertisement.

Barbados Crop Over Festival (1999). Advertisement.

Barbados Museum (1999). *1627 and all that* (advertisement).

Barbados National Trust (1999). *Barbados National Trust heritage passport*. Barbados: Barbados National Trust.

Barbados Tropical Spectacular (1994). Advertisement.

Beckles, H. (1981). Rebels and reactionaries: The political responses of white labourers to planter class hegemony in seventeenth century Barbados. *Journal of Caribbean History* 15: 1-19.

Beckles, H. (1982). Notes on the decolonisation of West Indian history: Towards the uncovering of the Barbadian revolutionary tradition. *Bulletin of Eastern Caribbean Affairs* 8 (2): 13-23.

Beckles, H. (1984). *Black rebellion in Barbados: The struggle against slavery 1627-1838*. Bridgetown: Antilles Publications.

Belle, G. (1983). The abortive revolution of 1876 in Barbados. *Journal of Caribbean History* 18 (1): 1-34.

Bennett, J. (1958). *Bondsmen and bishops: Slavery and apprenticeship on the Codrington plantations of Barbados 1710-1838*. Berkeley: University of California Press.

Best, L. (1968). Outlines of a pure plantation economy. *Social and Economic Studies* 17 (3).

Boissevain, J. (1996). Introduction. In J.Boissevain (Ed.) *Coping with tourists. European reactions to mass tourism*. (pp. 1-26) Oxford: Berghahn Books.

Brandes, S. (1988). *Power and persuasion. Fiestas and social control in rural Mexico*. Philadelphia: University of Pennsylvania Press.

Bruner, E. and Kirshenblatt-Gimblett, B. (1994). Maasai on the lawn: Tourist realism in East Africa. *Cultural Anthropology* 9 (2): 435-470.

Buck, R. (1978). Toward a synthesis of tourism theory. *Annals of Tourism Research* 5: 110-11.

Butler, M. (1984). Mortality and labour on the Codrington estates, Barbados. *Journal of Caribbean History* 19 (1): 48-67.

Burn, W. (1937). *Emancipation and apprenticeship in the British West Indies*. London: Jonathan Cape.

Cadbury, H. (1942). An account of Barbados two hundred years ago. *Journal of the Barbados Museum and Historical Society* 9 (2): 81-83.

Cadbury, H. (1943). A Quaker account of Barbados in 1718. *Journal of the Barbados Museum and Historical Society* 10 (3): 118-124.

Caldecott, A. (1898 (1970)). *The church in the West Indies*. London: Cass, reprinted.

Campbell, P. (1982). *The church in Barbados in the seventeenth century*. Garrison, St Michael, Barbados: Barbados Museum and Historical Society.

Chattel House Shopping Village (1999). Advertisement.

Coke, T. (1808-1811 (1971)). *A history of the West Indies*, 3 vols. London: A. Paris, reprinted London: Cass.

Coleridge, H. (1825 (1970)). *Six months in the West Indies*. London: John Murray, reprinted New York: Negro Universities Press.

Condé Nast Traveler (1998). Stop press. December: 54-56.

Condé Nast Traveler (1999). Places and prices. July: 134-144.

Crain, M. (1996). Contested territories. The politics of touristic development at the shrine of El Rocio in southwestern Andalusia. In J. Boissevain (Ed.), *Coping with tourists. European reactions to mass tourism* (pp. 27-55) Oxford: Berghahn Books.

Craton, M. (1974). *Sinews of empire. A short history of British slavery*. London: Temple Smith.

Craton, M. (1982). *Testing the chains: Resistance to slavery in the British West Indies*. Ithaca, New York: Cornell University Press.

Crick, M. (1989). Representations of international tourism in the social sciences: Sun, sex, sights, savings and servility. *Annual Review of Anthropology* 18: 307-344.

Cunard (1999). Advertisement. *Condé Nast Traveler*, September: 18.

Dann, G. (1998a). 'There's no business like old business': Tourism the nostalgia industry of the future. In W. Theobald (Ed.) *Global Tourism*, 2nd edition (pp. 29-43) Oxford: Butterworth-Heinemann.

Dann, G. (1998b). The dark side of tourism. *Etudes et Rapports*, série L, no. 14.

Dann, G. (2000). Differentiating destinations in the language of tourism: Harmless hype or promotional irresponsibility? *Tourism Recreation Research* 25 (2): 63-75.

Dann, G. and Potter, R. (1990). Yellow man in the yellow pages: Sex and race typing in the Barbados telephone directory. *Bulletin of Eastern Caribbean Affairs* 15 (6): 1-15.

Dann, G. and Potter, R. (1994). Tourism and postmodernity in a Caribbean setting. *Cahiers du Tourisme*, série C, no. 185.

Dann, G. and Potter. R. (1997). Tourism in Barbados: Rejuvenation or decline? In D. Lockhart and D. Drakakis-Smith (Eds.) *Island tourism. Trends and prospects* (pp. 205-228) London: Pinter.

Davies, H. (1993). Down to his last shack in the sun. *The Independent*, 25 May.

Davy, J. (1854 (1971)). *The West Indies before and since slave emancipation*. London: W. Cash; Dublin: J. Glachan and J. Gilpin; Bridgetown: J. Brown, reprinted London: Cass.

Dickson, W. (1789 (1970a)). *Letters on slavery*. London: J. Phillips, reprinted Westport, Connecticut: Negro Universities Press.

Dickson, W. (1814 (1970b)). *Mitigation of slavery*. London: Longman. Hurst, Rees, Orme and Brown, reprinted Westport, Connecticut: Negro Universities Press.

Drayton, K. (1983). Racism in Barbados. *Bulletin of Eastern Caribbean Affairs* 9 (2): 1-5.

Dunn, R. (1972 (1973)). *Sugar and slaves: The rise of the planter class in the English West Indies 1624-1713*. Chapel Hill, North Carolina: University of North Carolina Press, reprinted New York: Norton.

Durham, H. (1972). *Caribbean Quakers*. Hollywood, Florida: Dukane Press.

English, E. (1986). *The great escape. An examination of north-south tourism*. Ottawa: The North-South Institute.

Erisman, M. (1983). Tourism and cultural dependency in the West Indies. *Annals of Tourism Research* 10: 337-361.

Fermor, P. (1950 (1955)). *The traveller's tree: A journey through the Caribbean islands*. London: John Murray, reprinted.

Finney, B. and Watson, K. (Eds.). (1977). *A new kind of sugar: Tourism in the Pacific*. Santa Cruz: Center for South Pacific Studies, University of California.

Foley, M. and Lennon, J. (1996a). Heart of darkness. *International Journal of Heritage Studies* 2 (4): 195-197.

Foley, M. and Lennon, J. (1996b). A fascination with assassination. *International Journal of Heritage Studies* 2 (4): 198-211.

Froude, J. (1888 (1969)). *The English in the West Indies or the bow of Ulysses*. New York: James Scribner, reprinted New York: Negro Universities Press.

Goffman, E. (1973). *Asylums. Essays on the social situation of mental patients and other inmates*. London: Pelican.

Goldberg, A. (1983). Identity and experience in Haitian voodoo shows. *Annals of Tourism Research* 10: 479-495.

Goveia, E. (1965). *Slave society in the British Leeward Islands at the end of the eighteenth century*. New Haven, Connecticut: Yale University Press.

Goveia, E. (1970). The West Indian slave laws of the eighteenth century. In D. Hall, E. Goveia and F. Augier (Eds). *Chapters in Caribbean history 2* (pp. 9-53) Barbados: Caribbean Universities Press; Aylesbury, England: Ginn.

Gray, B. (1991). Jamaica for mature audiences. *Globe and Mail*, 9 November.

Graves, C. (1965). *Fourteen islands in the sun*. London: Leslie Frewin.

Greenwood, D. (1989). Culture by the pound: An anthropological perspective on tourism as cultural commoditization. In V. Smith (Ed.) *Hosts and guests: The anthropology of tourism*, 2nd edition. (pp. 129-138) Philadelphia: University of Pennsylvania Press.

Handler, J. (1967). Father Antoine Biet's visit to Barbados in 1654. *Journal of the Barbados Museum and Historical Society* 32 (2): 56-76.

Handler, J. (1972). An archeological investigation of the domestic life of plantation slaves in Barbados. *Journal of the Barbados Museum and Historical Society* 34 (2): 64-72.

Handler, J. (1974). *The unappropriated people: Freedmen in the slave society of Barbados*. Baltimore: Johns Hopkins University Press.

Handler, J. (Ed.). (1975). Memoirs of an old army officer. *Journal of the Barbados Museum and Historical Society* 35 (1): 21-30.

Handler, J. and Lange, F. with the assistance of Riordan, R. (1978). *Plantation slavery in Barbados: An archaeological and historical investigation*. Cambridge, Massachusetts: Harvard University Press.

Handler, J. and Sio, A. (1972). Barbados. In D. Cohen and J. Greene (Eds.) *Neither slave nor free* (pp. 214-257) Baltimore: Johns Hopkins University Press.

Harlow, V. (1926 (1969)). *A history of Barbados 1625-1685*. Oxford: Clarendon Press, reprinted New York: Negro Universities Press.

Harrigan, N. (1974). The legacy of Caribbean history and tourism. *Annals of Tourism Research* 2: 13-25.

Haynes, E. C., Haynes, P. and Haynes. E. S. (Eds.). (1910). *Notes by General Robert Haynes of Newcastle and Clifton Hall Plantations, Barbados, and other documents of family interest*. London: Argus Printing.

Haynes, R. (1934). *The Barbadian diary of General Robert Haynes 1787-1836*. E. Cracknell (Ed.) Mestead, Hampshire, England: Azania Press.

Higman, B. (1984). *Slave populations of the British Caribbean 1807-1834*. Baltimore: Johns Hopkins University Press.

Hills, T. and Lundgren, J. (1977). The impact of tourism in the Caribbean. *Annals of Tourism Research* 4: 248-267.

Hoyos, F. (1976). *Barbados: A history from the Amerindians to independence*. London: Macmillan.

Innes, F. (1970). The pre-sugar era of European settlement in Barbados. *Journal of Caribbean History* 1: 1-22.

Ins and Outs of Barbados (1999). *Ins and outs of Barbados*. Barbados: Miller Publishing Co.

Insiders' Jamaica (1999). *http://www.insidersjamaica.com.attractions.html*.

Karch, C. (1979). *The transformation and consolidation of the corporate plantation economy in Barbados 1860-1977*. PhD dissertation, Rutgers University, New Brunswick, New Jersey. (Available from University Microfilms, Ann Arbor, Michigan order no. GAX79-16145).

Labat, P. (1931 (1970)). *The memoirs of Père Labat 1693-1705*, trans. J. Eaden. London: Cass, revised edition.

Lennon, J. and Foley, M. (2000). *Dark tourism: The attraction of death and disaster*. London: Continuum.

Levy, C. (1980). *Emancipation, sugar and federalism: Barbados and the West Indies 1833-1876*. Gainesville: Center for Latin American Studies, University of Florida.

Ligon, R. (1970). *A true and exact history of the island of Barbadoes*, 2nd revised edition. London: Cass.

Littleton, E. (1689). *The groans of the plantations, or a true account of their grievous and extreme sufferings by the heavy impositions upon sugar and other hardships*. London: M. Clark.

Lowenthal, D. (1993). *The past is a foreign country*. Cambridge: Cambridge University Press.

Luke, H. (1950). *Caribbean circuit*. London: Nicholson and Watson.

McQueen, J. (1825 (1969)). *The West India colonies*. London: Longman, Hurst, reprinted New York: Negro Universities Press.

MacCannell, D. (1989). *The tourist. A new theory of the leisure class*, 2nd edition. New York: Schocken Books.

MacCannell, D. (1992). *Empty meeting grounds. The tourist papers*. London: Routledge.

Macdonald, J. (1991). Jamaica's white witch certainly was no lady. *Toronto Star*, 2 November.

Marshall, W. (1971). The termination of the apprenticeship in Barbados and the Windward islands: An essay in colonial administration and politics. *Journal of Caribbean History* 2: 1-45.

Marshall, W. (Ed.). (1977). *The Colthurst Journal*. Millwood, New York: KTO Press.

Matthews, H. (1977). Radicals and Third World tourism. A Caribbean focus. *Annals of Tourism Research* 5: 20-29.

Matthews, H. (1978). *International tourism: A political and social analysis*. Cambridge. (Massachusetts): Shenkman Publishing.

Maynard, G. (1968). *A history of the Moravian Church, Eastern West Indies Province*. Port of Spain, Trinidad: Yuilles Printerie.

Miller, R. (1992). Tennant's laager. *Sunday Times Magazine*, 1 March.

Morgan, N. and Pritchard, A. (1998). *Tourism promotion and power. Creating images, creating identities*. Chichester: Wiley.

Morley, S. (1972). There's no business like old business. *Punch*, 29 November: 777.

Morne Coubaril Estate (1999). (Leaflet). St Lucia: Morne Coubaril Estate.

Nash, D. (1989). Tourism as a form of imperialism. In V. Smith (Ed.) *Hosts and guests. The anthropology of tourism*, 2nd edition. (pp. 37-52) Philadelphia: University of Pennsylvania Press.

Oldmixon, J. (1741 (1969)). *British empire in America*. London: J. Brotherton, J. Clarke et al., reprinted 2nd edition New York: Augustus Kelley.

Palmer, C. (1994). Tourism and colonialism: The experience of the Bahamas. *Annals of Tourism Research* 21: 792-811.

Parris, E. (1983). Cultural patrimony and the tourism product: Towards a mutually beneficial relationship. Paper presented to the Organization of American States' regional seminar.

Paton, W. (1887 (1969)). *Down the islands: A voyage to the Caribees*. New York: Scribners, reprinted New York: Negro Universities Press.

Pattullo, P. (1996). *Last resorts. The cost of tourism in the Caribbean*. London: Cassell.

Perez, L. (1974). Aspects of underdevelopment: Tourism in the West Indies. *Science and Society* 37: 473-480.

Perez, L. (1975.) *Underdevelopment and dependency: Tourism in the West Indies*. El Paso: Center for Inter-American Studies, University of El Paso.

Pinckard, G. (1806). *Notes on the West Indies*, 3 vols. London: Longman, Hurst, Rees and Orme.

Plantation House, Bequia (1999). Advertisement.

Plantation Theatre (1999). *Tropical spectacular* (advertisement).

Playboy (1976). The best kept secret in the Caribbean. Thrills and romance in the Leewards and Windwards. May.

Pope-Hennessy, J. (1967). *Sins of the fathers: A study of the Atlantic slave Traders 1441-1807*. London: Weidenfeld and Nicholson.

Potter, R. (1995). Whither the real Barbados? *Caribbean Week*, 25 November-8 December.

Potter, R. (2000). *The urban Caribbean in an era of global change*. Aldershot: Ashgate.

Potter, R. and Dann, G. (1994). Some observations concerning postmodernity and sustainable development in the Caribbean. *Caribbean Geography* 5 (2): 92-107.

Potter, R. and Dann, G. (1996). Globalization, postmodernity and development in the Commonwealth Caribbean. In Yeung, Yue-man (Ed.) *Global change and the Commonwealth* (pp. 103-129) Hong Kong: Chinese University of Hong Kong.

Potter, R. and Dann, G. (Eds.). (1987). *World bibliographical series, vol 76–Barbados*. Oxford: Clio Press.

Puckrein, G. (1984). *Little England*: *Plantation society and Anglo Barbadian politics*. New York: New York University Press.

Ragatz, L. (1928). *The fall of the planter class in the British Caribbean 1763-1833*. New York: American Historical Association, reprinted New York: Octagon Books.

Richter, L. (1999). The politics of heritage tourism development. Emerging issues for the new millennium. In D. Pearce and R. Butler (Eds.) *Contemporary issues in tourism development* (pp. 108-126) London: Routledge.

Rojas, E. (1989). Human settlements of the Eastern Caribbean: Development problems and policy options. *Cities* 5: 243-258.

Rojek, C. (1997). Indexing, dragging and the social construction of tourist sites. In C. Rojek and J. Urry (Eds.) *Touring cultures. Transformations of travel and theory* (pp. 52-74). London: Routledge.

Savage, R. (1936). *Barbados, British West Indies*. London: Arthur Barker.

Schnayerson, M. (1998). The little island that could. *Condé Nast Traveler*, June: 98-105, 150, 160-163.

Seaton, A. (1996). Guided by the dark: From thanatopsis to thanatourism. *International Journal of Heritage Studies* 2 (4): 234-244.

Seaton, A. (1999). War and thanatourism: Waterloo 1815-1914. *Annals of Tourism Research* 26: 130-158.

Sewell, W. (1861 (1968)). *The ordeal of free labor in the British West Indies*. New York: Harper and Brothers; London: Sampson, Low, reprinted London: Cass.

Sheridan, R. (1970 (1976)). *The development of the plantations to 1750. An era of West Indian prosperity 1750-1755*. Kingston, Jamaica: Caribbean Universities Press, reprinted.

Soufriere Estate (1999). Advertisement.

Spencer, F. (1974). *Crop Over*: *An old Barbadian plantation festival*. Barbados: Commonwealth Caribbean Resource Centre.

Sturge, J. and Harvey, T. (1837 (1838)). *The West Indies in 1837*. London: Hamilton, Adams and Company (reprinted).

Suderman, J. (1991). Nightlife in Havana a slice of the past. *Globe and Mail*, 5 October.

Sunbury Plantation House (1999). Leaflet.

Sylvain, R. (1993). Beauty, history and value bring Cuba new invaders. *Toronto Star*, 9 January.

Thomas, J. (1889 (1969)). *Froudacity*. London: T. F. Unwin, second edition London and Port of Spain, Trinidad: Beacon Books.

Time (1970). Tourism is whorism. 3 August: 24.

Treves, F. (1913). *The cradle of the deep*: *An account of a visit to the West Indies*. London: Smith, Elder and Company.

Trollope, A. (1859 (1968)). *The West Indies and the Spanish Main*. London: Chapman and Hall, reprinted London: Cass.

Truman, G., Jackson, J. and Longstreth, T. (1844 (1972)). *Narrative of a visit to the West Indies in 1840 and 1841*. Philadelphia: Merrihew and Thompson, reprinted 2nd edition New York: Books for Libraries Press.

Turner, L. and Ash, J. (1975). *The golden hordes*: *International tourism and the leisure periphery*. London: Constable.

Tyrol Cot (1999). Leaflet.

Urry, J. (1990). *The tourist gaze. Leisure and travel in contemporary societies.* London: Sage.

Waller, J. (1820). *A voyage in the West Indies, containing various observations made during a residence in Barbados and several of the Leeward islands; with some notices and illustrations relative to the city of Paramaribo in Surinam.* London: Printed for Sir Richard Phillips and Company.

Washington Post (1972). Remarks made by Neville Linton at a meeting of the Caribbean Travel Association, 16 January.

Williams, E. (1942 (1969)). *The negro in the Caribbean.* New York: Associates in Negro Folk Education, reprinted New York: Negro Universities Press.

Williams, E. (1964 (1983)). *Capitalism and slavery.* London: André Deutsch, re-printed.

Young, R. (1977). The structural context of the Caribbean tourism industry: A comparative study. *Economic Development and Cultural Change* 25 (4): 657-672.

The Marketing of Slavery Heritage in the United Kingdom

John G. Beech

SUMMARY. This paper examines the promotion of slavery heritage sites in the United Kingdom in the context of an increasing interest in peace and reconciliation studies. With the exception of Hull, an abolitionist center, several sites have been developed within the last four years at slave trade ports. Their evaluation considers the strengths and weaknesses of the displays at Liverpool, Bristol and Lancaster, and comments on the significant omission of a major exhibition in London, an important slave trade port as well as a capital city. In the absence of previous research and theoretical frameworks in this area, the phenomenon of slavery is related to other heritage visitation sites, such as concentration camps, which are potentially embarrassing to the contemporary majority. Finally, the weaknesses of the conventional model of the slave trade are explored and an alternative is presented. *[Article copies available for a fee from The Haworth Document Delivery Service: 1-800-342-9678. E-mail address: <getinfo@haworthpressinc.com> Website: <http://www.HaworthPress.com> © 2001 by The Haworth Press, Inc. All rights reserved.]*

KEYWORDS. Slavery, heritage tourism, museums, Britain, reconciliation

INTRODUCTION

In the last five years there has been an increasing interest in Britain's participation in the slave trade in particular, and in the broader

John G. Beech is affiliated with Coventry Business School, Coventry University, UK.

[Haworth co-indexing entry note]: "The Marketing of Slavery Heritage in the United Kingdom." Beech, John G. Co-published simultaneously in *International Journal of Hospitality & Tourism Administration* (The Haworth Hospitality Press, an imprint of The Haworth Press, Inc.) Vol. 2, No. 3/4, 2001, pp. 85-105; and: *Slavery, Contested Heritage and Thanatourism* (ed: Graham M. S. Dann and A. V. Seaton), The Haworth Hospitality Press, an imprint of The Haworth Press, Inc., 2001, pp. 85-105. Single or multiple copies of this article are available for a fee from The Haworth Document Delivery Service [1-800-342-9678, 9:00 a.m. - 5:00 p.m. (EST). E-mail address: getinfo@haworthpressinc.com].

area of slavery in general. This growing awareness has manifested itself in several ways, especially in the development of permanent and temporary exhibitions. It is the intention of this article to consider how these displays present the slave trade and slave heritage. In order to provide a reasoned analysis and an evaluation of the process so far, the following strategy has been adopted.

The paper begins with a consideration of the academic context in which such an assessment needs to take place. An upsurge in the broader issue of reconciliation is reviewed, and the general lack of interest in placing the study of slavery in this wider framework is noted. The traditional models of the slave trade, variants on a common theme, are investigated and found to be wanting. A more complete alternative is proposed.

The primary local displays related to slavery are described in some detail, with Bristol, Liverpool and Hull being given prominence. Finally, these and smaller exhibitions are judged in relation to the proposed model in order to highlight the weaknesses in current approaches in Britain.

CONTEXT

Reconciliation and the associated concept of peace studies have become a respectable academic field of study in the United Kingdom. The Universities and Colleges Admissions Service handbook (UCAS, 1998) lists four undergraduate degrees in various formats of peace studies at the Bolton Institute of Higher Education, the University of Bradford, Lancaster University and the University of Ulster. Such programs are generally interdisciplinary, and usually set peace in a wider context which includes the study of conflict and of reconciliation. Often universities regard Peace Studies as more appropriate to Masters level or as a basis for postgraduate research. The University of Bradford has a Department of Peace Studies; Lancaster University's Richardson Institute (named after the Quaker Lewis Fry Richardson, and the first such center to be established in Britain, in 1959) is devoted to the study of peace and conflict; De Montfort University, Bedford has an Institute for the Study of War and Society; and Coventry University has a Centre for the Study of Forgiveness and Reconciliation.

These related issues of peace and reconciliation are, to some extent, reflections of the public psyche. Although the number of centers for study is too small to offer any meaningful statistical comparison, it is worth noting the variety of links offered from the Richardson Institute's web-site. The data are presented in Table 1 and, while being a measure of supply, do give some indication of their relative importance from a British perspective.

Any attempt to analyze these data and reach conclusions is, of course, fraught with difficulty. But the low figures for both Northern Ireland and Africa require some comment. Northern Ireland clearly presents a non-modal case in the United Kingdom context, and may well therefore arouse feelings of concern over political correctness and the issue of balance. This argument may also explain the complete absence–not even a title–of any reference to conflict in Kashmir or in Sri Lanka. It is easy for a British source to choose to avoid the Irish question as too contentious to risk involvement. The case of Africa is different.

It can be argued that reconciliation with historic issues is not within the remit of a site, and this point of view is not unreasonable. What is more difficult to justify is the general exclusion of the issue of reconciliation with involvement in the slave trade that has been largely missing from the contemporary British scene for two hundred years.

Until very recently, the UK has been in a state that can best be described as 'in denial.' The author's experience at school in the

TABLE I. URLs Given at the Richardson Institute's Web-Site

Group of links	Number of such links
Institutes involved in Peace and Conflict Studies	19
Conflict Transformation and Peace-Building NGOs[1]	0
Links to Middle East Sites	158
Links to Central and Eastern European Sites	27
Links to Former Yugoslavia	69
Links to Africa	0
Links to Northern Ireland	3
International Organizations	13
Links on Global Warming and Conflict Prevention	17

(Source: Gonzalez and Khrychicov, 1999)
1. Non-Governmental Organisations

1950s and 60s is quite typical. The story of the Atlantic Slave Trade was presented thus:

- bad Englishmen set up a trade in slaves in order to support the operation of American plantations;
- they transported large numbers of people from Africa to North America;
- some good Englishmen campaigned long and hard against this evil trade, and eventually Good, in the form of the anti-slavery movement and in the person of William Wilberforce, triumphed over Evil, not personified by any Englishman and not associated with any particular English port.

No attempt was made to explain how Evil arose on such a scale in the first place, scant effort was expended in order to explore the economic impacts of slavery on Britain, and no one tried to understand how some ports became intimately involved with the trade while others, which might have been expected to follow the lead of Liverpool and Bristol, in fact, took no part in the activity.

The reality of a post-war Britain that became increasingly multicultural has finally started to heighten awareness of the reality of a shameful past with regard to the slave trade and Britain's involvement in it. This consciousness has manifested itself in a number of ways, notably:

- a major television series on Channel 4 with a supporting book written by Martin (1999) that is now widely available;
- a growing presence of material relating to slavery in at least some of the ports which were the bases of Britain's slave traders;
- most recently, Prime Minister Tony Blair's decision to override the objections of Home Secretary Jack Straw that there be a national recognition of Britain's involvement in the slave trade (Watson, 2000). A news agency (Reuters, 2000) subsequently reported that Blair was considering the idea, and that no decision had yet been made.

It is clearly not the case that Martin's book constitutes a pioneering work to deal with the subject of slavery in the United Kingdom, since it is pre-dated in particular by Hugh Thomas's (1998) seminal account and James Walvin's (1992) earlier study. However, it is the first to generate any degree of mass appeal.

The promotion of slavery as part of British heritage is also not new, given that William Wilberforce's house at Hull has been open to the public since 1906. Nevertheless, it is only very recently that the slavery movement, in contrast with the anti-slavery movement, has been presented, let alone promoted, as part of the United Kingdom's heritage.

THE DRIVERS OF SLAVERY HERITAGE IN THE UNITED KINGDOM

Involvement in the slave trade is clearly an activity which was geographically determined. Operational considerations–the presence of an active commercial fleet–provided an entry barrier which resulted in the number of participating cities being restricted. The three major participants were, in order of scale, Liverpool, London and Bristol. In terms of relative significance, it must be borne in mind that these three ports were of different magnitude. When size is brought into consideration, it becomes clear that small ports which were active are underestimated if this factor is ignored. Table 2 provides data which quantify the effect.

The final column, derived from the division of the second by the third, offers a simplistic indication of the relative significance of slavery to the cities concerned. It suggests that Liverpool and Bristol were clearly centers of the slave trade, while slavery was important to London, but only as one of its many sources of income. The figures in the last column should be treated with caution, however, as populations changed during the eighteenth century, the year 1801 being chosen only for the reason that it was the first occasion in which a

TABLE 2. Scale of Involvement of Different British Ports

	Slave Voyages 1700-1807 *Source: Liverpool Maritime Museum display*	Population in 1801 *Source:* Great Britain Census Office 1970	Slave voyages during the period per thousand population
Liverpool	5300	77,653	68.25
London	3100	958,863	3.23
Bristol	2200	40,814	53.90
Lancaster	130	24,942	5.21

census was conducted in Great Britain. With respect to Bristol, for example, Morgan (1996) records that it was the third largest city in England (after London and Norwich) at the start of the eighteenth century, but that it had fallen to sixth position by the end. The figure for Bristol is thus an "under-representation" of slavery's significance, while the Liverpool and London data are "over-representations" due to rising populations. Even allowing for these shortcomings, there is clear evidence that Bristol and Liverpool were in a league of their own when considering the impact of slavery on a port's economic success.

Commercial and, presumably, ethical considerations played a part in determining those ports which, although strongly active in other maritime areas, did not participate in slavery to any significant extent. Glasgow, Cardiff and Plymouth are in this minor participation category, but exactly why they were different from Liverpool, London or Bristol is beyond the scope of this paper.

A major variable of analysis is thus geographical. Within each location there is a variety of forms in which slavery heritage might or might not be promoted. These options include:

- exhibition events
- permanent exhibitions
- heritage trails
- publications

and constitute a related set of factors.

A final consideration is the perspective from which slavery heritage is currently presented. Approaches might range from denial, through admitting to participation in a remote (geographically and historically) event, to full acceptance of the negative impact of the involvement of African peoples, and complete recognition of the positive economic impact on the home port along with the broader effects on its development.

Before pursuing this last avenue of inquiry as a way of analyzing and evaluating contemporary presentations, it is necessary to investigate the underlying model or models used to understand slavery activity in its original historical context. The traditional model has been the familiar triangle showing a flow of goods. Figure 1 supplies an unusual variant on this representation, taken from an educational pack produced by Mersey Tourism.

Ignoring the surreal geographical perspective (perfectly valid for a subterranean, but rather less familiar than the normal avian view), the

FIGURE 1. Model of the Slave Trade

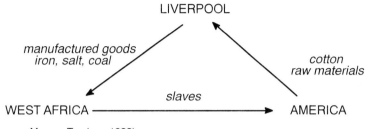

(Source: Mersey Tourism, 1999)

model is conventional, if rather lacking in detail. A more developed version, as published by Bristol Museums Service, is included in Table 3.

The increase in detail that the Bristol model offers in comparison to that of Liverpool results in a fuller picture. However, four basic problems inherent to the general model remain:

- each of the three legs is represented as essentially equal;
- no home port, and hence no commercial driver, is evident; commercial drivers must thus be assumed to exist equally in all three corners of the triangle;
- Africans are reduced to the level of a commodity and thus totally dehumanized;
- the flow represented is one of goods rather than of profits.

The last point makes no sense from an economic perspective. A model of trade should not in any case deal with a flow of goods. From a business studies perspective, the latter represents a supply chain, and is the domain of operations management specialists. A broader and more conventional business analysis would be to consider the benefits and costs to various stakeholders. Such a model would therefore be concerned with the profits rather than goods, as in Table 4.

By shifting the emphasis from goods to profits, a further improvement in the validity of such a model is evident–the triangle is no longer equilateral. Due emphasis is given to the British as both drivers of the trade and the major beneficiaries, and the role of the home port is seen as critical to the continuation of the trade.

TABLE 3. Products Associated with the Atlantic Slave Trade–Movement of Goods

	Liverpool (Mersey Tourism 1999)	Bristol (Bristol Museums and Art Gallery 1999)	Hull Source: Wilberforce House display
Outward passage	Manufactured goods; iron; salt; coal	Manufactured goods from Bristol (guns, textiles, alcohol and metalware) shipped to West Africa and sold or exchanged for human beings	Iron; firearms; spirits; cloth
Middle passage	Slaves	Enslaved Africans shipped and sold to supply labor for British plantation (sic) in the Caribbean and colonies in North America	Slaves
Homeward passage	Cotton; raw materials	Slave-produced commodities (sugar, rum, tobacco, cotton, cocoa and coffee) shipped to Bristol for refining and processing, and then sold on	Sugar; rum; tobacco; cotton

TABLE 4. Flow of Profits Associated with the Slave Trade

	British merchants (traders and/or manufacturers)	African traders	Plantation owners
Outward passage	✔	-	-
Middle passage	✔	✔	-
Homeward passage	✔	-	✔

A model of the slave trade should be based on profit flows, as Figure 2 illustrates in relation to the foregoing points.

The traditional flow of goods is represented by a flow of profits in the reverse direction and is shown by the white arrows. These profits accrued to land-based traders who sold their goods to those engaged in shipping. The latter–the slavers of the conventional view–made profits from buying from local manufacturers or, in the case of slaves, suppli-

FIGURE 2. Profits-Gained Model of Slave Trade

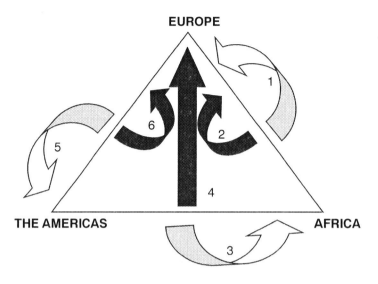

Key:
1 Profit to European manufacturer of sales of goods to European slave ship owner
2 Profit to European slave ship owner of sale of European goods to Africans
3 Profit to African slave trader of sales of slaves to European slave ship owner
4 Profit to European slave ship owner of sale of African slaves in America
5 Profit to American producer of sale of goods to European slave ship owner
6 Profit to European slave ship owner of sale of American goods in Europe

ers and then selling on the 'goods,' and did so from all three legs or passages of the trade. These profits are represented by the black arrows.

Two points in particular emerge from consideration of this model:

- the old equilateral model actually reflected profits made by land-based merchants rather than ship owners;
- Europe benefited doubly by the trade, with both manufacturers/suppliers and shippers gaining.

The raising of the level of sophistication in moving from the Liverpool to the Bristol model (Table 3) also highlights an area of exploitation not apparent in the former, that is, the use of slave labor to produce more cost-effective crops. However, the use of an economic basis for both models is significantly non-representational in one respect, since it takes no account of non-economic outcomes and, as a result, the human misery of enslavement and transportation is entirely overlooked, as is the appalling loss of life on the Middle Passage.

SLAVERY HERITAGE AS TOURISM

A preliminary review of the tourism products which have been developed around slavery heritage in the United Kingdom clearly shows their narrow geographical range in that they are limited to a handful of towns or cities. The range of products is also rather restricted:

- permanent exhibitions;
- temporary exhibitions;
- heritage trails with escorted walks;
- souvenir literature;
- education packs aimed at primary and secondary school markets, and reprinted posters and literature.

Of these products, all may be considered 'heritage,' but their identification as 'tourism' products varies. The heritage trails are certainly aimed at a tourist market, and the exhibitions are designed for both residents and outsiders. The souvenir literature is arguably incidental, in that visitors are not intended to be primary sales targets, although in reality they offer a significant source of sales through exhibitions and tourist offices.

CITY-BY-CITY SURVEY

Liverpool

Liverpool currently offers the largest display of slave heritage material in the United Kingdom. The Merseyside Maritime Museum has a major permanent exhibition on the history of the transatlantic slave trade. This exhibition is housed in the basement of the museum, which is located in a former bonded warehouse in the Albert Dock development. The latter additionally comprises a number of art and heritage organizations, including a museum dedicated to the Beatles, as well as several retail outlets aimed at the tourist market. It therefore attracts visitors with a range of interests in slavery heritage. The slavery exhibition shares the basement with a like-sized major exhibition on emigration, which is similar in concept and approach to the emigration display at Cobh, in the Republic of Ireland. The rest of the museum is dedicated more directly to shipping, especially the great liners of the early years of the twentieth century.

The display broadly covers the three legs of the triangular trade, although the principal emphasis is on Africa, the Middle Passage and plantations in the New World. The impact of slavery on Liverpool is represented mainly by the appearance of black people as sailors, servants or slaves. A single board among several hundred records a few examples of economic impact. The political impact is also evident, in that members of the Gladstone family, of whom the Victorian Prime Minister William Ewart Gladstone was the most famous, were Liverpool slave traders. The lead of Liverpool in the slave trade is explicitly stated in the museum's guide book. For example, the following excerpt states that:

> The main European countries involved in slaving were Portugal, Spain, France, the Netherlands and Britain. In Britain, it started in the 1640s, and up to about 1730 London and Bristol took the lead. Liverpool dominated the trade after 1750.
>
> *(Anon., 1999: 8)*

The scale of the exhibition is large. Included is a re-creation of the Middle Passage which is extensive enough for the visitor to move around without sensing the limits of the display and one which incorporates clever use of audio material.

The emphasis in the accompanying publications is on the black population of Liverpool, especially in the twentieth century. The issue of racist clashes is well-documented (e.g., Murphy, 1995), and several older texts, including contemporary accounts of Liverpool's active participation in the slave trade, have been republished. For instance, a 1985 reprint of the book *Liverpool and Slavery* by 'Dicky Sam' (1884) remains in print. The educational material on offer sets a broader context of the slave trade, covering all aspects thoroughly, with the economic impact being given a fair showing; certainly there is much more coverage of it here than in the museum displays.

A Slavery History Trail has been developed, and guided tours take place throughout the year, lasting on average about one and a half hours. A variety of impacts–social, economic and architectural–are noted in the course of these tours.

London

London's contribution to the marketing of slave heritage is conspicuous by its absence. There are no exhibitions, temporary or permanent, and no heritage trails. No publications specifically on London and the slave trade have been traced. Although Sue Webber of the Later London History and Collections of the Museum of London did kindly conduct a search of the Museum's computerised record system for the author, she was able to locate only two related items:

1. One 17th century cloth seal made of lead alloy, stamped with the arms of the Company of Royal Adventurers of England to Africa.
2. An 1807 medal stamped 'Abolition of the Slave Trade'; obverse showing a man in western-style dress shaking hands with a man in loin cloth and cape, with huts, dancers and men working in fields in the background.
                    (Personal E-mail communication, 23 December 1999)

For a city so deeply involved in the slave trade, and with such a significant minority of Caribbean and African origins with a desire to see their heritage recognized, this omission is quite amazing.

The National Maritime Museum at Greenwich, in the outer suburbs of London at Greenwich, does, it must be noted, have a display on the slave trade, but this is, as the museum's name indicates, not a London-specific exhibition, but a national one.

Bristol

Bristol has been promoting its connections with the slave trade on an active basis since 1997, when an exhibition was opened in the

Georgian House in Great George Street. This edifice, which is part of the city's museum infrastructure, was built around 1790 by John Pinney, a Bristol merchant who made his fortune from sugar plantations in the West Indies. The most recent displays contextualize the Pinney family's business activities in the Caribbean and set the slave trade in its broader social and economic settings.

The interest that these exhibits generated encouraged the Bristol City Museum and Art Gallery to arrange a series of events during the summer of 1999. From 6 March to 1 September of that year, a program of exhibitions, workshops and events was organized under the banner of *A Respectable Trade?* Although the focus of the program was the slave trade, a wide exposure to Caribbean culture was provided, and, to a lesser extent, to African culture. In particular there was a series of "community-led exhibitions on current issues relevant to African-Caribbean (sic) communities in the city" (Source: 'A Respectable Trade?' promotional leaflet).

The Georgian House is open to the public only during the months from April to October. Consequently, and in spite of all the progress in marketing slavery heritage that had been achieved, in the winter of 1999/2000 there were suddenly only the exhibits in the main Bristol Museum and Art Gallery on view. The latter were by then very few, since several had been removed for display elsewhere and were distributed round the museum. There was thus no coherent exhibition of slavery items available until the Spring of 2000.

However, a *permanent* display opened at the beginning of April 2000 in Bristol Industrial Museum. This museum is housed in a former warehouse on the waterfront in the old docks, a setting not unlike the Merseyside Maritime Museum. Other exhibits here emphasize both the social and the commercial history of Bristol, and future plans aim to enlarge the portrayal of the city's role in a variety of trades, both maritime and land-based. There are also items relating to Bristol's land and air transport history alongside the major display of maritime history.

The Museum and Art Gallery has been very active in publishing material on Bristol's role in the slave trade. Publications number almost a dozen and cover the direct involvement in the trade, its economic impact and the abolition movement, all from a local perspective. A teacher's guide to the *A Respectable Trade?* exhibition remains in print, and was designed to be used in developing classroom activities.

A slave trade trail has also been developed (Dresser et al., 1998), consisting of no less than forty-two points of call. It has attracted national press attention, which has helped to encourage both visitation and a general awareness of the issues (Rowe, 1999).

Other British Cities Which Engaged in the Slave Trade

It has not been possible to conduct a series of visits to all the British cities and towns which participated in the transatlantic slave trade. However, at least one has been identified which has publicly acknowledged its involvement–Lancaster. This recognition consists primarily of a small permanent exhibit in the city's museum, entitled *Black Ivory–A History of British Slavery*. The display of material culture is unusual in that it focuses sharply on the port's involvement, rather than the more usual Middle Passage emphasis. Exhibits relate to slaves who were brought to Lancaster, and the economic growth in Lancaster that was fueled by the profits of slavery is explored. There is no emphasis on any anti-slavery movement within the city.

The economic impact of slavery is more widely recognized in authors such as Andrew White (1992), who comments in a book which looks at the broad context of Lancaster's Georgian architecture that Lancaster was heavily involved in the slave trade. Melinda Elder's (1994) study of Lancaster's commitment to the slave trade is one of the few works available at Britain's slavery heritage centers that records the decline of the slave trade as being attributable to hostilities, outright war and economic conditions rather than to any impact of abolitionism.

Among other cities which display slavery artefacts in their museums, there is Glasgow (not a major port of slave trade activity). However, it should be noted that the majority of cities and towns which did have a small-scale involvement with the transatlantic slave trade (compared to Liverpool, London and Bristol) remain, at least in terms of what they display in their museums, in denial.

Hull

Hull enjoys a unique position in the United Kingdom, as a city which markets its slavery heritage from the particular perspective of being a center of the anti-slavery movement. Here it was that a major abolitionist, William Wilberforce, was born and was a local Member of Parliament for the early part of his political career. Hull was not in fact a participant in the slave trade because of its position as an East coast port with fishing and Baltic trade activities rather than Atlantic interests.

As well as a monument to William Wilberforce, Hull has opened the Wilberforce home to the public as a museum of social history (see Table 5). Originally opened as a museum in 1906, it was further restored in 1922 and 1950. The present arrangement of displays derives from 1983, the 150th Anniversary of both Wilberforce's death and emancipation under British rule. Iain Rutherford's (undated) account of the building's history gives a clear overview of the broader intentions of the museum. Within the display area it describes itself as "home to the city of Hull's social history collection," and the house thus contains exhibits which relate to slavery and others which do not.

The non-slavery displays may strike the student of slavery heritage as incongruous, but the attempt to link Wilberforce with a broader context of social history is effective for the average visitor if the positive comments in the museum's Visitors Book are accepted as evidence of their satisfaction.

At the time the author visited, patrons were greeted with two display boards. One noted that Hull is twinned with Freetown in the Gambia and that the Museum has active research links with the Na-

TABLE 5. Displays at Wilberforce House, Hull

Displays which focus on slavery	Displays which do not relate to slavery	Displays which link slavery with the broader social context
Display on the Atlantic slave trade Display on the anti-slavery movement centered on the life story of William Wilberforce Collection of anti-slavery memorabilia	Display of clay pipes, china and kitchen items in the original kitchen Display of dolls and toys Recreation of a Victorian parlor and a Victorian drawing room Restored Banquet Meeting Room Display of locally produced silverware Display of locally produced costumes	Recreation of two Georgian rooms as if Wilberforce were resident, including visitor-activated audio readings from his diary

tional Museum in Banjul, the capital of the Gambia. The other was sponsored by Jubilee 2000, the organization campaigning in the United Kingdom to have Third World debt cancelled, and pointed out that Hull was the first local authority to support Jubilee 2000. The visitor is thus introduced to the museum with a sense of contemporary social history that is largely absent in the exhibits of the slave trade ports.

The display on the anti-slavery movement stresses the role of Wilberforce, a reasonable enough emphasis in his original home. In spite of the evident attempts to give due credit to others in the movement, such as Granville Sharp and the Quakers, it is nevertheless made clear that William Wilberforce was drawn to the already-established Society for the Abolition of the Slave Trade because he was seen as a likely and useful supporter, being both a Member of Parliament and a recent convert to evangelical Christianity. Although throughout the display the movement is presented as much wider than a movement in which Wilberforce dominated, there is virtually no attempt to continue the story of the fight after 1833, the year of his death. The final panel in the slave trade display is all that is offered:

The Shadow of the Plantations

Britain congratulated herself for giving freedom to the slaves and turned her attention to her growing Empire in India and Africa. In the West Indies the plantations were in decline before Abolition and the land was overworked and overpopulated. Descendants of slaves migrated to America and Britain to escape poverty.

The evils of slavery did not end with Abolition. Colour and racial prejudice, built up by centuries of black slavery, is still with us today.

Such cursory acknowledgement of any problem after 1833 stands in stark contrast with the attempts at the entrance of the museum to give the exhibits a contemporary flavor.

The displays are not simply promoting a Wilberforce cult since there is criticism of his various political stances. He is taken to task, for example, over his lukewarm concern for the problems of the British poor, for his support of the 1815 Corn laws and for the harsh public order measures following the Peterloo Massacre.

Some points are made in panels that are not mentioned in the displays of the slave trade ports described above:

- It was not just the slave ports that were advantageous to Britain; specifically, Halifax's wool trade and West Midlands gunsmiths and cutlerers benefited.
- The trade was conducted in spite of heavy loss of life experienced by white traders and clerks stationed in Africa. A "slavers' rhyme" is quoted:

Beware and take care
of the Blight of Benin,
one comes out
and forty goes in.

- Plantation owners often became absentee owners by the second generation, building extensive mansions in Britain. Examples quoted are Harewood House in Leeds, built by the Lascelles, and an extensive town house in Bristol built by the Pinney family.

In spite of obvious attempts to present slavery heritage in a balanced and objective way throughout the displays, the eye is drawn on leaving the museum to a statue of Wilberforce, the caption of which concludes with the less-than-objective statement:

The World owes to him the Abolition of Slavery

The statue is not of recent origin and a generous interpretation might be that it allows today's visitor to reflect on the changed perception of the significance of Wilberforce within the Abolition Movement!

ANALYSIS AND CONCLUSIONS

The promotion of a heritage of which people are far from proud has been covered generically by authors such as Foley and Lennon (1997), who use the term "dark tourism." Tunbridge and Ashworth (1996) have drawn attention to such heritage under the label "dissonant heritage." This writer (Beech, 2000), too, has explored the problematic issues related to visiting a site of dissonant heritage, specifically a

Nazi concentration camp, by investigating the competing needs of very different types of patrons. Attendance at British slave trade sites and displays is a significantly less extreme example of this kind of visitation, and is at least once removed in comparison, since British sites (unlike their American counterparts, many of which have a highly developed tourism associated with them, and African sites, which are as yet largely undeveloped for tourism) did not witness the brutality and death that are associated with these two other corners of the triangle.

In the case of Buchenwald, this writer (Beech, 2000) has pointed out that there are two distinct types of visitors, those with personal associations with camps, often, but certainly far from exclusively, Jewish, with needs related to remembrance, and the general public, with needs relating to education. These differing expectations can be met to some extent by geographically distinct areas, but, in the main, both types intermix in the central areas of the visitor site. In the case of slavery heritage sites in the United Kingdom, the distinction between two types of visitor is less obvious in some respects, although more evident in one other, in that it is based on race. The two groups are white Britons, who, for the most part, are visitors in unconscious denial, or to put it more bluntly, in a state of ignorance, and black Britons, most born and brought up in Britain, who identify with the slaves and see them as part of their heritage. The white Britons, however, rarely identify with the slave traders.

Perhaps the most significant point about these initiatives to promote slavery heritage in Britain is that, with the exception of the abolitionist-centered example of Hull, none had made any significant attempt to do so until the last five years. The fact that they are now engaged in major efforts is therefore to be applauded. Even so, and on closer scrutiny, a number of important points need to be made. In particular it should be noted that:

- There is a lack of any concerted attempt by London to reflect on its slavery past. This significant omission is doubly extraordinary, first as a port which was the second most active participant in the slave trade (in terms of number of slave voyages), and second as the capital of a country on which the slave trade made a profound economic and social impact.
- The efforts of Liverpool and Bristol are to be commended, but, in the case of the former especially, more could be done to promote

the economic impact that slavery had, at both primary and secondary levels.

- Lancaster has demonstrated clearly that even the smaller participants can play a role in educating the British public about slavery.
- There is still the possibility for a memorial day, at present reported, but not widely received, to be under consideration by government.
- There is scope for a more physical manifestation to symbolize an acknowledgement of the evils perpetrated by earlier generations of Britons. In particular, there should be a greater awareness of the direct loss of life as well as loss of freedom that arose from the transatlantic slave trade. A perpetual flame in the capital city would not be inappropriate as such recognition.

As John Willis so helpfully pointed out at *The Plantations of the Mind* conference in Charleston, South Carolina, where the original version of this paper was delivered, in considering the presentation of slavery heritage in general and the slave trade in particular, it is necessary to address the question: 'Whose heritage is it anyway?' The displays in the United Kingdom are clearly positioned in a maritime context, as evidenced by both the two major ports which accept their legacy of slavery and the national attempt to address a slavery past (Hull being the only exception to this approach, presenting slavery in a social history context for very particular reasons). This "maritimization" of slavery leads to two uncomfortable conclusions:

1. It effectively defines slavery as essentially the slave *trade*, and thus locates it firmly in the past, something temporally distant which has only limited applications for present-day Britain.
2. It defines slavery as a *maritime* activity. Arguably, such accentuation is as insensitive as it is misleading. It is hard to imagine that any German recognition of the Holocaust would be placed in a railway museum simply on the basis that trains were used to transport victims to the concentration camps. "Maritimization" results in the defining of the slave trade as a subset of transport and is thus a process which places slavery in the mobile context of white heritage. Slavery is not statically defined from any kind of black perspective.

While major advances have undoubtedly been made in the presentation of slavery heritage in the United Kingdom in the last few years, it is clear that much still remains to be accomplished, and that most of what has been achieved could be done better. In particular, the longer term impacts of slavery need to be openly recognized, both the positive direct and indirect economic impacts on broad swathes of white British society and the negative impacts on the black Caribbean, American and British peoples.

REFERENCES

Anon. (1999). *Maritime Liverpool. The guide to Merseyside Maritime Museum, HM Customs and Excise Museum and the Museum of Liverpool Life.* Liverpool: Merseyside Maritime Museum.

Beech, J. (2000). The enigma of holocaust sites as tourist attractions. The case of Buchenwald. *Managing Leisure* 5(1): 29-41.

Bristol Museums and Art Gallery. (1999). *A respectable trade? Bristol and transatlantic slavery. A teacher's guide to the exhibition with extra information for use in the classroom.* Bristol: Bristol Museums and Art Gallery.

Dicky Sam. (1884). *Liverpool & slavery* (1985 reprint by Scouse Press). Liverpool: A. Bowker & Son.

Dresser, M., Jordan, C., and Taylor, D. (1998). *Slave trade trail around central Bristol.* Bristol: Bristol Museums and Art Gallery.

Elder, M. (1994). *Lancaster and the African slave trade.* Lancaster: Lancaster City Museums.

Foley, M. and Lennon, J. (1997). Dark tourism. An ethical dilemma. In M. Foley, J. Lennon and G. Maxwell (Eds.), *Hospitality, tourism and leisure management* (pp. 153-164). London: Cassell.

Gonzalez, G. and Khrychikov, S. (1999). *The Richardson Institute online links.* Available: http://www.lanks.ac.uk/users/richlinks/inst/index.htm [2000, 22 February 2000].

Great Britain Census Office. (1970). *1851 Census of Great Britain.* Shannon: Irish University Press.

Martin, S. (1999). *Britain's slave trade.* Basingstoke: Macmillan.

Mersey Tourism. (1999). *Tourism on Merseyside student information pack.* Liverpool: Mersey Tourism.

Morgan, K. (1996). The economic development of Bristol. In M. Dresser and P. Ollerenshaw (Eds.), *The making of modern Bristol.* Tiverton: Redcliffe.

Murphy, A. (1995). *From the empire to the Rialto. Racism and reaction in Liverpool 1918-1948.* Liverpool: Liver Press.

Reuters. (2000). Britain says considering commemoration of slaves, 3 March.

Rowe, M. (1999). A city faces up to its shady past. *The Independent on Sunday,* 12 December: 3.

Rutherford, I. (n.d.). *History of the Wilberforce House.* Hull: Hull City Museums and Art Galleries.

Thomas, H. (1998). *The slave trade. The history of the Atlantic slave trade 1440-1870*. London: Papermac.

Tunbridge, J. and Ashworth, G. (1996). *Dissonant heritage. The management of the past as a resource in conflict*. Chichester: Wiley.

UCAS. (1998). *UCAS handbook entry 1999*. Cheltenham: UCAS.

Walvin, J. (1992). *Black ivory*. London: Fontana.

Watson, R. (2000). Blair supports plan to remember slaves. *The Times*, 3 March.

White, A. (1992). *The buildings of Georgian Lancaster*. Lancaster: University of Lancaster Centre for North-West Regional Studies.

Sources of Slavery–
Destinations of Slavery:
The Silences and Disclosures
of Slavery Heritage in the UK and US

A. V. Seaton

SUMMARY. This study seeks to account for differences between the UK and US in including sites of black slavery as part of their heritage tourism and museum agenda. Both countries were heavily involved in the slave trade and both currently have immigrant communities with an appreciation of their origins. However, and unlike the American situation, it is only recently that Britain has opened the contentious issue of slavery to public gaze. In this regard, attention focuses specifically on the mounting of a pioneering Slave Exhibition at Liverpool's Maritime Museum and, by interviewing its chief curator, various insights are gained as to the potential and pitfalls of such a permanent display of an inglorious past. Further interpretation is added by references to the general literature on heritage tourism, the emerging context of "thanatourism" and the framework of a Force Field model that can usefully accommodate the competing interests of rival stakeholders. *[Article copies available for a fee from The Haworth Document Delivery Service: 1-800-342-9678. E-mail address: <getinfo@haworthpressinc.com> Website: <http://www.HaworthPress. com> © 2001 by The Haworth Press, Inc. All rights reserved.]*

KEYWORDS. Liverpool, slave exhibition, slavery heritage tourism in the UK and US, thanatourism, force field model

---

A.V. Seaton is affiliated with the International Tourism Research Institute, Luton Business School, Putteridge Bury, Hitchin Rd, Luton.

[Haworth co-indexing entry note]: "Sources of Slavery–Destinations of Slavery: The Silences and Disclosures of Slavery Heritage in the UK and US." Seaton, A. V. Co-published simultaneously in *International Journal of Hospitality & Tourism Administration* (The Haworth Hospitality Press, an imprint of The Haworth Press, Inc.) Vol. 2, No. 3/4, 2001, pp. 107-129; and: *Slavery, Contested Heritage and Thanatourism* (ed: Graham M. S. Dann and A. V. Seaton), The Haworth Hospitality Press, an imprint of The Haworth Press, Inc., 2001, pp. 107-129. Single or multiple copies of this article are available for a fee from The Haworth Document Delivery Service [1-800-342-9678, 9:00 a.m. - 5:00 p.m. (EST). E-mail address: getinfo@haworthpressinc.com].

INTRODUCTION

In November 1999, the UK's Channel 4 television for the first time broke a silence that had pervaded the electronic media for 50 years–in its coverage of the extent and scale of British involvement in the slave trade during the 18th century. Over four weekly episodes of this new series documented the critical role that slavery had played in the economic development of five cities and the foundations it had laid for the fortunes of several individual families whose lineage extends to the present day. The program, and the book which accompanied it, breached a lacuna in popular culture that paralleled the temporal abyss which had existed in UK museum and heritage culture until only seven years ago in 1994 when the Maritime Museum in Liverpool had mounted the first major permanent exhibition to narrate the history of the British slave trade. Needless to say, the TV program makers extensively consulted with the museum staff in making their series.

This situation contrasts with the United States, where slavery had been on the heritage tourism and museum agenda for some years, and wider aspects of black cultural issues had featured for much longer (Austin, 1982; Dickerson, 1988; Ruffins, 1992). Why, then, the differences in the scale and pace of development in the two countries? Why were the slavery sites in the US more developed touristically than heritage in UK cities that had provided the economic foundations for the development of slavery? Though the focus of the slave trade was on the plantations of America and the West Indies, much of this trade was financed, managed and controlled from Britain. Records are available of this involvement so that, at face value, it would seem to have offered an obvious subject for heritage development as part of the burgeoning trend to animate social and economic history, particularly industrial heritage at the local and national levels, as a tourist attraction. In Britain, as in the US, there is a large minority population of blacks that could be interested in the story, as well as many non-blacks in the general population. But it is only very recently, and then in just a few places, that museum and heritage development has begun to engage with this particular element in British urban, economic and national history.

This study, which has been prepared with the assistance of the Slave Museum by means of an interview with its chief curator, Mr. Tony Tibbles, explores the differential status of slavery as a heritage theme in the two countries, and attempts to offer explanations as to why it exists. It indicates the extent of Britain's involvement in the slave trade, and the current levels of heritage development focused on it, with particular reference to the pioneering slave exhibition in the Maritime Museum, Liverpool. Drawing on concepts and critical perspectives from the literature of heritage and thanatourism, the analysis highlights a number of issues that affect differences between the UK and US. It concludes with a model of heritage development as a "Force Field," structured, over time, by the varied interests and power resources of four main groups.

BRITAIN'S INVOLVEMENT IN THE SLAVE TRADE

Until the last decade, and for most people in the UK, perceptions of Britain's relationship to slavery were mainly directed, in as far as they occupied the public consciousness at all, to the role of social reformers, particularly that of William Wilberforce, in the campaign for abolition. The William Wilberforce Trust in Hull (see article by Beech in this volume) was the only heritage attraction that dwelt on slavery, and its dominant remit had been to narrate the drama of reform, rather than that of slavery's economic and social importance to Britain's industrial wealth from the seventeenth century onwards. The absence of heritage development was maintained through the 1970s, 1980s and early 1990s, the period of government encouragement of the service sector and tourism. The heritage industry expanded, particularly industrial heritage, as traditional industries such as shipbuilding, mining and manufacturing contracted or disappeared as going concerns to be metamorphosed as museums, exhibitions and theme parks (Hewison, 1987). Yet, in spite of all this growth, slavery did not feature in this blossoming of economic and social history.

Slavery could claim to be a key contender for portrayal within industrial heritage development since it had played such a vital role in Britain's economic history, particularly in London and the west. The main coastal cities that faced west including Bristol (Richardson, 1986-1990), Liverpool, Glasgow, Whitehaven, Lancaster, Chester and even Lyme Regis (Thomas, 1997; Tattersfield, 1996) were involved to a greater or lesser extent in the slave trade which provided the basis for much of their wealth in the 18th and early 19th centuries.

Historical data highlight the quantitative extent of the British slave industry, as well as qualitative evidence of participation. The Royal African Company, set up with a royal warrant from Charles II in 1672, was responsible for the shipping of some 90,000 slaves by 1689. In 1712, the South Sea Company was founded, and its shareholders included Queen Anne and her successor, George I. By 1720, the social roll-call of membership included a substantial number of Britain's ruling elites, as Hugh Thomas's litany forcefully indicates:

> Subscription in 1720 reads like a directory of contemporary Britain. Most of the House of Commons (462 members) and 100 members of the House of Lords (out of its total of 200) were included. So were Alexander Pope, Sir John Vanbrugh, John Gay, and all the Royal Family, including the bastards. The Speaker of the House of Commons, Black Rod in the House of Lords, and Lord Chancellor were all on the list. The Swiss canton of Berne had a large holding of South Sea stock. So had King's College Cambridge, and Lady Mary Wortley Montagu. (Thomas, 1997: 241)

Thomas (1997: 805) leaves open the question as to whether all knew what the South Sea traded in, but comments that, in the UK, more than any other country in the world except Portugal, it certainly didn't need great imagination to guess. Between 1715 and 1731, the South Sea Company sold 64,000 slaves and, in 1720, had 150 ships involved in the business. Between 1721 and 1730, Britain carried over 100,000 slaves to America. In the 1730s, British ships took approximately 170,000 slaves to America, Jamaica, Cuba and the Caribbean colonies (Thomas, 1997: 241, 244, 246). By 1775, there were 331,000 blacks in British North America, 190,000 in Jamaica and 60,000 in Barbados (Walvin, 1996: 9). In total, Britain may have been responsible for transporting up to 2,600,000 slaves.

After the early supremacy of London and Bristol and, to a more limited extent, Glasgow, from the mid-eighteenth century, Liverpool became the dominant slave port:

> Huge fortunes, which would later become the building blocks of banks and manufacturing interests had their origins in the Liverpool slave trade. (Martin, 1999: 55)

Direct involvement in Liverpool included the Heywood Brothers who founded the Heywood Bank, later absorbed by St Martins, and then, Barclays Bank. Leyland was another Liverpool bank involved. There were also slave auctions in Whitehaven, Chester, Dartmouth and, as Tattersfield has recently illuminated, in the genteel, Jane Austen resort town of Lyme Regis.

The stereotypical view of the trade in English mythology has always been that of entrepreneurial villains financing ships that directly bore slaves from Africa to the New World. However, the reality was different and more pervasive. Since the financing of a slave ship cost £10,000-£20,000, few were underwritten by single individuals. They tended to be joint speculations by consortia of venture capitalists, each of which would have had small amounts invested in several vessels. But slavery was not their only business. In fact, it often represented just one investment, not necessarily the largest, alongside others. Slavery interests were thus only one element in a portfolio managed by investment capitalists who saw themselves as entrepreneurs rather than as slave owners (Hancock, 1989).

Moreover, benefiting from the slave trade did not just consist of direct involvement by groups of proprietors and/or speculators. There were more indirect forms of association. First, there was the economic interdependency factor, whereby some British goods were exported and used to barter for slaves, and were conveyed to Africa on the same ships that subsequently transported that human cargo to America and the West Indies. These goods included guns, other weaponry and, particularly, textiles. Second, indirect involvement could come from being the beneficiary of slave profits, in ways that created tainted national legacies. Slave exploitation financed great country houses, art collections and libraries that were regarded, then and later, as jewels of Britain's cultural patrimony. In short, slavery was not just a limited circuit of cruel exploitation, but a widely dispersed network of interlocking economic, social and cultural relationships which profoundly influenced the evolution and shape of British society (Tibbles, 1994b). What prevented the history of this major industrial phenomenon being packaged as heritage in the same way that, between the 1970s and 1990s, other industries of the past (mining, shipbuilding, the Industrial Revolution itself) became the subject of exhibitions? Before trying to answer that question, it is first necessary to examine the slave heritage situation in the US.

SLAVE HERITAGE ATTRACTIONS
IN US AND BRITAIN
1950-1990s

Slave Heritage in the US

The course of slavery in US history, culminating in the Civil War, and its subsequent abolition, is too well known to require additional comment. Instead, attention here focuses on its legacy in Afro-American heritage development.

A recent study by Crew (1996) dates the portrayal of Afro-American history and culture in museums and exhibitions to the first two decades after World War II. These displays were largely regional initiatives pioneered by small groups in specific cities that included the Elma Lewis School for the Arts in Boston (1950), the San Francisco Negro Historical and Cultural Association (1956), and the Ebony Museum of Negro Culture, Chicago (1961). Such ventures multiplied through the 1960s but made little impact upon national museum and heritage agenda. By the end of the 1960s, the United States had entered upon a period of political activism which led to a defining moment in American museology–a black protest at the annual meeting of the Association of American Museums in 1970:

> Activists disrupted the conference by questioning the relevancy (sic) of work done by those museums. They felt the activities of these museums often ignored a very large segment of their constituency and the issues of significance to them. The protesters demanded that museums of all types pay greater heed to the communities in which they existed and the challenges inherent to these areas. (Crew, 1996: 85)

The Smithsonian Institution responded in the early 1970s with two exhibitions that not only celebrated African American issues, but did so with the collaboration of black advisors and managers. In 1978 the African American Museums Association was formed.

However, none of these developments focused specifically on slavery. The watershed event on this issue occurred in 1979 at the flagship heritage town of Colonial Williamsburg, Virginia's capital from 1699 to 1780. Prior to 1979, Williamsburg had been presented as a settlement with no black presence, despite the fact that 52 per cent of its population in the 18th century had been black. The role of slavery in that city's history was brought on stage, almost literally, when the management group in Williamsburg invited administrators and faculty at what was then the Hampton Institute, now Hampton University (a black university), to assist in revising the narrative and making black participation a central element of its enactment. The story of the problems, controversy and final success of this venture has been well-documented (Martin, 1984; Matthews, 2000).

In the decade that followed the Williamsburg re-launch, Afro-American issues played a larger part in the cultural life of the nation. In 1988, at the Valentine Museum Richmond, the Richmond African American community mounted two exhibitions on slavery in successive years: in 1988 "In bondage and freedom: Antebellum black life in Richmond," and in 1989, "Jim Crow and reaction in the New South." Both of these displays embraced the emerging practice of active involvement of black groups in delivering their own heritage (Crew, 1996: 89).

By 1994, the American Visions study of black heritage in the US, a book almost 600 pages long, included more than 40 attractions with slavery associations in the South, excluding those of the Civil War (Chase, 1994). They comprised plantations, museums, commemorative sites, battlefields involving black combatants, cemeteries and slave market sites.

Black Heritage and Slavery in the UK

The US was ten years ahead of British slave heritage. Apart from the previously mentioned Wilberforce Trust in Hull, a traditional museum that had existed since the turn of the century and had mainly highlighted abolition history, there had been no major museum or heritage development focused on slavery, except as an element of other narratives.

The breakthrough came in 1994 with the establishment of a permanent Slavery Exhibition in Liverpool. Like the Williamsburg site, it was a modification of an existing heritage attraction–the Maritime Museum–which had been in existence since the turn of the century, and had previously featured slavery as a minor element in a discourse about the port of Liverpool's development which came to be recognized as inadequate (Tibbles, 1996). The initiative to produce a more comprehensive alternative came in 1991 from the head of a private charity, The Peter Moores' Foundation, a philanthropic endowment by a member of a family which had made its fortune in football pools. Peter Moores had become aware of British ignorance about slavery from his travels to Barbados and approached the Maritime Museum with a proposal to part fund a permanent exhibition. As in Williamsburg, the planned development attracted initial controversy and suspicion, particularly from black groups in Liverpool and, as in the US, a wide process of consultation and involvement with them took place that was facilitated by the appointment of a special outreach manager with responsibility for community participation and relations.

The exhibition opened in 1994 in the basement of a four storey building on the Albert Dock, itself a recent heritage development utilizing early Victorian buildings as an office, retail and leisure complex. The exhibition, which is one of seven permanent displays, is called "Transatlantic Slavery: Against Human Dignity." It comprises artifacts, graphic materials and a walk-through Middle Passage experience. The main narrative tells the story of slavery as an unholy, tripartite conjunction of European capital, African labor and American land. One of its aims is to dispel the racist imaging of history that, prior to the slave trade, blacks were childlike, intellectually primitive and incapable of grasping conceptual issues (Cummins, 1996: 93-94). The exhibition addresses the issue that calling people "slaves" collectivizes them in a way that strips them of any individual features or culture. As the curator later explained:

> One of the main intentions was to get across the point that Africa should not be portrayed only as a place where Europeans got "slaves." To remind visitors that Africa . . . had a diversity of states, societies and cultures. (Tibbles, 1996: 98)

To meet this objective the program notes emphasized the differentiated origins of slaves:

> To refer to the Africans who were enslaved only as "slaves" strips them of their identity. They were, for instance, farmers, merchants, priests, soldiers, goldsmiths, musicians. They were husbands and wives, fathers and mothers, sons and daughters. They could be Yoruba, Igbo, Akan, Kongolese. (Tibbles, 1994a: Program notes)

As part of the attempt to reconstruct the cultural variety of slave populations, the museum devotes considerable effort to presenting artifacts of African cultures, and to general issues of representation and naming (Small, 1994). In apportioning responsibility the museum narrative identifies local figures and families, local and national commercial organizations including banks, and also named families with historic houses who established themselves on slave profits. The Slavery Museum exposes these networks of exploitative privilege by identifying beneficiaries such as All Souls Oxford, the textile industry and the arts in Britain, and by drawing attention to fashions, such as a predilection for mahogany furniture, that was almost entirely supported by slave labor in Brazil (Tibbles, 1994b).

The museum attracts 250,000 visitors per year, of whom 59 per cent are from the surrounding area. The slavery exhibition is the second most popular exhibition after the Customs and Excise display. It has increased black visitors from 1 per cent to 4 per cent of the total, still a disappointing proportion. The museum has been a public success, focusing international and national media coverage, stimulating debate about the issues (Small, 1997), and attracting VIP visitors, including the Minister of Culture for Senegal. Educational programs have been developed and the museum hosts an annual slavery seminar for final year high school students. The exhibition's success has also allowed the museum to extend its remit from purely maritime matters to other questions of race and culture. In 2000, it hosted a rotating exhibition on the history of Jamaican music, *Reggae Explosion*, which was also shown in Birmingham and Bristol. The museum has additionally influenced museum agendas elsewhere, acting as a stimulus to slavery heritage in other cities. Bristol mounted its own six-month exhibition in 1999, which doubled its normal attendance figures. It now operates a slave trail that is supported with a well-designed 28-page booklet that comprises 42 slave-related sites in the city. The trail deploys a number of the strategies of the Liverpool exhibition through the use of its program notes that offer a radical rewriting of heritage at some of the city's existing monuments, buildings, and commercial and charitable institutions. It records participation in slavery by religious groups including the Quakers, banks (National Westminster, philanthropists such as Edward Colston and Thomas Daniel, whose monument is in Bristol Cathedral). The trail also reveals the slavery profits that financed a number of the city's most famous architectural features and heritage buildings: Queen's Square, the Theatre Royal, King Street, the Corn Exchange and Tailor's Court House. In addition, the trail relates aspects of the abolitionist narrative at sites associated with key figures in the reform movement: Thomas Clarkson, Hannah More and Mary Anne Schimmelpenninck (Anon, 1999).

The Maritime Museum at Greenwich has introduced a slavery section to its "Trade and Empire" exhibition, a major new development that attracted criticism. The Liverpool exhibition has also stimulated overseas work. In 2002 the Mariner's Museum, Virginia, is to mount a Transatlantic Slavery Exhibition based on the Liverpool one but with new materials. It may tour the US (Tibbles, 2000). Nevertheless, these initiatives are still restricted to a few places in the UK, and they are not representative of all heritage efforts. In one of the smaller slave ports, Whitehaven, a new "rum trail" is to be opened that has so far not included engagement with slavery as part of its narrative (Robinson, 2000).

SLAVE HERITAGE IN AMERICA AND BRITAIN: WHY THE DIFFERENCES?

The discussion so far indicates differences in the timing and spread of American developments, compared to those in Britain. How should they be explained?

The Problem of Physical Evidence

Economic history is inherently difficult to animate since, as Marx would have been the first to emphasize, it operates back-stage where issues of ownership and control are decided, and such processes are difficult to present as museum theater. What passes for economic history, in heritage presentations has often been the front-stage recovery of industrial sites and buildings, or the hardware of industry transacted in them. An example of the former is New Lanark, a world heritage site in Scotland featuring the restoration of the model mills managed by Robert Owen; of the latter there is Beamish Open Air Museum, an outdoor site which exhibits a comprehensive catalog of industrial artifacts, re-constructions of the working environment in which they were used and simulations of the everyday social life of the workers. These efforts have occasionally been censored for offering a

"Disneyfied" kind of techno-nostalgia in which the historical relationships of production have been lost or suppressed under the prettified quaintness of mechanical verisimilitude and sanitized heritage theater. The temptations of artifacts in heritage exactly parallel those of costume Barthes identified in dramaturgical representations of history:

> It should be recalled that there are two kinds of history: an intelligent history which rediscovers the profound tensions, the specific conflicts of the past; and a superficial history which mechanically reconstructs certain anecdotic details; costume has long been a favourite realm for the exercise of this latter history. (Barthes, 1972: 42)

Even techno-nostalgia is an excluded option with slavery heritage, since slavery, compared with other industries, had no extensive paraphernalia of production. There are generally few equivalents to the nostalgia-producing engines, extractive gadgets, looms, frames, winding gear, transport forms and archaic instruments, that charm and seduce in other kinds of industrial reconstruction, although, admittedly, in Charleston some attempt has been made to narrate the technical history of cotton processing, and in Barbados that of sugar production. One of the sinister and poignant features of slavery is that it is a phantom industry that leaves scant traces; its capital lies in people, long since dead, not machinery.

America was almost as constricted by this absence of physical evidence as the UK, except in one key respect. There were physical locations that had been associated with slavery, most notably plantation houses and estates, but also sites of slave markets, battles and memorials involving slaves. However, even plantations and other locations are polysemic signs, capable of many different interpretations, unless they are scripted, coded and marked to anchor meanings to slavery. One of the major issues, perhaps the key one in plantation heritage discussions, is the question of scripting of slavery in order to ground the significance of buildings and landscape. Where there is an absence of such textualizing, it can be seen as suppression by omission, since audiences lacking historical perspectives may be unable to make those connections for themselves.

In the UK, there are few important locations which signify in this way. Not one eighteenth century dock remains, an omission that frustrated the media eager for a photo opportunity at the time of the opening of the museum in Liverpool (Tibbles, 2000). One of the problems of establishing the Slavery Museum was therefore finding artifacts. Many of those selected for display have no intrinsic association with slavery (e.g., African works of art, Benin jewelry, maps, guns, paintings and engravings), but were included to contextualize the culture of Africa from which slaves came. In short, the absence of physical evidence is more acute than in the US and may be seen as one inhibitor of slavery heritage development.

The Differences in the Number and Patterns of Black Settlement in the US and UK

The second major difference is that of the size of ethnic minority populations, and therefore their influence in the US and UK. As Tibbles (2000) observes, 'minorities in the past have tended not to be represented in museums.' The likelihood of minority representation increases as the size of the minority increases. In Britain there are over 3 million black people, making up 5.5 per cent of the population. In England the black population is 6.5 per cent, and in London it is 20 per cent. However, over half of these populations are Indian and Pakistani rather than Afro-Caribbean (Owen, 1992-1995). Moreover, as the Channel Four program demonstrated, even those Afro-Caribbean people in the UK and ex-colonies may not be aware of their slave roots. Hence the question of Afro-Caribbean representation in slavery is less of an issue in Britain than in the US.

In the United States the non-white ethnic population is greater, and the Afro-Caribbean population both as a proportion of the population (up to 70 per cent in parts of some cities like Washington), and in absolute numbers is much greater than in the United Kingdom. Thus the dimensions of excluded history would be greater if slavery were not a heritage issue. The audience factor raises the question as to whether heritage developments should be determined by financial considerations, put in place either to maximize tourism revenue, or to placate minority opinion when a historical conflict achieves sufficient pull on collective memory to generate demands for some kind of historical memorial. In the UK neither kind of market force has yet exerted a big enough drawing power to expand slavery as a form of tourism heritage. The developments have all been initiated by well-intended heritage planners and policy makers, rather than significant lobbies in the black population.

Moreover, there may be socio-demographic factors that differentiate the UK and US in heritage terms. In both countries it is known (Seaton, 1992, 1999; TIAA, 1997) that the main market for heritage and cultural tourism comprises educated, relatively affluent, middle-class groups. There are many more middle-class black people in the US than in the UK, and their concentration in some cities, such as Washington, has already impacted upon culture and heritage planning, through, for example, the initiatives within Smithsonian museums to create black cultural trails and heritage exhibitions.

History also discloses not simply differences in numbers, but different patterns of Afro-Caribbean settlement in the US and UK, and thus the relationship of black people to slavery. In the US, although black immigration has continued in the twentieth century, the main Afro-Caribbean population was originally formed through direct descent from slave enclaves created from the late seventeenth to the nineteenth centuries. In Britain there were two distinct patterns of settlement. The first, comparable to the American situation, consisted of enforced settlements of black slaves in the eighteenth century, but it involved much smaller numbers of people when contrasted with the industrialized scale of slave immigration in America. Since Thomas (1997) estimates that only about 200,000 slaves were brought to Europe, there are consequently very few black people in the UK who are descended directly from slaves introduced to Britain in this first period. Moreover, those who did arrive worked mainly as domestic servants, rather than as agricultural and industrial laborers, and often enjoyed conditions less punitive than those experienced in the American or West Indian plantations. It was the second settlement that brought the majority of the black Afro-Caribbean population to the UK in the 1950s and after. They came by choice as British citizens through subject membership of the Empire. This wave of immigration took place mainly from the 1950s (van Helmond and Palmer, 1991; Fryer, 1984). It does not mean that the new arrivals did not have slave origins in the West Indies before reaching Britain, rather that they might have been unaware of them. Indeed, even if they were so aware, many did not consider such origins as a defining factor for their presence in Britain.

The Role of Slavery in Official Versions of National History

The third major difference is the structural role of slavery in the history of the two countries. The modern American state was created out of the trauma of the Civil War, whose antagonists were polarized on the question of slavery. There is no way of avoiding the issue for any coherent version of history. The surprising thing may be that, with this structural break in its history, so little was done for 100 years to animate and explore the issues that had created the nation.

In Britain there was no comparable event or watershed to give slavery a similar historical significance. The zenith of Britain's imperial power was after the abolition of slavery, so that the story of the Empire can, and certainly has been, told without significant attention to slavery, except for a positive narrative about Britain's role in its abolition in 1833. Indeed, by doing away with slavery before America, Britain was even able to claim a moral high ground that formed part of the Victorian mythology of an ethical empire.

The contrasting relationship between official history and slavery in the US and UK means that the legacies of slavery in the two countries are very different. Slavery, though a discomforting inheritance in the US (particularly in the south), is nevertheless acknowledged as an undeniable fact. This realization makes it a safer subject in the US, since it is a recognized landscape whose transformation can be positioned as part of progressive history, a source of pride for American citizens, though probably more easily so for those in the north than in the south. In the official history of America the triumph over slavery and the evolution of a "land of the free" are central to the grand narrative of national development.

In the UK, by contrast, the true dimensions of the slave trade and Britain's part in managing it have never been emphasized in standard historical texts, and there has been no public awareness coming to terms with its effects. Because Britain was so far removed from the physical locations of slave trafficking, it was possible for entrepreneurs, and indeed whole geographical communities in London and on the west coast, to benefit economically, without having to have first hand contact with the mechanisms of oppression that produced their wealth. In the novels of Jane Austen and other nineteenth century writers, the shadowy fortunes that lie behind characters who have prospered through interest in the colonies are rarely explicitly linked to slavery. Moreover, while the American Civil War ruined many southern families who derived their wealth from slavery, in the UK the corresponding economic and social legacies continue. As pointed out earlier, the direct and indirect beneficiaries of slavery included families and institutions that still exist today.

The result is that Britain's involvement in slavery has not been a subject for heritage development since it may have been seen to have more potentially socially and politically divisive results than in the US, where slavery forms an essential part of mainstream historical narrative. In Britain, one of the consequences of slavery heritage development might, ironically, be to subvert, or reposition one existing kind of heritage attraction that has been a central feature of British tourism–the country house. Not just the manor itself, but the great painting collection, the famous library, and the "men of taste" associated with it, once revealed to have been built upon "real foundations" of slavery, would inevitably be looked at in a different way by visitors. Harewood House and Font Hill in Wiltshire, associated with the notorious dilettante author William Beckford, are two examples of heritage built on the huge family fortunes made through slavery. In developing the Slavery Museum in Liverpool, the promoters encountered some resistance when trying to obtain photographs of a location with a slavery background. The attribution of slavery associations inevitably changes perceptions of families, places and history.

Slavery as Thanatourism and Dissonant Heritage

Many of the issues raised by slavery heritage are common to a whole category of heritage that has been variously described as "dark tourism" (Foley and Lennon, 1996; Lennon and Foley, 2000), "thanatourism" (Seaton, 1996, 1999) and "dissonant heritage" (Tunbridge and Ashworth, 1996). Its related attractions are ones that have in the past been associated with crime, violence, disaster and death, many involving questions of historical guilt and blame that resonate down to the present (see articles by Beech, Dann and Potter, Dann and Seaton, and Eskew in this volume).

Ashworth (1991, 1999) has noted that all heritage development is a form of appropriation in the sense that it is always owned and staged by someone about some subjects, which means that it inevitably excludes or marginalizes others. Heritage attractions, through their design, exhibits, scripting and performative features, offer *a preferred view of history* that suppresses, marginalizes or minimizes alternative versions. Moreover, the development of heritage sites always involves not just issues of what actually happened in the past, but the relations of people in the present to them. Just because something is a historical event does not mean that contemporary communities, who had played no part in it, want to see it celebrated or memorialized. Nor does it imply that the audiences, to whom any heritage development must appeal in order to be sustainable, will be attracted.

Dark tourism embodies the dilemmas inherent in all heritage development to an extreme degree. It raises difficult questions: the extent to which historical crimes and disasters of the past should be perpetuated through memorials and heritage presentations in the present; for whom they should be perpetuated; for what reasons; and with what consequences? Dark tourism may open new, or intensify old sores, create divisions within geographic communities and have unexpected consequences. One unintended outcome may even be litigation, as has already happened with historically oppressed minorities in the US (Native Americans), in Australia (the Aborigines) and New Zealand (the Maoris). It is not inconceivable that, if the fate of specific African families and tribes could be exactly documented from capture to enslavement, and those responsible individually or collectively identified, that similar claims for damages or compensation could be made by their Afro-Caribbean descendants.

These issues render certain kinds of thanatourism in general, and slavery heritage in particular, a sensitive and problematic area to develop. In both Williamsburg and Liverpool there was controversy at the outset that was negotiated through prolonged and intensive consultation with ethnic groups. In Liverpool the match funding necessary to complement the Moores' donation that stimulated the development was difficult to raise from other sponsors. In North Carolina the plantation at Somerset Place has been censored in a black heritage guide for its failure to engage with slavery in offering 'an interpretive framework . . . oriented toward "the Great Family" and the Great House'(Chase, 1994: 119). When the Maritime Museum in Greenwich launched a slavery section, as part of its Empire Exhibition, there were angry letters in the press from people claiming that it was opening up historical wounds that had no place in the present.

The Heritage Force Field

One way to engage with the kind of cross currents just described is to conceptualize heritage development, following Ashworth and Tunbridge (1996), as a site of different collective interests that may be convergent, divergent or a mixture of both. These concerns may not be equally weighted, since some groups may have more power to influence events than others. Moreover, the interests may not be static, but change over time, and so too may the balance of power among the various factions. This perspective can be modeled by representing heritage as the product of a "force field" in which four distinct groups potentially operate within a milieu of power over time: the *subjects* of heritage or their representatives; the *owners* and *controllers* of heritage; the *spatial host communities* of heritage development; and the *audiences* (see Figure 1).

FIGURE 1. The Heritage Force Field

Owners/Controllers • Goals/interests of institution? • Goals/interests of financial backers? • Goals/interests of animators–researchers, creatives, etc.? • Other groups/interests (e.g., governmental)?	**POWER** **and** **TIME**	*Host Community* • Their relationship to heritage narrative and subject groups, and to owners/controllers? • Their participation in, and benefit from, heritage development? • Their acceptance of visitor numbers?
POWER **and** **TIME**	**HERITAGE** **DEVELOPMENT**	**POWER** **and** **TIME**
Subject Groups • Their benefit from narrative? • Degree of participation? (Whose story? Whose blame? Whose heroic narrative? Whose exclusions/silences?)	**POWER** **and** **TIME**	*Visitor Groups* • Their relationship to subject narratives/ silenced narratives? • Their relationships to, and with, subjects, owners/controllers, and host communities? • Their tastes–aesthetic, historical, etc.?

Some brief comments may be made about Figure 1.

The Owners/Controllers: These are the often institutional agents behind a heritage development. They fulfill an allocative and operational function, even though the two roles may not necessarily be separated. If they are divided, then the allocative controllers are financial backers and the operational controllers comprise managers and any support specialists whom they may employ to research, design, build and furnish the attraction. In some instances the allocative and operational controllers may have, or develop, different objectives and thus constitute two, rather than one, group within the force field.

The Subject Groups: These are the subjects about whom the heritage narrative is told. Exactly how they are constructed within heritage narratives will depend upon their involvement and participation. They may be represented or misrepresented (from their own perspectives) not just by what is included, but through silences.

Host Communities: These are residents located near heritage sites. Like the subjects of heritage, they are most likely to approve an attraction if they have been involved in its development, if they approve of the subject groups and narratives within it, and are willing to accept its visitors.

Visitor Groups: Virtually all heritage sites, those related to thanatourism as well as others, must command a market, since even the most publicly subsidized attraction comes under fire if it is seen to have too few visitors. The market holds permanent power to shape heritage and attraction development, that is often ignored in the more puritanical critiques voiced by custodians of "authenticity," opposed to any form of popular translations of heritage stories.

The interests and goals of the four groups may produce a wide permutation of different relations and alignments, ranging from harmony through common interests, to hostility through unresolved conflicts of interest that may lead to contestation or opposition to a heritage development, or even spoliation, once it is in place. The least contentious kind of heritage is one where the allocative/operational controlling group behind the development is itself the sole subject of the narrative, is staging it within its own spatial community, and expects its main visitors to be from the surrounding area (a small local museum, established by voluntary effort within a village, would be a good example). The most contentious heritage is that where the allocative/operational controllers are unilaterally representing subordinated groups, in localities not their own, and framing narratives that do not reflect the subjects' views of themselves (a military exhibition by an invader in an occupied country, depicting the indigenous population in derogatory ways, would be an example). Between these two extremes there is an infinite number of permutations of interaction within the Force Field.

The model suggests how conflict may not simply arise from discrepancy between subjects and controllers, but also between communities and controllers. The location of a slavery museum might, for instance, be perfectly acceptable in some places but resisted elsewhere. In Washington, for example, although the idea of a Holocaust Museum was supported by both Jewish audiences and backers, questions were raised by other groups as to why it should be in the US capital as part of the Smithsonian complex. Ashworth (1999) has reported objections to Holocaust sites in Poland where currently nearby residents are post-war immigrants who had played no part in the wartime persecution of Jews, and resent having it memorialized in their neighborhoods. In Liverpool the locating of the Slavery Exhibition was uncontentious, since the site in the renovated Albert Dock had no surrounding community, and an existing Museum, the Maritime Museum, was already well-established.

The nexus of power and interests between the four main groups is dynamic, not static, and its configuration may change over time. Subject groups who have been excluded, marginalized or subordinated in previous narratives may increase in social power to change the way that they are represented; audiences may alter their tastes, rejecting what they formerly liked (e.g., wax work galleries of historical celebrities, or glass case museums) and demand more dynamic displays; owners and controllers may modify their goals and intentions (e.g., at military museums and battlefield sites in western Europe, heritage groups are now tending to downplay nationalistic themes, and to emphasize European unity and reconciliation).

Heritage is, then, as much a product of present perspectives as past events. Indeed, a recent study concluded:

> Present needs seemed to reshape past remains in a fashion strikingly analogous to revisions of memory and history . . . I began to realise that the pasts we alter or invent are as prevalent and consequential as those we try to preserve. Indeed, a heritage

wholly saved or authentically reproduced is no less transformed than one deliberately manipulated. 'Recreated pasts ought to be based on the knowledge and values of the present,' writes Kevin Lynch; they should 'change as present knowledge and values change, just as history is rewritten.' Such change is in fact unavoidable. (Lowenthal, 1985: xviii)

The result of all these impacts over time is that heritage is never a stable, finally completed process but a constantly evolving process of accommodation, adjustment and contestation. This perspective contrasts with that of heritage development as a battle between unproblematic, historical truth and various kinds of bad faith–ranging from commercial to political. It is easy to produce a comic strip, Manichaean view of heritage that conceives it as structured by, on the one hand, wicked tourism exploiters, enforcing suppression or distortion, and contested on the other by dominated or excluded minority victims, trying, with the help of academic voices, to bring truth to light. The Force Field model seeks to depict how the agencies and social actors involved in heritage development, and the political and temporal environments in which they interact, may produce a more complex configuration of influences than the assumption of this two-cornered fight between truth and falsehood. In heritage debates more than one side may have their own myths to promote. It has recently been argued that some aspects of slavery may have been exaggerated, including the significance of the Underground Railway of escape, which emerged in the late 1990s, associated, according to one writer, with film presentations, liberal guilt and a novel (Kammen, 1998). Lowenthal (1998) has questioned the existence of slave breeding farms, and perhaps the most difficult of historical findings to accommodate is the recent academic emphasis on the role of black African élites in the slave trade, without which the system would have been unworkable (Tattersfield, 1998).

CONCLUSION

This analysis has sought principally to provide a comparative focus on variance in the pace and nature of slavery heritage development in the US and UK. The contrasts in the status of slavery heritage in the two countries can be seen as a function of differences in physical evidence, the dissimilar position of slavery in relation to historical national discourses, as also to variation in the numbers of black people and their relationship to slavery in the two countries. The greater development in the US is less a function of a more liberal climate, than to the effect of this nexus of conditions that operates to make slavery a more visible and inescapable issue, than in Britain, even though the latter's role historically was at least as culpable. As Crew suggests, the dimensions of the multiracial population of the US have exerted pressures to animate what was previously called "minority" history:

> Pragmatism, demographics, and a sense of social responsibility have all helped to bolster the case for including the history of African Americans in museum exhibitions and programmes . . . Both African Americans and museums benefited from the recognition by these institutions that residents of local communities had histories worth sharing. Museums became more representative and African American histories became more of an integral part of the history learned by visitors to these institutions. (Crew, 1996: 90)

This study has also sought to explore the problems of memorializing slavery within wider questions of thanatourism and dissonant heritage, through a model that focuses on the different stakeholding groups that have to reach an accommodation in any heritage development, and the issues of power and change that may affect their relations. Heritage is an elusive and contested concept. Lowenthal (1998: 37) reminds us that those who drafted the National Heritage Act in Britain 'could no more define national heritage than we could define, say, beauty or art.'

If the potential need to accommodate all the stakeholders identified in the Force Field model is accepted, then one of the implications is that the historical significance and interest of a phenomenon alone–whether the importance of slavery in British and US history, or of the Nazi Death Camps in Europe–does not inevitably authorize its status as a heritage theme in *any place*. Nor where it does legitimate, does it necessarily indicate how that heritage should be represented. The cases in Britain and America offered in this study suggest some of the complexities involved in slavery heritage decisions, their relationship to present communities and the problems of finding forms of representation that, in addressing the issues of the past, accommodate to the needs of many audiences in the present.

REFERENCES

Anon (1999). *Slave trade trail around central Bristol.* Bristol Museums and Art Gallery.

Ashworth, G. J. (1991). *Heritage planning.* Groningen: Geo Pers.

Ashworth, G. J. (1999). Heritage dissonance and holocaust tourism: Some cases from European planning, *Conference 95th Annual Meeting of the Association of American Geographers,* Honolulu, Hawaii, 23-27 March.

Ashworth, G. J. and J. E. Tunbridge (1990). *The tourist-historic city.* Chichester: Wiley.

Austin, J. F. (1982). Their face to the rising sun: Trends in the development of black museums. *Museum News,* January/February: 29-32.

Bankes, G. (1994). Museum ethnography and communities. *Journal of Museum Ethnology,* 6: 1-6.

Barthes, Roland (1972). *Critical essays.* Evanston: Northwestern University Press.

Chase, Henry (1994). *In their footsteps: The American visions guide to Africa-American heritage sites.* New York: Henry Holt.

Crew, Spencer R. (1996). African Americans, history and museums: Preserving African American history in the public arena. In Kavanagh (pp. 80-91).

Cummins, A. (1996). Making histories of African Caribbeans. In Kavanagh (pp. 92-104).

Dickerson, A. J. (1988). *The history and institutional development of African American museums.* Unpublished MA thesis, The American University, Washington DC.

Foley, M. and J. J. Lennon (1996). JFK and dark tourism. *Journal of International Heritage Studies,* 2 (2): 195-197.

Fryer, Peter (1984). *Staying power: The history of black people in Britain.* London: Pluto.

Hancock, David (1995). *Citizens of the world.* Cambridge: Cambridge University Press.

Hewison, Robert (1987). *The heritage industry: Britain in a climate of decline.* London: Methuen.

Kammen, Carol (1998). The underground railroad and local history. *CRM* 21 (4). US Dept of the Interior, National Park Service, 1849 C Street, NW, Suite 350NC, Washington, DC 20240.

Kavanagh, Gaynor (1996). *Making history in museums.* Leicester: Leicester University Press.

Lennon, J. J. and M. Foley (2000). *Dark tourism.* London: Cassell.

Lowenthal. David (1985). *The past is a foreign country.* Cambridge: Cambridge University Press.

Lowenthal, David (1998). *The heritage crusade and the spoils of history.* Cambridge: Cambridge University Press.

Martin, S. I. (1999). *Britain's slave trade.* London: Channel Four Books.

Martin, Z. (1984). Colonial Williamsburg: A black perspective. In S. Nichols (Ed.). *Museum education anthology, 1973-1983: Perspectives of informal learning: A decade of roundtable reports.* Washington DC: Museum Roundtable.

Matthews, Christy Coleman (2000). Twenty years interpreting African American history: A Colonial Williamsburg revolution. February 25.

Owen, D. (1992-1995) 1991 *Census statistical paper 1-9,* Centre for Research in Ethnic Relations, University of Warwick; Ethnic Minorities in Britain, CRE Fact Sheet, 1997.

Richardson, David (1986-1990). *Bristol, Africa and the eighteenth century slave trade*. Bristol: Bristol Record Society, nos. 38, 39, 42.

Robinson, Mike (2000). Personal communication.

Ruffins, F. D. (1992). Myths, memory, and history: African American preservation efforts. 1820-1990. In I. Karp and C. Kreamer (Eds.). *Museums and communities: The politics of public culture*. Washington DC: Smithsonian Institution Press.

Seaton, A. V. (1992). Social stratification in tourism choice and behaviour. *Tourism Management*, 13(1): 106-111.

Seaton, A. V. (1996). Guided by the dark: From thanatopsis to thanatourism. *International Journal of Heritage Studies*, 2(4): 234-244.

Seaton, A. V. (1999a). War and thanatourism: Waterloo 1815-1914. *Annals of Tourism Research*, 26(1): 130-159.

Seaton, A. V. (1999b). Why do people travel? An introduction to tourist behaviour. In L. Pender (Ed.). *Marketing for travel and tourism*. Cheltenham: Stanley Thornes.

Small, S. (1994). Concepts and terminology in representations of the Atlantic slave trade. *Journal of Museum Ethnology*, 3: 7-21.

Small, S. (1997). Contextualising the black presence in British museums: Representations, resources and response. In E. Hooper-Greenhill (Ed.). *Cultural diversity: Developing museum audiences in Britain*. (pp. 50-66). Leicester: Leicester University Press.

Tattersfield, Nigel (1998). *The forgotten trade*. London: Pimlico.

Thomas, Hugh (1998). *The slave trade. The history of the Atlantic slave trade 1440-1870*. London: Papermac.

Tibbles, Anthony (1994a). *Transatlantic slavery: Against human dignity*. Liverpool: National Museums and Galleries on Merseyside.

Tibbles, Anthony (1994b). *Transatlantic slavery: Against human dignity*. London: HMSO.

Tibbles, Anthony (1996). Against human dignity: The development of the transatlantic slavery gallery at Merseyside Maritime Museum, Liverpool. *Proceedings, IXth International Congress of Maritime Museums* (pp. 95-102) National Maritime Museum and National Museums and Galleries on Merseyside.

Tibbles, Anthony (2000). Interview with author, February 24, Liverpool.

Travel Industry Association of America (TIAA) (1997). Profile of travelers who participate in historic and cultural activities. *Travelscope Survey*, Washington.

Tunbridge, J. E. and A. J. Ashworth (1996). *Dissonant heritage–The management of the past as a resource in conflict*. Chichester: Wiley.

van Helmond, M. and Palmer, D. (1991). *Staying power: Black presence in Liverpool*. Liverpool: National Museums on Merseyside (NMGM).

Walvin, J. (1996). *Black ivory. A history of British slavery*. London: Fontana.

Aunt Jemima
and Uncle Mose Travel the USA:
The Marketing of Memory
Through Tourist Souvenirs

Kenneth Goings

SUMMARY. This paper extends an earlier analysis of black collectibles to the realm of tourism. It argues that the elite practice of bringing back cultural trophies from travels abroad has been replaced by the phenomenon of middle class tourists returning home with souvenirs. One particular type of memorabilia in the United States is the portrayal of Afro-Americans on a number of tourist-related items. The article traces their origin, continuation and decline within an ideological framework that both promotes and institutionalizes racism. The slave-like images of mentally deficient, indolent, though happy blacks, as epitomized in the stereotypical figures of Aunt Jemima, Uncle Mose and their pickaninny offspring, while predominant from post-emancipation to the 1950s, have not entirely disappeared today. *[Article copies available for a fee from The Haworth Document Delivery Service: 1-800-342- 9678. E-mail address: <getinfo@haworthpressinc.com> Website: <http://www. Haworth-Press.com> © 2001 by The Haworth Press, Inc. All rights reserved.]*

KEYWORDS. Black collectibles, tourist souvenirs, racist representations, Afro-Americans, Uncle Mose and Aunt Jemima

---

Kenneth Goings is Professor and Chair, Department of African American and African Studies, the Ohio State University, 486 University Hall, Columbus, OH 43210.

[Haworth co-indexing entry note]: "Aunt Jemima and Uncle Mose Travel the USA: The Marketing of Memory Through Tourist Souvenirs." Goings, Kennneth. Co-published simultaneously in *International Journal of Hospitality & Tourism Administration* (TheHaworth Hospitality Press, an imprint of The Haworth Press, Inc.) Vol. 2, No. 3/4, 2001, pp. 131-161; and: *Slavery, Contested Heritage and Thanatourism* (ed: Graham M. S. Dann and A. V. Seaton), The Haworth Hospitality Press, an imprint of The Haworth Press, Inc., 2001, pp. 131-161. Single or multiple copies of this article are available for a fee from The Haworth Document Delivery Service [1-800-342-9678, 9:00 a.m. - 5:00 p.m. (EST). E-mail address: getinfo@haworthpressinc.com].

FROM TROPHIES OF TRAVELERS
TO SOUVENIRS OF TOURISTS

Tourists have always collected "souvenirs" to remind them of their travels and to let those left behind know what the trip was like and what the visual experience really resembled. Crusaders came home with pieces of the "true cross," Columbus returned to Spain with plants, animals and people in order to prove that he had indeed discovered a new world, Lord Elgin brought back a large number of the marble statues and friezes from the Parthenon in Greece, and the Vanderbilts and Carnegies reassembled in the United States a collection of paintings and furniture from their European adventures. Until the late 19th century, most leisure travel was restricted to this kind of élite. However, after that time, changes in the economy and in transportation made such travel increasingly affordable to others in terms of both time and money. Furthermore, these economically liberated and democratically created tourists, like their more affluent counterparts, also wanted to bring back mementos of where they had been. Indeed, it is from this period that the beginning of a souvenir industry emerged for the middle-classes. Unlike Lord Elgin or the Vanderbilts and Du Ponts, these new tourists brought back postcards, ashtrays, trinkets, and other kinds of knickknacks from their exploits abroad.

BLACK COLLECTIBLES AS SOUVENIRS

Given the era in which they were produced, it is not surprising that many tourist souvenirs belonged to a genre of material now called "black collectibles" (Goings, 1994: chapter one), each conveying powerful messages about a supposed past and a hoped-for future in new vacation-lands. However, before examining the content of these communications, it is first necessary to define black collectibles (see the end of this article for Image Section.)

They are generally understood to be commercial items made in or with the image of a black person (see Image 1). There were literally tens of thousands of such articles produced in the United States and elsewhere from the 1880s to the late 1950s, and they were almost always without exception derogatory, with racially exaggerated features. Another common characteristic was that most were intended for daily use–objects such as advertisements, postcards, household ware, toys, games, ornaments and decorations. This paper will only discuss a small segment of these collectibles–tourist souvenirs.

The quotidian nature of these items meant that they were used constantly (the wear and tear on the surviving collectibles attest to this). Furthermore, it is suggested that, by employing them so routinely, users consciously and unconsciously grew to accept the cruelly exaggerated stereotypes they represented. These common articles of material culture, which consistently depicted blacks in servile roles, thus gave a physical reality to the ideas of racial inferiority. Collectibles were the props that helped reinforce the new racist ideology that began emerging after reconstruction. They helped to "prove" that African-Americans were indeed "different" and inferior.

FROM THE 1880s TO THE 1930s

The Appearance of Aunt Jemima and Uncle Mose

Aunt Jemima, Uncle Mose and their kin were first portrayed from the 1880s to the 1930s. This period, which encompasses the true origins of black collectibles, coincided with the emergence of mass tourism in the US.

For African-America, these fifty years also included the retreat from reconstruction, the disfranchisement movement, the rise of the second Klan, lynchings and the great migration north. It is within this post-emancipation era that new structures and new routines had to be respectively developed and practiced in order to create and sustain a "new" or different racial ideology, one that was not based on slavery, but rather on the concepts of racial inferiority. During this period, which the great historian Rayford Logan has termed "the nadir," every institution in the United States–the academy, the church, courts, sciences, and even foreign policy–gave vent to the most violent forms of racism, including torture and random executions by vigilantes. Although black people have always been exposed to violence–from their initial capture in Africa, to the "breaking in" or "seasoning process" in British North America, and then to the master's whip under slavery–one noted scholar argues that the violence displayed in the south in this period following emancipation was "distinctive." He writes:

> To count the lynchings and burnings, to detail the savagery, the
> methodical torture prolonged for the benefit of the spectators, to

dwell on the voyeuristic sadism that characterized these ritual murders and blood rites in the name of enforcing deference and submission is to underscore the degree to which many whites by the late nineteenth century had come to think of black men and women as less than human. (Litwack, 1987: 321)

The Myth of the Old South/New South

Combined with the growing belief about the sub-human nature of African-Americans was the creation of a "new" tradition. This way of thinking included the myth of the gothic "old south/new south" where, supposedly, all white people had retained black servants and slaves (particularly a mammy), and where all members of this servile class were *happy* to be working for the master. As can be seen, the tourist souvenirs clearly followed this pattern. As one author has noted:

> In persuading the north to view the 'quaint darky' through south-ern eyes, the mythmakers accomplished at least two important goals. First, by convincing northerners that relations between the races were kindly and mutually beneficial, they removed a prin-cipal obstacle in the way of sectional harmony. Second, the ac-quiescence by the north in the southern scheme of race relations permitted the south to deal with, or fail to deal with, its race problems unmolested. (Boskin, 1986: chapter 14)

Humor became the "device" to placate the northern conscience. As a result, black people could be pictured in their "natural" state as happy clowns or Sambos, and then of course, it would only be the bad "niggers," those black brutes who allowed their base animal instincts to take over, who would have to be lynched.

The Role of Publicity

Manufacturers and their publicity agents easily tapped into these sentiments. Amidst a mounting array of competing product claims, many advertisers shifted their focus from presenting information to attracting attention. What better way to evoke interest, arouse humor, and provide the tourist with a therapeutic sense of comfort and racial superiority than with the stereotypical old south/new south myth of the loyal *happy* servant just waiting to carry out the master's–now the consumer's/tourist's–bidding (Lears, 1983: 17). These contented darky images were then applied to many of the souvenir products of the day. Yet there was still the lingering idea of sub-human beings, creatures that must have constituted another race because they surely could not be the same as "normal" men and women. In this regard, and toward the end of the nineteenth century, J. Stanley Lemons (1983: 17) noted, in an article on Negro stereotypes that:

> . . . Common was the image of the Negro as a servant and maid. There was old Uncle Tom or Uncle Remus, Aunt Jemima or Mandy the maid, Preacher Brown and Deacon Jones, Rastus and Sambo, and the ole 'mammy'. . . they were so familiar that few people had any notion that they degraded Black Americans. Most people thought the caricatures were funny . . . (after all who could be upset with the image of a mammy or Sambo?)

But in addition to these images, Lemons (1977: 104) observed that:

> In the 1880s coarse, grotesque caricatures began to dominate. Ugly, animal-like features were displayed. These images showed black people as pseudo-devils, or with big mouths, big ears, oversized hands and feet, and with sloping foreheads, that were meant to indicate a limited intelligence, and behaving in exaggerated and ridiculous fashion.

These beings were not members of the majority "race"; they were clearly from another race–that was the message delivered by these collectibles. Such a communication was further reinforced by another phenomenon that was taking place.

Retrogression

In the 1880s and 1890s many race propagandists began promoting an idea called "retrogression." This was the belief that with emancipation the restraints on the "unchanging Africans" had been dropped, and these black people were reverting to their former selves–savage heathens. This retrogression was to be seen most clearly in the family life, morals, and sexual practices of black people. African Americans were thought to have little or no sense of family, to place no value on the institution of marriage, and to be carrying and transmitting venereal diseases at an alarming rate.

The greatest advocate of what would become a very popular theory was Philip A. Bruce, who articulated these notions in his book *The Plantation Negro as Freedman* (1899 (1976)). He went on to say that the "average" black parent was "morally obtuse and indifferent" to her children (Bruce, 1976: 35). Hence all the abandoned pickaninny images in the first period of the collectibles. As the Charleston *News and Observer* related in 1898:

> . . . Everybody knows that when freed from the compelling influence of the white man he reverts by a law of nature to natural barbarism in which he was created in the jungles of Africa. (*Charleston News and Courier*, 1898: 514)

This language and the ideas it contained were too great to waste, particularly because the U.S. had its own jungle–Florida.

The Promotion of Florida

In light of the foregoing, it is appropriate to start with a discussion of the Sunny State since it was the recipient of so much of the early mass tourism in the U.S. Its full contextualization, however, comprised the kinds of items that welcomed northerners to the sunny climes of Dixie.

This multi-part postal sleeve with a series of pictures inside provided the visual messages that southern promoters wanted to convey to the north (see Image 2). First, there were the images on the outside cover–The Happy South–no atrocities here.

Just grey-haired older black men–no wild bucks–along with cotton plants which they happily picked, watermelon which they happily ate and the old slave cabins in which they now happily lived as free people. Turning to the inside cover, the image was of the old-time southern darky: The former slaves were curiosity pieces, the younger generation was also not threatening, and no matter what their age they were happy to be working picking that cotton. Come on down for a great time (see Image 3).

On the reverse of this sleeve, typical southern products were featured–watermelons (can't have darkies without watermelon), razorbacks (how they liked their pork!) and pickaninnies (everybody knew what they were really good at). These were some of the mass-market images sold to northerners (see Image 4).

As for Florida in particular, this was the region that in the 1920s and 1930s became the preferred destination of more and more vacationers. Of all the southern tourist spots no other state was more represented in tourist collectibles than Florida. Shown are some images from the first period of the collectibles, the 1890s to late 1930s, from the Sunshine State. The first item is a fairly innocuous spoon and, as can be seen on the handle, there is the happy darky just waiting to serve the tourist (see·Image 5).

However, the following were more typical of the Florida images. Bearing in mind the "retrogression" theory, what are shown here are abandoned babies brought by the stork, since, of course, the freed people had no idea how babies were made or from where they came (see Image 6). Image 7 shows an abandoned baby awaiting his fate.

These cute and amusing cards were nonetheless sending the message that, although the darkies down here were stupid, lazy, and harmless, they were still content with their lot. Remembering that they never really knew how to take care of their own children, it comes as no surprise to learn that in the "jungles" of Florida alligators would capture one or two of the pickaninnies. This retrogression theory also helps explain why so many of these people were shown up in trees. Like their "cousins," the monkeys of Africa, these all but mentally deficient beings at least knew that alligators could not climb (see Image 8).

In Image 9, abandoned pickaninnies are out for a joy ride, completely oblivious of Aesop's fable about the fox and hare.

In Image 10, the slothful pickaninny is engaged in what darkies love to do: fish by the banks of a river when, lo and behold, there is something else expecting a bite.

Image 11 is included in order to underline the fact that some days the alligator wins and other days it loses.

However, more often than not, as this item in Image 12 from Biloxi, Mississippi, reveals, the alligator ends up victorious.

Symbolic Slavery

From the late 1880s, when the collectibles originated, to the late 1930s, is a period that various scholars of black memorabilia have termed the "time of symbolic slavery" or the "freezing" of the Sambo Jemima slave image. Such "freezing" meant that those items conjuring up the happy mythical old southern slave (the contented darky) who was retrogressing, were associated with the tourist souvenirs of the period. And perhaps no item has been more linked with the darky of yesteryear than the watermelon. Sliced watermelon, of course, was seen as a mirror image of the happy darky's grin. Since it is difficult to eat watermelon in a genteel fashion, scenes of darkies savagely biting into the fruit were seen as additional proof of "retrogression" to heathenism. Additionally, of course, there were all those fondly told and tenderly recalled stories of darkies slipping into the watermelon patch at night for their favorite treat. Thus, one should not be surprised to see barefoot pickaninnies feasting on watermelons (see Image 13), pickaninnies driving watermelons (see Image 14), pickaninnies thinking about watermelons (Image 15), or moody pickaninnies suffering from watermelon withdrawal (see Image 16).

By producing and using in advertising everyday items that clearly depicted black people as inferior, as objects worthy of torment and torture, manufacturers and consumers were providing a physical reality for the underpinning ideology, confirming what the racist propagandists were saying all along (these beings were not people like themselves). African-Americans, male and female, were portrayed as very dark, generally bug-eyed, nappy-headed, childlike, stupid, lazy, deferential– *but happy.* This last characteristic was an important dimension of the collectibles, for as Neil McMillen notes in *Dark Journey,* rigidly following and obeying the cast rituals was not enough. He writes:

> Lest they appear 'sassy' or 'sullen' . . . blacks had to show ready acquiescence by inflection and gesture, to appear by every outward sign to be 'willingly' and 'cheerfully' humble. (McMillen, 1989: 12)

Black people could not *just* be second class citizens. They were required to *actively* acknowledge their subordinate position, and the collectibles reflect this asymmetry. Moreover, they had to keep reassuring the north that things were just fine down in Dixie.

THE 1930s TO THE 1950s

In the second period of the collectibles attitudes changed, and racial tensions began to relax. From the late 1930s to the late 1950s, the hardened stereotypes of the preceding era were replaced with lighter and even happier images. And as can be seen, these images of the second period originated not just in the south, but from all over the country.

During this second latter epoch, tourism was a growing nation-wide phenomenon as destinations across the whole of the United States tapped into a ready reservoir of stereotypes to sell themselves as places from yesteryear, where the living was good and all the darkies were happy. Coterminously, Aunt Jemima, Uncle Mose and their kin reached a new stage of development, one could say almost an adult maturity. The bulk of the items during this time were articles of house-ware. However, some postcards, a few advertising motifs and a number of "decorative" items were also produced. This period encompassed the Great Depression and World War II. The strictures of the former and the production demands of the latter meant that most items manufactured during this era had to be functional as well as decorative. In addition, the war brought about a softening of racial attitudes. Since *blacks* had fought overseas to destroy Nazism and Fascism, it was a bit more difficult to reinstate the hardened racism of the earlier period. Part of the change in the image of African-Americans thus reflected the increasing challenge launched against the old south/new south mythical Negro in the 1920s and 1930s.

At this time, Coon Chicken Inns appeared. They were actually established in order to let every one know that urban black folk were just as foolish and comical as their country Jim Crow brethren (see Image 17).

Smiling happy faces also dominated this second period: for example, a compact for women's make-up (see Image 18), a salt and pepper shaker from a restaurant in Ohio (see Image 19) happy canoeists from Florida (see Image 20, and a condiment set from Biloxi (see Image 21). These tourist souvenirs clearly reflected a toning down of racial attitudes brought about by the Depression and World War II.

FROM THE LATE 50s
TO THE EARLY 60s AND BEYOND

By the late 1950s and the early 1960s the manufacturing of these collectibles ceased. It was during this decade that African-Americans began to call themselves "black." Furthermore, the activism of the modern phase of the Civil Rights movement with its non-violent acceptance of beatings and resistance to police brutality, linked with the assertiveness of the growing black power movement, made it *almost* impossible to portray African-Americans as the loyal, servile, but *happy* Aunt Jemima and Uncle Mose. All Americans had to do was to turn on their television sets, and it was obvious that Aunt Jemima and Uncle Mose were out marching, battling police dogs, burning down Watts and securing their vote.

The exaggerated characteristics of the collectibles began to disappear, as it became patently illiberal, if not downright racist, to possess such items. However, while their manufacture appeared to have ceased, as a visit to almost any truck stop quickly illustrates, tourist mementos were being reproduced in record numbers, the reasons for which have been discussed elsewhere (Goings, 1994: chapter 4).

Black collectibles can thus be regarded as a window into the history of tourism in America. As the nation changed and its attitude about race underwent modification, those items used to promote tourism through racially charged materials altered as well. These tourist souvenirs, like the other pieces of black memorabilia, were/are props in the racial ideology that has engulfed America from the late 19th century to the present. When people travel to see the USA, they are often experiencing more than just historical sites and natural wonders. They are seeing how a nation has constructed and is still constructing its concept of race.

REFERENCES

Boskin, J. (1986). *Sambo*, New York: Oxford University Press.
Bruce, P. (1889). The Plantation Negro as Freedman.
Charleston News and Courier (1898). 11 January.
Goings, K. (1994). *Mammy and Uncle Mose: Black collectibles and American stereotyping*, Bloomington, Indiana: University of Indiana Press.
Gutman, H. (1976). *Black family slavery and freedom 1750-1925*. New York: Pantheon Books.
Lears, T. (1983). From salvation to self-realization. In R. Fox and T. Lears (Eds.), *The culture of consumption*. New York: Patton.
Lemons, J. (1977). Black stereotypes as reflected in popular culture 1880-1920. *American Quarterly*, 29, Spring, 104.
Litwack, L. (1987). Trouble in mind: The Bicentennial and the Afro-American Experience. *Journal of American History*, 74, 2.
McMillen, N. (1989). *Dark journey*. Urbana: University of Illinois Press.

IMAGE SECTION

IMAGE 1

IMAGE 2

142

IMAGE 3

Greetings from the Happy South.

✶→➤◉╬◉⟨←✶

To the average Northern tourist the old time southern darky is an interesting subject for observation. The younger generation with their peculiarities are extremely funny, while the older ones are thrifty and ambitious to some extent. In the far South they are employed in the cultivation and picking of the enormous cotton raising industry. Thoroughly acclimated to the extreme heat prevailing in this section, they are better able to endure the extremities of this country than our white brethren. The shiftless and worthless darky although prevalent in some sections is fast disappearing. Through the valiant efforts of the late Booker T. Washington they are enabled to receive that higher education which places them in a position to avail themselves of responsible and lucerative employment.

Descriptive Matter by Joseph Kaufmann.

IMAGE 4

SOUTHERN PRODUCTS. WATER MELONS. RAZOR BACKS AND PICKANINNIES.

From _old Point Comfort_
Joslee, Monroe Spa

144

IMAGE 6

IMAGE 7

IMAGE 8

IMAGE 9

A Joy Ride in Florida

IMAGE 10

IMAGE 11

TAKING HOME A SOUVENIR ST. PETERSBURG FLA   THE SUNSHINE CITY   603

IMAGE 13

IMAGE 14

EVERYTHING IS BIG AT THE VAN WERT COUNTY FAIR.

IMAGE 15

157

IMAGE 18

IMAGE 19

IMAGE 20

IMAGE 21

Whitewashing Plantations:
The Commodification
of a Slave-Free Antebellum South

David L. Butler

SUMMARY. This article begins with a brief explanation of personal experiences on plantation tours. It follows with an empirical examination of tourist brochures from over 100 plantations and a textual analysis of their data. A frequency count of keywords is created, serving to highlight that "slavery," "slaves" and "slave cabins" occur less often than such expressions as "owners," "landscapes" and "furnishings." Reasons for this imbalance are sought. More specifically, the investigation asks why plantation owners and their operations under-emphasize slavery and what this situation means for the contemporary tourist. In so doing, the inquiry attempts to answer the question as to whether or not such marginalization of slavery is a legitimate concern now and in the future. *[Article copies available for a fee from The Haworth Document Delivery Service: 1-800-342-9678. E-mail address: <getinfo@haworthpressinc. com> Website: <http://www.HaworthPress.com> © 2001 by The Haworth Press, Inc. All rights reserved.]*

David L. Butler is affiliated with the Department of Economic Development and Planning, University of Southern Mississippi, Hattiesburg, MS 39406-5051.

Grateful acknowledgement is made to the University and Grants Office at the Department of Transportation for funding which enabled this study to be presented. Thanks also to Richard Shein at the University of Kentucky for an introduction to critical museum research and to Byron Miller at the University of Cincinnati for suggesting the title of this paper.

[Haworth co-indexing entry note]: "Whitewashing Plantations: The Commodification of a Slave-Free Antebellum South." Butler, David L. Co-published simultaneously in *International Journal of Hospitality & Tourism Administration* (The Haworth Hospitality Press, an imprint of The Haworth Press, Inc.) Vol. 2, No. 3/4, 2001, pp. 163-175; and: *Slavery, Contested Heritage and Thanatourism* (ed: Graham M. S. Dann and A. V. Seaton), The Haworth Hospitality Press, an imprint of The Haworth Press, Inc., 2001, pp. 163-175. Single or multiple copies of this article are available for a fee from The Haworth Document Delivery Service [1-800-342-9678, 9:00 a.m. - 5:00 p.m. (EST). E-mail address: getinfo@haworthpressinc.com].

KEYWORDS. Plantation tours, Louisiana, South Carolina, textual analysis, promotional material, slave versus owner words, marginalization of slavery

INTRODUCTION

Approximately five years ago, this research began after a visit to New Orleans. Due largely to the appeal of some advertisements in local publications, an excursion was taken along the River Road in Louisiana in order to explore some of the plantations and to join the various tours on offer. Although each tour left something to be desired, it was very difficult to pinpoint or define what was missing. It was not until a visit to the Laura Plantation, a home that had been recently purchased without yet undergoing "renovation" to the immaculate standards of most tourist sites, that it became clear what was absent from the other plantations–the realization that they had either removed or marginalized slavery. Most of them, in their tour narratives, did not even utter the words "slave" or "slavery," far less establish their connections with the landscape in such features as slave graveyards and former slave cabins. Nor, for that matter, did they mention their contribution to the total antebellum plantocratic infrastructure. The Laura Plantation, by contrast, since it had not yet been "restored," still bore the bare, dilapidated traces of the slaves who had worked, lived and died on this property. Upon reflection, it appeared that the other plantation tours were deliberately misleading the tourist by not adequately representing the history of slavery. It was this awareness of under-representation and significant omission that acted as a catalyst for this research by stimulating an inquiry into whether or not all plantations on the River Road had either marginalized or removed slavery from their environments.

About two years ago, on this occasion in Charleston, South Carolina, another trip was undertaken to visit some plantations in the area. The purpose of the outing was to determine whether or not the Louisiana experience was unique. It wasn't. These plantations either sidelined or overlooked slavery just as the Louisiana ones had done. It became clear that most of the former also ignored the realities of slavery during the tours and in their presentation of the landscape. With this twofold plantation odyssey complete, the question then became how to research the phenomenon, how to demonstrate that the Louisiana and South Carolina plantations constituted the touristic norm rather than the exception.

RESEARCH PROJECT

Since plantations sell themselves by means of pamphlets and advertisements targeted at tourists, a textual analysis of this promotional material appeared to be the most rational method to initiate this first phase of the inquiry.[1] The plantation tours in question included most of the narrative related during a tour, as well as references to any markers of the landscape found within the publicity. In fact, at times, it appeared as though the guides were reciting from the brochure script. Therefore, brochures seemed to be a logical starting point to discover what plantations, labeled as historical plantation experiences, were actually marketing.

The research began with a call to every southern state's tourism bureau in order to request its official travel guide and any other supplements that highlighted plantations.[2] Another resource was Fodor's *The South* (1998). Within this book there were many plantations, along with their phone numbers and addresses. After receiving the state travel guides, a file of all the cited plantations was created. Once all of the publications had been examined, a list of approximately 150 plantations and phone numbers was drawn up and the telephoning began (see Table 1). During these initial contacts with the plantations, requests were made for all brochures that reflected the information included in their tours.

Data Collected

After receiving 102 plantation brochures, it was time to analyze them. In sifting through this material, it was clear that the authors had used a simple writing model that included highlighting and explaining a few pivotal concepts that they had found relevant to the plantation.

TABLE 1. Plantations Contacted and Brochures Received

Total number of plantations found:	153
Total called:	153
Total of brochures received:	102

Understanding this model made it easy to look for specific keywords. Common expressions included the Civil War, architecture, people's names, crops produced, and so on. All of these terms would have encouraged the reader (or tourist on the tour) to imagine specific items. The goal of this study was to compare these expressions, and the images they conveyed, to the word "slave" and to see which of the two appeared more often. After perusing the publicity, a list was made of the most common ideas that appeared. For example, reference to the original owner was a very common feature. A list of the nine most utilized words was drawn up, including "slaves," and then examined in each pamphlet. First a brochure would be read through in its entirety. Then it would be re-examined, this time with a pen, making a mark where any of the nine keywords was found. Each keyword was counted only once in each leaflet even if it were repeatedly mentioned.

TEXTUAL ANALYSIS

Keywords

Table 2 shows how often each of the keywords occurred. Interestingly, the words "slave," "slavery," "slave cabins" and the like yielded the least frequency, as could be justifiably anticipated from the past plantation tour experiences. If a brochure did not allude to slavery in the text but had a map featuring a slave cabin without any related commentary, it was still counted. Nevertheless, the findings indicated

TABLE 2. Frequency of Keywords in Plantation Brochures

Topic	Frequency
Architecture	72
Original Owners	80
Current Owners	51
Crops	43
Slaves	30
Furnishings	36
Gardens/Grounds/Landscape	45
Civil War	45
Heritage/Politics/Public Office	43

that slaves were referred to less often at plantations than even the furnishings. It is also worth noting that, in the rare instances where it was mentioned, slavery was typically associated with generosity.

States

Among the first questions to be asked was where the majority of the tourist plantations were located. Given that not all of them were tourist attractions, it could not be assumed that most would be in the Deep South. Table 3 lists not only the number of plantations, but also how many brochures were received from each state.

Second, one wished to discover whether there were regional variation in terms of portraying slavery at plantations. In particular, did the more northern southern states represent slavery more frequently than did the Dixie South (see Table 4)?

Ownership

Plantation ownership proved a crucial factor in determining what was the emphasis or lack of focus on slavery in the brochures. Originally it was not clear as to the significance this factor played in how slavery was, or was not, portrayed. Informal conversation with several owners, directors and historians on the staff at the plantations indi-

TABLE 3. Tourist Plantations by State and Brochures Received

State	Plantations Listed	Brochures Received	Percent
Alabama	9	3	33%
Arkansas	1	0	0%
Delaware	2	1	50%
Florida	4	0	0%
Georgia	19	7	37%
Kentucky	9	6	67%
Louisiana	33	22	67%
Maryland	3	2	67%
Mississippi	10	4	40%
Missouri	1	0	0%
North Carolina	9	11	122%
South Carolina	9	7	78%
Tennessee	10	7	70%
Texas	5	3	60%
Virginia	29	23	79%
Totals	153	102	

TABLE 4. Plantation Brochures Mention of Slavery by State

State	Brochures Received	Mentions of Slaves(ery)	Percent
Alabama	3	0	0%
Arkansas	0	0	--
Delaware	1	1	100%
Florida	0	0	--
Georgia	8	2	25%
Kentucky	6	2	33%
Louisiana	22	7	32%
Maryland	2	0	0%
Mississippi	4	2	50%
Missouri	0	0	--
North Carolina	11	2	18%
South Carolina	7	3	43%
Tennessee	7	1	14%
Texas	3	2	66%
Virginia	23	8	35%
Totals	102	30	Mean 29%

cated how important it was as to who controlled the dissemination of information, and what they wanted to achieve in choosing what to market and what not to promote. Five basic ownership styles of plantations were identified: state owned, federally owned, foundation owned, society owned and privately held. In general it was found that:

1. if federally owned, the plantation had an extensive collection of slave related history associated with the plantation.[3]
2. if state owned, it usually had some research on slavery completed, but this feature in itself did not guarantee that it would form part of the tour narrative, or that slavery would be exhibited as an element of the tour landscape.
3. if privately owned, slavery was usually not mentioned, although it might have been if the information were at hand. Most owners were curious about the history of slavery at their property and were delighted to speak at length about all the data they had accumulated over the years regarding the history of the plantation and its occupants, including slaves.
4. if society owned, especially if by a historical society, there was some reference to slavery, always assuming that the society had the money to conduct the research.

5. if owned by a foundation, slavery was ignored. Why? Because the employees who worked there were in the business of enhancing and protecting an individual or family reputation. A sure way to reveal a potential flaw in a person was to point out that s(he) was a slaveholder.

As Table 5 shows, most of the plantations contacted were privately owned. The second largest group was state owned, and the smallest, federally owned.[4]

QUESTIONS ASKED

The textual analysis just completed showed that the Louisiana and South Carolina plantation tour experiences constituted the norm, rather than the exception. Slavery was for the most part ignored or marginalized at the tourist plantations throughout the historic slave-owning South. From this conclusion, a number of further questions had to be asked:

1. Why did plantation tours exclude slavery?
2. Did individuals who toured plantations assume that the terms "plantation" and "slavery" were synonymous and thus that slavery was embedded within the tour, even if not mentioned?
3. Did it really matter that slavery was marginalized or ignored in plantation tours?

Each of these issues was examined through the lens of critical literature on museums, places, and plantations.

TABLE 5. Ownership of Plantations

Type	Percent
State Owned	30%
Foundation Owned	13%
Privately Owned sometimes no tours	43%
Society Owned	10%
Federally Owned	3%
Total	99%

Why Do Plantations Exclude Slavery?

Why do plantations exclude slavery? The simplest answer to this question is that the people in charge of creating the image of a plantation to be shown to the public deliberately choose to exclude slavery from their meta-narrative (Sherman and Rogoff, 1994: xi). The plantation curators are agents who invest resources to preserve, erase, strengthen, or weaken boundaries between documents and exhibits (Azoulay, 1994: 90). Similarly, every plantation, as a museum, may act as a site for the construction of a fictitious history, thus responding to the unconscious desire, including the hope, of the custodians that slavery did not happen, especially at this location. Furthermore, plantations act as a place for the collection of historical myths that serve to legitimate present ideologies (Hoffmann, 1994: 16). This observation is particularly valid in terms of the plantations owned by foundations whose sole task it is to preserve the reputation of a person or family as far into the future as possible.

In some instances, mentions of "slaves," "slavery" or "slave cabins" were included in the tour or in the brochure, but only tangentially. How should one account for this situation? It is argued in the literature that when a museum or historical display is established there are four main subjects:

1. the exhibiting subject.
2. the exhibited subject.
3. the person to whom the exhibition is addressed.
4. the "other" who has been excluded from the exhibition (Urry, 1995: 100).

This model certainly holds true for plantations. The exhibiting subject (1) is either a person or group of people who are in charge of (re)creating an image of the important historical person who lived there (2). This mostly fictitious meta-narrative is constructed for the tourist (3) as a part of capital accumulation on the part of the people or persons who own the plantation. The fourth subject is the excluded Other, in this instance the thousands of slaves (4) who were purchased, born and sold, and who worked, lived and died on the plantation. Their labor was the system that allowed the whole political-economic construct known as the plantation to exist. Without slavery, the plantation could not (and did not) survive.

Are Tourists Ignorant of Plantations and Slavery?

Before examining the position of the tourist, it is first necessary to clarify the concept of a plantation. According to the *Oxford English Dictionary (OED)*, the most commonly used definition is "an estate or farm, esp. in a tropical or subtropical country, on which cotton, tobacco, sugar-cane, coffee, or other crops are cultivated, formerly chiefly by servile labour" (*OED*, 1989). In other words, plantations are tied to the concept of servile labor in the form of slavery.

On the other hand, and as far as the tourist is concerned, there may be many different processes occurring at the same time. First, the term plantation today is not as narrow as the *OED* suggests. It has (d)evolved[5] to the point where various land holdings, motels, hotels, restaurants and other sites have all borrowed the name. Indeed, one "plantation" contacted as part of this research turned out to be a children's amusement park. When asked why she had designated it a "plantation," the owner replied that it was a common name in the area and that it was one likely to attract tourists. It can thus be seen that the term "plantation" is undergoing a major revision. It is no longer a stigmatized concept automatically associated with slavery. Instead it has been bestowed on places at which to stay, eat and be entertained in a grand fashion. The term now connotes opulence because of its connection with Great Houses and the derived wealth of the original owners and their descendants, much of which is highlighted on the tours. This observation is no more evident than in the most popular and highest grossing (taking inflation into account) movie in American cinema, *Gone with the Wind*.

Second, it has been suggested that an important motive of tourists is to seek experiences that contrast with the quotidian and mundane (Urry, 1995: 132). They thus choose places that they can anticipate in a fantasy of pleasure that they do not usually encounter in their daily lives. This means that, for the most part, tourists visit plantations in order to see the items most often mentioned in the brochures: architecture, heritage, gardens, furniture and the like. They are not there to have the seedy side of plantations–slavery–shown to them, thereby destroying the very dream that formed part of their pre-trip anticipation. By presenting slavery, too much of the ugly, historical reality of daily life in the past would be brought into the picture.

Third, the literature also indicates that the tourist gaze is sign-laden. When tourists visit a location, they want signification. The most frequently cited case is the example of a couple kissing beneath the Eiffel Tower in Paris (Urry, 1995: 8). Here the signs connote that, "Paris is for lovers." The question then becomes: What semiotic messages are the plantations transmitting? What does the tourist expect? Probably most visitors to plantations have seen *Gone with the Wind* and/or dozens of movies that adopt a similar formula. By the same token, when someone visits a plantation, a common conscious or unconscious comparison may be made to other plantations represented in the media. The plantation thus comes to signify wealth and opulence, and a life that few, if any, of the tourists who patronize them could ever come close to attaining. Nevertheless, they love to bask in the glow of the fantasy 'If only I lived here . . . ', a familiar enough strategy in the world of advertising.

As a final instance of how situated tourists are when it comes to expectations and signs on a plantation, it is worthwhile examining a few lines from Shipler's (1998) *A Country of Strangers*. Here the writer contrasts two different interpretations of tourists when they look at the same sight on a plantation. One of them is white and visiting a plantation in order to gaze upon the opulence. The other is an African-American who has slavery in his veins and is hoping to obtain a sense of heritage:

> A double image shimmers beneath the towering trees. One is for those who do not consider the history; beauty shrouds the shame. The other is for those who recognize that they have come upon the site of a great crime and can feel the shiver of remembrance. . . . The canal they created is a lovely river of sorrow; it marks the divided in America between those who see the beauty and those who feel the chill. (Shipler, 1998: 147)

Does It Really Matter?

In short, "Who cares?" It is not surprising that plantation owners, in trying to attract tourists, present them with a rosy side of a semi-fictitious history, all the while leaving the dark side of slavery out of the fantasy. Most tourists are on vacation to relax and enjoy themselves. Why, then, would they want to visit a plantation if all they are going to be shown is how terrible slavery was and how many people were bought, sold, tortured and died on the very ground on which they stand? Likewise, do they really wish to know that most of the magnificent architecture of the house, its construction and furnishings, and the planting and caring of the gardens was all brought about by slave labor? Probably not. Why, then, does it matter whether these plantations have excluded or marginalized slavery?

First, a plantation is a museum. Museums by their very existence are locations where members of the public are able to learn about objects and events, position them within their view of society and thus extrapolate this vision into the past (Azoulay, 1994: 88-90). In other words, people see, feel, and touch objects and, in so doing, confirm their belief that this is an actual recreation of what took place. They therefore now know how life was in the 1700s and 1800s. Plantations act as a crossroads between claiming and preserving the past, where efforts to represent that past and integrate it into the daily life of the present are channeled. That is to say, tourists walk away from a plantation with a sense of authenticity. If slavery or slaves are missing, then the extrapolation process and the production of verisimilitude are also denied. If plantations falsify or remove slavery from prominence in their museums, the result is a lost opportunity for a nation to learn from its past mistakes. The following emphasized passage reinforces the point:

> By purging *German Art Museums* of '*degenerate art*' . . . and by staging the *Great German Art Exhibition* to promote *paintings* and sculptures that were loyal to the *party line*, the *Nazis* hoped to make it possible for visitors to the *art museum* to feel in harmony with their purified history. The price to be paid for this was denial of the complexity not only of *art* but also of history. Appearance was sold as reality–and thereafter became reality, with the brutal consequence that reality was transformed by *political terror* into appearance. (Hoffmann, 1994: 13)

Translating this excerpt to the matter under investigation, it now reads:

> By purging *Plantations of 'slavery'* . . . and by staging the *Plantation Tours of the South* to promote *history* and *heritage* that were loyal to *dominant culture*, the *Plantation Owners* hoped to make it possible for visitors to the *plantation* to feel in harmony with their purified history. The price to be paid for this was denial of the complexity not only of *the plantation system* but also of history. Appearance was sold as reality–and thereafter

became reality, with the brutal consequence that reality was transformed by *commodification* into appearance. (modified from Hoffmann, 1994: 13)

The answer to the question "Does it matter?" is thus an emphatic "Yes!" It is necessary for people, both as individuals and as members of a society to see, touch and feel their past errors, so that when they are confronted with a similar evil in the present or the future, they can challenge it before it becomes institutionalized and the surrounding culture becomes desensitized to its dangers.

FUTURE RESEARCH

Even though this preliminary study demonstrates the extent to which many plantations eradicate the history of slavery from their own worldview, it fails to answer many questions regarding the tourist. For example, who actually visits plantations, where are they from and what are their demographic profiles? Do these tourists bring with them pre-conceived notions of slavery at plantations? The attempt to speculate on this issue needs to go beyond the realm of conjecture and to ask, if yes, how do they perceive the version of history that is presented? If not, do they believe everything that they hear on these tours? How many visitors go to plantations to learn about slavery and how many would be disillusioned if plantations actually represented the history of slavery? These are just some items for a future agenda that this research has attempted to highlight.

ENDNOTES

1. For the sake of space full details of brochure operator samples have not been provided. However, they are available on request from the author.
2. For the purpose of this paper, the South is defined as the southern slave-holding states during the US Civil War.
3. There was only one federally-owned plantation represented.
4. The cross-tabulations between ownership and the mention of slavery are not yet complete.
5. A further study stemming from this project is to examine the term "plantation" and when, where and how it is most frequently used.

REFERENCES

Azoulay, A. (1994). With open doors: Museums and historical narratives in Israel's public space. In D. Sherman and I. Rogoff (Eds.) *Museum culture: Histories, discourses, spectacles* (pp. 85-109) Minneapolis: University of Minnesota Press.

Cabasin, L. and Knight, C. (1998). *Fodor's: The South, the best of old and new, with Civil War sites and plantations, city walks and country drives.* New York: Fodor's Travel Publications.

Hoffmann, D. (1994). The German art museum and the history of the nation. In D. Sherman and I. Rogoff (Eds.) *Museum culture: Histories, discourses, spectacles* (pp. 3-21) Minneapolis: University of Minnesota Press.

Oxford English Dictionary (1989). Oxford: Oxford University Press.

Sherman, D. and Rogoff, I. (1994). Introduction: Frameworks for critical analysis. In D. Sherman and I. Rogoff (Eds.) *Museum culture: Histories, discourses, spectacles* (pp. ix-xx) Minneapolis: University of Minnesota Press.

Shipler, D. (1998). *A country of strangers: Blacks and whites in America.* New York: Vintage Books.

Urry, J. (1995). *Consuming places.* London: Routledge.

Gloria and Anthony Visit a Plantation: History into Heritage at "Laura: A Creole Plantation"

Elli Lester Roushanzamir
Peggy J. Kreshel

SUMMARY. The promotion and marketing of Louisiana 19th century plantation life is fraught with contradictions since plantation agriculture depended on slave labor and a rigidly hierarchical class/caste system. How, then, can that history be commodified as heritage and marketed effectively as a tourist destination? Drawing on Said's thesis of Orientalism and historians Hobsbawm and Ranger's concept of invented traditions, the marketing efforts are examined of a St. James Parish, Louisiana plantation called Laura: A Creole Plantation. With access to scripted guided tours, as well as promotional materials directed at tourists and travel professionals, a textual analysis is undertaken of the four ways in which history becomes heritage. These are: emphasizing genealogical continuity; connecting a little-known site with major events in US history; promoting Creole culture as particularly enigmatic; and highlighting women as owner/managers. It is argued that these are tactics that construct the tourist site positively, as primordial and exotic, but also as a precursor of modern practices of business and gender/race relations. These strategies combine, representing the plantation through the discursive activity of objectifying, containing, and commodifying the other, while concomitantly inventing the Laura persona as contem-

---

Elli Lester Roushanzamir and Peggy J. Kreshel are affiliated with Grady College of Journalism and Mass Communication, University of Georgia, Athens, GA 30602, USA.

[Haworth co-indexing entry note]: "Gloria and Anthony Visit a Plantation: History into Heritage at 'Laura: A Creole Plantation.'" Roushanzamir, Elli Lester, and Peggy J. Kreshel. Co-published simultaneously in *International Journal of Hospitality & Tourism Administration* (The Haworth Hospitality Press, an imprint of The Haworth Press, Inc.) Vol. 2, No. 3/4, 2001, pp. 177-200; and: *Slavery, Contested Heritage and Thanatourism* (ed: Graham M. S. Dann and A. V. Seaton), The Haworth Hospitality Press, an imprint of The Haworth Press, Inc., 2001, pp. 177-200. Single or multiple copies of this article are available for a fee from The Haworth Document Delivery Service [1-800-342-9678, 9:00 a.m. - 5:00 p.m. (EST). E-mail address: getinfo@haworthpressinc. com].

177

porary heroine. *[Article copies available for a fee from The Haworth Document Delivery Service: 1-800-342-9678. E-mail address: <getinfo@haworthpressinc. com> Website: <http://www.HaworthPress.com> © 2001 by The Haworth Press, Inc. All rights reserved.]*

KEYWORDS. Laura, Creole, plantation, Louisiana, textual analysis, tour narrative, gender, race

INTRODUCTION

The marketing of 19th century American plantations as tourist attractions is fraught with contradictions. Plantations, as locations of slave labor and rigidly hierarchical class and caste systems pose dark and challenging questions to recreational visitors. Yet, such sites have proven popular as they are increasingly targeted at diverse audiences in terms that many find satisfactory. How can such a compromised *history* be commodified as *heritage* and be promoted effectively as tourist destinations? What are the implications of such a transformation?

New Orleans is known worldwide as an appealing, tourist-friendly city, where visitor activities range from casino gambling to cultural touring. In contrast to what one travel writer (Mitchell, 1999) calls the self-consciously promoted vision of New Orleans–its colorful celebrations and parades, pageantry, dance, drunkenness, music, sexual display, and social and political bombast–the nearby plantations offer another dimension to the tourist experience. Within this environment, located in the already developed nearby tourist plantation community, "The River Road," Laura: A Creole Plantation (Laura) has been open to the public since 1994 (see article by Butler in this volume). Originally built in 1805, it comprises twelve extant buildings still surrounded by sugar cane. Six slave quarters, two manor houses, a kitchen, and what the promotional literature describes as "Creole cottages" are listed on the National Register. The standing slave quarters are noted as especially rare.

In this paper, the marketing efforts of Laura are examined, since they supply rich evidence to help answer questions about heritage tourism. Promotional materials directed towards tourists and travel professionals, and scripted, on-site, guided tours provide textual evidence of the discursive strategies that transform lived experience into a saleable commodity. Among these questions are: How does a text create the tourist? How is the relic of a vicious social formation tamed and transmuted into a successful and favorably viewed tourist site? Has heritage overwhelmed history, confining it to the single dimension of nostalgia?

These issues derive from several theoretical influences. Said (1979, 1993), Baudrillard (1983, 1988), Jameson (1991, 1997) and Barthes (1972) all articulate ways in which to show the relationship between mediated communication and the hegemony of a capitalist worldview. Said's development of the themes of Orientalism, Baudrillard's description of a hyper-reality cut from ties to a formerly understood reality,[i] and Jameson's insistence on tying textual content to the consolidation of finance capital each offer a basis for understanding Laura's integrated marketing communication from a critical perspective. Barthes' insistence on the power of myth to convey hegemonic ideology informs Said's, Baudrillard's and Jameson's work, and is central to this study as well. Hobsbawm and Ranger (1983) provide an historical model of invented traditions. Using the critical textual analysis first developed by Hall (1975), the evidence emerges from a close reading of the Laura Plantation promotional materials (i.e., those available to tourists and the trade, as well as the scripts from the Laura tours).[ii]

As the analysis proceeds, it is interesting to note the particular ways in which history becomes co-opted as heritage. It is argued here that specific discursive tactics construct the tourist site positively, as primordial, exotic, and interestingly dangerous, and also as a precursor of modern (safe and acceptable) practices of business and gender/race relations. In this paper, the investigation is situated within tourism studies, in particular, cultural/heritage tourism; a background in media studies helps highlight the relationship between discourse and tourism. Subsequently, a necessary digression is made into a description of the linguistic and cultural history of two key words for the study (and at Laura): plantation and Creole. Next the text is analyzed, which comprises the promotional message and scripted tours. Finally, there is an assessment of the potential for a plantation heritage tourist destination to engage tourists in terms of recreation and historical inquiry.

MEMORY AND NOSTALGIA: LITERATURE REVIEW

In *The Beautiful and Damned*, Fitzgerald (1922) narrates his protagonists' visit to the Arlington, Virginia home of General Robert E. Lee. Swarms of tourists, leaving trails of peanut shells and crowding around restored attractions, lead Gloria and Anthony to a final indignity: 'a pleasing sign . . . in large red letters "Ladies' Toilet."' Moved to tears, Gloria protests the impetus to tart up old places into tourist destinations. Anthony sides with the preservationists and promoters, noting that without them historic sites would eventually vanish. Gloria responds:

> Beautiful things grow to a certain height and then they fail and fall off, breathing out memories as they decay. And just as any period decays in our minds, the things of that period should decay too, and in that way they're preserved for a while in a few hearts like mine that react to them. . . . The asses who give money to preserve things have spoiled [them]. Sleepy Hollow's gone, Washington Irving's dead and his books are rotting in our estimation year by year. . . . Trying to preserve a century by keeping its relics up to date is like keeping a dying man alive by stimulants. . . .
>
> It's just because I love the past that I want this house to look back on its glamorous moment of youth and beauty without poignancy and there's no poignancy without the feeling that it's going, men, names, books, houses–bound for dust–mortal . . . (pp. 166-7)

The terms in which Gloria frames "memory" are eminently anti-capitalist; she describes the *longue durée*, i.e., that of the moldering relic quietly crumbling into the ground and disappearing, losing its value altogether. In this, she articulates a clear concept of memory diametrically opposed to the one that propels heritage tourism. Tourism, whether "cultural" or not, always raises issues of authenticity and location: geographical, psychological, functional, etc. Frow (1997) identifies three common approaches to conceptualizing tourism/ist. As he explains, one is to regard tourism as an inauthentic pastime where a tourist, contrasted with a traveler, summarily passes over the other, perhaps rarely really attending to experiences along the way. This approach effectively condemns tourism out of hand. Another more subtle view is that tourism represents a quest for authenticity.

UCB Summer Row Library

Tel. 0121 243 0055
Birmingham B3 1JB

Borrowed Items 21/11/2011 15:30
Odedra, Retha

Item Title	Due Date
163351 Slavery,	28/11/2011
168377 The darker side	28/11/2011
158179 New horizon	28/11/2011
106024 Dark tourism	12/12/2011
178731 The dark tourist	28/11/2011

Amount Outstanding : £5.00

Thank you for using this unit
www.ucb.ac.uk

Noting the work of MacCannell (1976, 1992), Frow suggests that in this model, concepts of authenticity are problematized by references to conditions of production. The tourist is consciously looking for a "real" experience different from the norm. A third configuration begins by questioning the constitutive role of representation. Here, immediately upon labeling something/someone as authentic, that thing/person has automatically been mediated, and thus compromised. An example is described by Baudrillard (1983: 14) in which the ancient Tasaday society, protected by ethnologists, is paradoxically no longer "authentic"; the pristine native has been compromised by the representation.

Contemporary tourism is less a process of travel and discovery, than an industry. In this regard, Frow (1997) cites Kirshenblatt-Gimblett and Bruner (1989):

> [The travel industry comprises] travel agents, tour operators and guides, hotels and resorts, transportation networks and information and communication systems, mass media marketing, tourist regions and attractions, travel gear and souvenirs, travel literature and films, educational institutions that train industry personnel and foster scholarly research on tourism, regulatory and policy-making bodies, government agencies, professional associations. and international travel organizations and clubs. (p. 99)

The product of the industry is double: both material (travel gear, souvenirs, etc.) and immaterial (a commodified relationship between the tourist and the other). The latter is both provider and object, implicated in the industry and the attraction.[iii] As Frow (1997) observes:

> The commodification of reciprocal bonds . . . are moments of that logic of contemporary capital which extends private appropriation and ownership from material to immaterial resources, and whose paradigm case is the commodification of information. . . . [T]his appropriation can take place without any requirement of formal consent. (p. 100)

The logic of the tourist industry perpetuates retrograde relations, whether as underdevelopment in the Third World (since lack of development is the marker of difference, hence, the "attraction") or, in the case of plantations and other heritage sites, as explication of or even

mimed performance of former social relations. The tourist is invited to
re-live or stimulate a non-existent memory, thereby reifying the commodified version of the past. Heritage tourism is part of a broader
category of "cultural tourism" in which industry professionals depend
of necessity on a variety of culture specialists: historians, archivists,
archaeologists, etc. Heritage tourism has been investigated from different perspectives, e.g., surveys of visitors to a site, sources of heri-
tage-site funding, etc. In most cases, research suggests that the varied
interests engaged in this sort of tourist development are far from a
match made in heaven. As Kurin (1998) observes in his foreword to
Walle's (1998) recent *Cultural Tourism: A Strategic Focus:*

> Cultural tourism is a form of cultural production. It takes place
> through several media–tours, festivals . . . reenactments, theme
> parks. . . . [and] [v]arious aspects of someone's culture are repre-
> sented to visitors by tradition bearers, actors, tour guides, ex-
> perts, and others. Someone pays–tourists, sponsors, govern-
> ments, or organizations. In the mix, a complex production
> emerges, a new form of culture that often reflects the varied . . .
> goals . . . of those involved. (p. xiii)

According to Frow (1997), interest in heritage tourism has grown
significantly among the American public in the last decade. As such,
heritage tourism has increasing relevance to a number of interests,
both supply and demand oriented. Heritage tourist destinations, like
any other tourist sites, are obliged to promote and protect a brand
while providing expected services in an unexpected but commodious
way. The intention is that historical detail, combined with carefully
targeted marketing, will create an authentically satisfying tourist experience. Cultural tourism, especially heritage tourism, presupposes a
relationship between historical authenticity (itself a complex notion)
and an authentically satisfying tourist experience.

One approach to assessing tourism is to focus on its environmental
effects. While all tourism impacts on the local environment, culture
and heritage tourism make particularly deeply felt impressions; economic change is only one. Cultural and heritage tourism utilize local
community resources almost by definition, and therefore clashes of
interest predictably occur. One case study of cultural tourism in the US
suggests a model of three criteria for tourism that emanate from the
local culture's perspective: power, payoffs and tradeoffs (Peck and

Lepie, 1989). In another study, Becker (1998) examines one of this century's most prominent "folk revivals"–the reemergence of Southern Appalachian handicraft traditions in the 1930s. Through an analysis of the concepts of folk and tradition, she finds that the consequences of those labels are to obscure tradition in favor of middle-class taste and consumer culture. "Heritage" can be too easily converted from contested engagements with history to a commodity intentionally fabricated for a consumer audience.

Tourists themselves provide information about the meaning of heritage tourism. In a survey of 1,200 British heritage tourists, McIntosh (1999) offers the concept of "insightful tourism" as an appropriate paradigm for the investigation of the essentially personal, emotive, and symbolic context associated with cultural tourism encounters, from which visitors derive valued insights, along with an appreciation of the meaning of life. In other words, cultural tourism is an individualized experience, and therefore, should be analyzed at that level rather than at the community or institutional levels. Other researchers have concurred, suggesting that the growth of heritage tourism is linked to an increasing desire for personal fulfillment through multi-tasking vacations and leisure. Colonial Williamsburg, cited as one of the most successful heritage tourist destinations in the US, stresses its educative function and has aggressively developed links with other brands that do the same (e.g., Mattel's American Girl Dolls). The Williamsburg success indicates that perhaps the UK data can be generalized to the US industry.

Critical research literature most often draws on UK examples for advancing arguments about the construction of heritage. However, *Colossus of Roads* (Marling, 1984) provides an early US study which examines how roadside kitsch in the mid-West evokes responses of nostalgia and historical memory. In another US treatment, *On the Beaten Track: Tourism, Art and Place* (1999), Lippard explores the points of convergence between heritage tourism displaying culture for profit and artists portraying tourism as social critique.

The business of tourism has been found to be problematic with respect to the unique requirements of cultural display. In his examination of the partnerships necessary for a heritage site, Walle (1998) elaborates on how commercial and cultural interests almost inevitably clash due to the competing priorities of each. He argues that cultural tourism professionals should adapt, rather than lift wholesale, the strategies and tactics of other types of tourism. However, marketing efforts must remain sensitive to the special requirements of cultural tourism, among which are the appearance of authenticity and the relationship between ongoing real (local) lives and a frankly commodified past. Walle explains that in the dialogue between cultural tourism professionals and business professionals, the latter often exert an inequitable advantage. 'Because cultural tourism professionals are nested between host cultures and the business community, their actions are likely to dissatisfy at least some of the stakeholders with whom they work' (p. 3). Walle (1998) observes that 'public funding is being profoundly reduced and cultural tourism . . . [is] being forced to merge with the private sector' (p. 2). The *raison d'être* of heritage tourism is to connect a people's experiences in the present with a common past, and its explanatory power regarding who they are (and are not). The broadening of corporate control over heritage tourism/tourist sites must signal a changed focus in some fundamental manner.

Interdisciplinary insights provide ways to help synthesize some of the conflicts encountered in the study of heritage tourism. For example, a collection of essays (with contributions from environmentalists, consultants and academics) and edited by a folklorist (Wells, 1996), explores marketing heritage from the vantage-point of culture workers. Wells states in her introductory essay that heritage tourism has become a new type of product that 'could be called "public culture"–a mediated, interpreted, and "packaged" version of custom or tradition . . . ' (p. vii). From this perspective the difference between heritage and history lies in the processes of commodification and the transformation of the very notion of "public culture" into consumer goods. It is unclear as to whether, in this framework, public culture means anything more than a marketplace of cultural products.

In short, heritage tourism marketing faces distinctive challenges which can be perceived as a conflict between long-term business goals (authenticity of strategic planning) and preservation/restoration of a moment or moments from the past (historical/cultural authenticity). The latter is always further contested by all the social variables with which history is analyzed, most notably class, race/ethnicity, and gender. The former, by contrast, can be reduced to a formula, although it too is contested among the groups who produce it (e.g., business professionals, culture workers).

Authenticity and progress are key concepts related to successful heritage tourism promotion. A number of researchers have claimed that the increase of heritage tourism is in part a response to the anxieties endemic to a hyper-mediated social formation; but the response to such tourism leads to an increasingly mediated "self." Searching for roots is more than a fad in US culture, yet heritage tourism may actually distance the seekers from their goal. The tourist experience, the commodified heritage, is one more mediation. Hughes (1995) argues that authenticity in tourism should be re-theorized and 'assessed against the relative social meaning that continues to be vested in an artifact. . . . [It may be] possible to find manifestations of authenticity through individual's assertion of personal identity' (p. 799). This argument suggests a break between historical integrity and "authenticity." Hughes claims that '[a]uthenticity continues to reside in the resistances, choices, and commitments that individuals express within the opportunities and constraints provided by . . . markets and . . . imagery to which . . . tourism is an increasingly major contributor' (p. 800).

A working assumption of heritage tourism appears to be that contemporary society has evolved from a past that remains linked to its members through sites, material objects and personal testimony. Progress is treated as an inevitable natural process. This notion of progress is linked to the liberal pluralist perspective in which formerly divergent interest groups (e.g., class, race and gender) achieve ever-greater access to power and the fruits of a democratic society. Modernization is the process of progressively diffused social benefits accruing to an increasing number of persons.

For progress to occur, there must be a former time (defined as both long ago and worse, but not so bad as to prohibit evolution towards the more egalitarian present) from which to develop: '[i]nventing traditions . . . is essentially a process of formalization and ritualization, characterized by reference to the past. . . . ' (Hobsbawm and Ranger, 1983: 4). According to Hobsbawm and Ranger (1983), elements of the past are used 'to construct invented traditions of a novel type for novel purposes' (p. 6). As Hall (1994) suggests, tourism is an aspect of policy agendas at a number of different levels, from the local to national and even international decision-making. 'The political nature of tourism at both the macro- and the micro-political level' is, he argues, significant and under-acknowledged (p. 4); tourism entails the elements of politics: power, distribution of wealth, etc. Heritage tourism resurrects various pieces from the past, reforms them into palatable and sell-able parts, and reintegrates them into a "tourist site" that will prove viable in the marketplace. As part of that procedure, traditions are invented that serve the new purposes of a satisfactory tourist experience coherent and viable with the present. Part of the work of texts (brochures, guided tours, sites) is to create an audience, more properly, to create a subject for whom the text fabricates its specific message.[iv] However, audiences are notoriously intractable; effective advertising must strive for limiting meaning without restricting appeal.

DIGRESSION:
A REVISIT TO "PLANTATION"
AND "CREOLE"

Williams' (1976) insight, that certain key words contain within their meaning traces of ongoing social struggle, is particularly germane to this study, especially as regards the two central words "plantation" and "Creole."

The Laura Plantation is promoted as "LAURA: A Creole Plantation." The words "plantation" and "Creole" are frequently used in the promotional literature of a variety of Louisiana tourist attractions, and seemingly cover widely divergent types of products and destinations.

The meaning of "plantation" is dependent on relations of dominance and subordination. In *The New Shorter Oxford English Dictionary (SOED)* (Brown, 1993 (1973)), "plantation" is defined as 'an estate or large farm, esp. in a former British colony, on which cotton, tobacco, etc., are cultivated, formerly chiefly by slave labor.'[v] Hence the fascination with the Laura Plantation because it is described as having long been a women-managed productive farm, and its location in Louisiana, along with its association with Creole culture, is intriguing.

It is also interesting to discover that the notion of "Creole" is, by definition, intertwined with that of plantation. Again referring to the *SOED's* definition of plantation, one finds the following: 'Plantation Creole is a Creolized language arising amongst a transplanted and largely isolated Black community, as slaves in the US.' Without plantation there is no Creole; Creole too is implicated in the relations of dominance that define the plantation. The *SOED* notes the links between plantation as a site of oppression and the creation of localized cultures. This suggests that an examination of how the Laura Plantation is promoted as a tourist destination can lead to potentially intriguing insights about the relationship between memory, historic preservation, and variables such as gender, race and class.

Describing a site as a "plantation" marks it as belonging to a former period in US history. The antithesis of current society in which the family-fun farm is portrayed just short of nonviable, plantation more nearly conjures up images of Tara in *Gone with the Wind*. However, in the past, plantations were precisely large family farms having much in common with the contemporary beleaguered family farm, the single major difference being plantations' dependence on slave labor.

Plantations in Louisiana typically originate from the period during and just after the American Revolution, a significant difference from those of Virginia and other Deep South states that date to the late 17th century. As an historian of Louisiana plantations and genealogy notes, '[t]he settling of the earliest Louisiana colony was somewhat different . . . as that in the far south was the outcome of a plan of the King of France to scheme that country out of debt' (Seebold, 1971: 2). Historians describe the settling of Louisiana by French aristocrats displaced by the French Revolution and Spanish aristocracy similarly attracted to Louisiana. Often these immigrants traveled by way of the West Indies, there also learning the solid return of farming sugarcane and other crops with slave labor, i.e., the plantation for production.

The concept of "Creole" is identified with the Gulf area, and specifically with Louisiana, and the term has come to have a number of sometimes-contradictory meanings and connotations. O'Sullivan et al. (1994: 66-67) define Creole as a 'language which develops out of a pidgin language to become the native language of a group. . . . [f]or example the Africans who as slave labour were captured and transported to the "New World" developed . . . a contact language [which took] on all the complexity of an established language.' In this, and similar definitions, "Creole" contains within its definition reference to oppression and resistance as well as specifically to race and place or origin. It is a linguistic term, describing both conditions of experience and the process of language formation.

On the other hand, for Herrin (1952: 27), an historian apologist of aristocratic culture, such associations are mere 'fanciful legend, utterly incredible, a product of the grossly misinformed. . . . ' Herrin defines Creole as a racial construct; it refers to "white" people of Spanish and French descent, 'never to be used to identify persons with both white and Negro blood. . . . ' (p. 28). Herrin identifies other "racial strains," characteristics that are "natural" to Creoles. He distinguishes Creoles not only by blood, but by their shared, striking physical characteristics, their common lively sense of aesthetics, gallantry and adventure, and preference for administration of large business ventures to trade or physical labor, among others. He stresses that these are traits which emerged from a lineage and caused the rich, highly advanced, intellectual and aesthetic culture.

The *Cambridge International Dictionary* (2000) defines a Creole person as one who is related to the original group of Europeans coming to the West Indies or the southern US, or a West Indian of mixed African and European origin who speaks Creole. This definition highlights not race, but history and culture, suggesting that "Creole" refers to conditions of experience. Finally, common usage also applies "Creole" as an adjective linked to products of the Gulf area such as specific spices and other foods, architecture and artifacts.[vi]

This analysis suggests that plantation is a relatively stable term, denoting and connoting historical relations of dominance and subordination as well as describing processes of production. Its malleability is limited. Creole, however, is an extraordinarily de-stable term, providing pliant material with which to construct a variety of social meanings. Its meanings vary from strong connotations of resistance, to enslavement by Europeans, to strong associations with European aristocratic culture. Its use as a linguistic term is complex. Its description of people, in whichever particulars of race or class/caste, is ambiguous. Moreover, its attachment to many aspects of material culture, geographic location, etc. demonstrates its enormous utility for a wide variety of applications. This lack of stability, the open-ended possibilities of meaning, removes "Creole" from the constraints of its historically contested uses, thus making it relatively easy to co-opt.

PROCEDURES

Adapting the method first described in Hall's (1975) valuable introduction to *Paper Voices*, it is first necessary to become familiar with materials ranging from Laura Plantation's promotions to the pamphlets of nearby plantations and Louisiana tour groups specializing in plantation destinations. The text for analysis is confined to the visual and verbal elements of Laura Plantation (and the related "Le Monde Creole courtyard tours") brochures, promotions to the industry and the scripts of on-site guided tours. "Deep readings" of the text are conducted with attention directed first at overall stylistic matters (amounts of copy and graphics, design, etc.), later to uses of language, metaphor, references and thematic focus.

In the initial readings of the promotional material for the Laura Plantation, it can be noted that representations use two related strategies: the exotification of the other and the codifying of tradition. Creating an other as exotic involves processes which distance that other in time and space, reifying differences of experience (and therefore of power) as abstract, often primitive reminders of someone else's authentic past. Codifying a tradition suggests both that versions of history are being constructed and that specific relations of power enable an hegemonic version to predominate. In analyzing an advertising text (within an integrated communication system) one can also continually observe how advertising techniques partner with the other strategies. Hall's method of analysis focuses radically on the text, but the text is always linked theoretically to conditions of production; it theorizes the audience as constructed by discourse, i.e., every narrative constructs its preferred reader. As such, textual evidence is always understood within the larger context of its social formation.

CRITICAL INTERROGATIONS: LAURA AS TEXT

Why Laura? Laura Locoul was not the first owner of the land and farm that bears her name, nor were her family original owners. The St. James Parish, Louisiana website[vii] describes the site as first a Colapissa Indian village, later an Acadian refugee settlement, and finally, a plantation built in 1805 by Gullaume DuParc, native of Normandy. Thomas Jefferson granted DuParc part of the 12,000-acre sugar cane estate because DuParc was a veteran of the American Revolution. The plantation's history is traced through "DuParc's Creole wife," who managed the business; to her daughter, Elizabeth, who later married Raymond Locoul; and finally to Laura, who eventually sold the property to the Waguespack family. That family held the property, not always inhabited, until 1984. The website information reiterates the history as told by the current owners and forms part of the tourism promotion.

The National Register of Historical American Buildings Information (2000) differs slightly:

The land on which Laura stands was originally owned by André Neau, who obtained it in a French royal land grant in 1755. The plantation became the property of the Dupare family in the late 1700s . . . [and] the main house appears to have been built around 1820. The plantation was divided between two family members in 1876. The house continued in the hands of Dupare heirs until 1891. In that year, Dupare descendant Laura Locoul sold the property to A. Florian Waguespack. However, a condition of the sale was that the plantation and house should continue to be called "Laura." The house was passed down through the succeeding generations of the Waguespack family until 1980, when the final Waguespack residents moved out.

Four key discursive strategies differentiate the promotional (commodified) from the archival (documentary) information: highlighting genealogical continuity; connecting this little-known site with major events in US history; promoting Creole culture as particularly enigmatic; and spotlighting women as owners/managers.

These four strategies add cachet to "Laura: A Creole Plantation" as a tourist destination, and are the foci of a constructed mythic past. Therefore, it can be seen how they help form Laura as different from other tourist destinations. Laura is promised to be a uniquely exotic island of "authentic" Creole experience, without abrogating Laura's relevance to how its visitors conceive Creole history.

The tourist business, *Le Monde Créole*, along with many other tourism operators, places its brochures in hotel lobbies and other likely locations. The brochures, one for the Laura Plantation itself, the other for New Orleans' courtyard tours (Laura lived in the French Quarter during the social season), are designed similarly to attract attention. Indeed, they do stand out among others with their uniform design concept: portrayal of the dark, direct gaze of (initially unidentified) Laura. The "Le Monde Créole: French Quarter Courtyards Tour (cemetery visit and voodoo tales)" depicts this woman faded over with pictures of cast-iron balconies. In effect, this is a collage in which the Laura persona stands behind the still-contemporary architecture of New Orleans. 'No existing place in New Orleans preserves more of her magical & haunting flavor than in her courtyards . . . '. The photo, paired with the quote, suggests the unidentified woman exemplifies a

Creole Everywoman–hinting at the centrality of women to this cultural milieu and at a barely suppressed sexuality.

Inside the brochure, again using a collage/montage design approach, are sepia-toned photographs superimposed over a modern-day color photo, with insets of copy in both English and French. Top and bottom contain a descriptive text of the courtyard tour, printed against hunter green background bars in a script typeface. Between those bars, a lush background of semi-tropical vegetation is shot from knee-height and centered is an extravagantly carved bird bath and statuary lion resting on broken brick tiles. Superimposed over that are four other elements: what appears to be the scene of a 19th century ball (or is it a slave auction?), an African-American boy balancing a basket on his head standing on a dirt road, a sheaf of documents (letters? a diary?) along with a photo of three more black children, and to the left, a photo of a woman (Laura?) cut away from her background, so that behind her are the plants from the modern-day courtyard. This woman, again dark (same woman as the cover photo?), is smiling and dressed in fancy clothes, maybe even a costume. She holds a devil's pitchfork, wears an elaborate headdress and her upper arms are circled by bracelets (is it Mardi Gras? a masked ball?). Superimposed over the woman's picture, the copy block ends with the words: "Laura Locoul (1861-1963)" as if identifying the picture. Part of this copy block reads:

> Based on Laura's Memoirs and some 5,000 pages of documents from the National Archives in Paris, relive compelling life stories of passion and devotion as well as rejection and denial. Feel the strength and tenderness of a world bound by an incredible love that still crosses today's boundaries of time, race and moderation!

Time, race, and extravagance are the elements used to entice the tourist to the Laura Plantation and the courtyard tour, while scholarly evidence bolsters the credibility of the *mise en scène*. The accompanying photos, reproduced in earthy sepia tones, combined with the verdant vegetation growing lush around the plaster lion also suggest an atmosphere that positively contrasts with a mundane concrete modern suburban life. The photos are "old" but the courtyards may still belong to "distinctive private homes of the French Quarter" conveying titillating vestiges of the class/caste society and past indiscretions that may still exist behind contemporary walls.

The front panel of the Laura brochure looks just like the courtyard tour brochure which promotes the Laura Plantation and vice versa. The same picture of Laura graces both, although on the Plantation pamphlet she is pictured alone. Thus, clearly visible are her white bodice, cinched belt and black lace demi-glove on the one hand which is showing.

The inside pages, also with the collage/montage technique, use a background color picture of (contemporary) growing sugarcane. Superimposed over that are a lovely, colorful woman's dress fan; a picture of the main house; an "old looking" cameo painting of an "old fashioned" woman holding a baby; a black-and-white photograph of farm outbuildings with several African-American working men standing nearby; a color photo of what are apparently slave houses; and over that a cartoon silhouette rabbit. No apparent theme connects these disparate pictures except as they convey a multiplicity of real items from the past. Their historical authenticity alone unites them; even their individual time periods seem different.

Like the courtyard tour pamphlet, the plantation brochure focuses on the authority devolving from access to Laura's memoirs. The back cover, with its picture of two white women driving a small, horse-drawn vehicle, reiterates the grounding of this tourist experience in fact. Photography, with its apparent ability to record reality, is used as shorthand for the integrity and authority behind the tour. Photography is also used in both pamphlets as a signifier of the serious reality of race relations; but the cartoon rabbit undercuts that seriousness by imbuing slave culture with a cheery aspect.

In short, the execution of the tourist information maintains a consistent image and is not excessively slick. Its serious, toney image is compatible with conveying that this destination meets the high standards of true heritage tourists, interested in "real history." The use of subdued colors, old photos and pictures of artifacts, references to archival research, and the recording of folk tales send a unified and convincing persuasive message to a niche audience.

These brochures stand in stark contrast to the many other New Orleans area tourist advertisements for similar destinations. Other publicity tends to show clear, crisp photos of the tourist site and to tout modern conveniences and comforts. The 'Charmed and tragic lives' of Creole men, women, slaves, and children who 'lived apart from the

American life-style for 200 years' mentioned in the Laura promotions provide both an imaginative narrative and promise material lessons.

Among the scripted tours, the "Manager's Tour" is the most generalized tour, and exemplifies the strategies of the other tours. In it, the history of the land, the buildings and the people who lived at the Laura site are detailed. Through it, an over-arching theme of difference links the strategies exotifying the other and codifying tradition, by which a complex history becomes a comprehensible tourist attraction.

The tour guides clearly identify themselves as "Creole," an expression which is immediately defined as non-Anglo culture. Thus, the escorts are "native guides," persons who understand foreign cultures (those of the visitors) but whose lives are centered in Creole culture. Tourists are the aliens. Repeatedly, it is made clear that the United States and Americans have been interlopers in Louisiana/Creole culture and politics, exerting both military and economic force to extend an unwelcome hegemony over local preferences and ways of life. The local present is transformed into a highly idiosyncratic locale, almost a separate nation, populated by a distinctive racial/ethnic group. The frequent use of expressions such as "foreign," "non-Anglo," "we" (as opposed to English speakers), "French customary law," "Creole pragmatism," "Anglo vulgarity," and many more, attest to the purposive construction of (separate) national identity (an alternative to the commonsense notion of Louisiana as one of 50 states).

"[T]his Creole thing" is exemplified in the tour as a caste culture, where Europeans dominated but also allowed other original (Native American) and imported (slave) cultures to 'pick and choose what worked for them.' The ruthlessness of "Creole culture" is not denied, but rather infused with an exotic and exciting primordial essence. Furthermore, its existence is explained and naturalized by statements comparing life at Laura with life in the Caribbean, Indian Ocean, South America and Africa. The tale is told that Leopold Senghor, the former (20th century) president of Senegal, collected in his country the same stories of the rabbit and the fool that Fortier (1969; dignified by mention of his later role as president of Tulane University) gathered at the Laura Plantation slave quarters. This reference is used in the text to show that Sengalese culture and African family life were allowed to persist and thrive. It celebrates both cultural strength and the absence of ultimate cruelty of the plantation owners.

The family-orientation of Creole life is stressed repeatedly. Its importance is perhaps best captured towards the end of the script with the following anecdote that begins with the comments of a French visitor to the Plantation:

> [O]ne of Laura's cousins from Paris . . . said, 'It is a shame that you never knew Laura. She was a gentle and warm person. But, my family never approved of Laura marrying an American.' Laura's family had been in Louisiana since 1699 and, though they lived here for 200 years, they still considered themselves to be something other than American. It is that difference that we call Creole.

Here, as elsewhere, the straight genealogical line helps construct an engaging narrative while obviating disjunctures and conflict. Any confrontation described within the text revolves around the family inheritance issues and is abstracted from more generalized social relations. The one exception is the positioning of Creole culture against an American (i.e., the tourist's own) standard; in this instance larger historical trends are noted, but only as they pertain to the eventual suppression of Creole social norms.

However, the narrative weaves in allusions to non-controversial, positively construed events/personages in U.S. history. Signifiers of positive American values such as George Washington and mentions of well-known peccadilloes associated with Louisiana state politics (with its reputation for colorful corruption) help show that plantation history is intertwined with familiar reference points. Indeed, the founding fathers of the US are said to have been instrumental in helping the original family establish its fortune on this site.

The significant roles women played in plantation life are also attributed to the lack of Anglo-dominance. This feature, too, is used to tame the outlandishness of Creole culture by suggesting that gender relations were egalitarian. The script recalls that '[b]y 1900 there were still as many women as men running farms and plantations along this River. And then, in the 20th Century, as we became more Americanized, the women here took the back seat like everywhere else.' The text highlights the values of pragmatism and meritocracy, linking those currently popular values to life on the plantation.

The elements of outlandishness are also used in a positive way, tamed, but nonetheless endowing a certain rogue glamor on the plantation, and on Creole life that the plantation is meant to exemplify. For example, one of the earliest owners is described as a former murderer then governor-commandant of central Louisiana. *'If that's not good Louisiana politics, I don't know what is!'* [italics in the original]. Plantation life is described as strictly business; the "real" residential life of this plantation family is centered in New Orleans. 'Creoles did not believe that moderation is a virtue.' This claim is supported with titillating tales of family pressures, parties, Prohibition-era shenanigans, etc., which occurred on the plantation itself and in the New Orleans homes where the family spent the social season. One particularly gloomy anecdote concludes tragically: 'For 20 years, there was a woman incarcerated on the men's side of the house.' More droll is the story that describes one former owner as 'a third-generation Creole; a devout Catholic, of pure French blood, a plantation president for 47 years [who] believed in Voodoo like her slaves.'

The "Back Tour" focuses on slave life and is specifically marketed as an African-American heritage experience. It introduces difference in two ways: by characterizing the plantation as a business rather than as a permanent home (describing the kitchen as 'the company kitchen serving the manor house and some meals for the workers') and by noting peculiarities in architectural style. Those are also linked to enterprise: 'workers/slaves could not read and, so, there was no signage . . . the Creole plantation business was painted one of the colors that you see on the Big House.'

Plantation efficacy is based on slavery; both tour scripts confirm that. The slave registry is pointed out, as is its post-Civil War entries that note that the entire year's wages of each worker were paid back to the plantation. The terms "slave" and "worker" are used interchangeably. Owner cruelty is detailed and always juxtaposed with compassion. For example, in one case the separation of a mother and child is described, along with the story that the proprietor's son kindly reunited them. Another instance details the branding of a former escapee and the horror of a young white child who witnessed it. That story concludes with a quote from a documentary source: The child's mother explains that 'the people of this plantation, all 200 of them, are no better or worse than you will find anywhere else.'

Gender, race and class relations are linked throughout the tours, again always softening the horror with panaceas such as the following:

As hard as she seems to us today, Elizabeth [the plantation own-
er], by and large treated her slaves according to the old French
colonial slave laws, the so called "CODE NOIR," (sic) the
BLACK CODE. [caps in orig.] Created in the 1720s to civilize
the treatment of slaves, the code was still a brutal system. Before
Louisiana became part of the US in 1803, the Black Code was in
effect and slaves were not allowed to be separated from their
immediate families . . . Male slaves were allowed to carry arms
(for hunting).

In short, the scripted tour poses an "us versus them" relationship in
which the plantation belongs to a foreign other. That other, although
highly privileged, is somehow made more palatable by being positioned as an underdog, with characteristics that are both pragmatic and
chivalrous. The culture, while based on slave labor and an inviolable
class system, nonetheless had some "modern" notions of race and
gender relations. All of these qualities come together in the persona of
Laura, who, as the text indicates, declared her intention of becoming a
"modern, liberated American." These attributes are personified by the
tour guides who consistently refer to themselves as Creole, and use the
first person when describing cultural practices, while remaining associated with current US and tourist culture. The guide's persona exemplifies a hybrid cultural background and serves as a link between
heritage and the tourist's present: 'This is the way we lived in Louisiana . . . There still exists this difference [of the Anglo language and
religion, and the Creole] . . . I hope that . . . you were able to glimpse a
little of that difference, a difference we call CREOLE [caps in orig.].'
The guides emphasize their genealogical ties, their own felt connections to significant historical events, their joyfulness in celebrating the
oddities of Creole culture, and their pride in what are described as
innately progressive aspects of this plantation's social formation.
Thus, the foreign becomes familiar.

DISCUSSION

To what does "the past" refer? The past may be the sum of its
histories and its representations as Brett (1996) suggests. Furthermore,
he says that "heritage" as distinct from "history" is particularly
rooted in the imaginative figures of representation. Heritage, then, as a

kind of representation, proposes a certainty which history, as critical inquiry, can never promise. Can heritage ever achieve more than a strictly representational status? Has heritage so engulfed members of society that history as such is no longer relevant to them?

The Laura Plantation is an exemplar of a first-rate heritage site by industry standards. Restored by professionals who are committed to preserving their own history (which they understand as coterminous with the plantation's) and to researching it through primary resources when possible, Laura is an entertaining and educational tourist destination. Its success testifies to its appeal.

Three styles of representation increase Laura's attractiveness. The strong narrative, the techniques of association and the practice of simulation objectify and commodify the time/space designated "Laura: A Creole Plantation." Every piece of Laura promotional material, from the brochures and trade information to the scripted tours, proposes a heroine, Laura, as an historical personage around whom other aspects of the site come into being. Laura's story is what ignites interest. The narrative, while it provides conflicts, tensions and surprises, centers around one person and, in so doing, leads attention away from community or structural issues. Laura lives and dies; her successes and failures frame the representation. The level of critique remains at the individual level. The sense of the familiar, that Laura is a person in many ways "like us" (if far more compellingly exotic and chillingly dangerous) is heightened by the degrees of association fostered between some of the clearly negative aspects of the past (caste, slavery, gender relations), and present values. The text creates Creole culture as an underdog culture, within which, and despite its vagaries, exist precursors of modern values. The cultural, political and economic struggles are essentialized. Rather than stimulating discomfort, the discourse constantly allays it. The excesses of Creole culture are explained in terms of a blameworthy, yet natural, escape from the rigors of plantation life and the incursions of a dominant American culture.

The terms "plantation" and "Creole" are thoroughly domesticated into a kind of old-fashioned business vocabulary. The dependence on slave labor and the harsh family and gender relations that span both master and slave cultures are tempered by stories of escapades and idiosyncrasies.

Simulation is a practice that tends to prohibit critical response by reifying an historical material reality as myth. Bits and pieces of the past are combined into a new reality, a new past. Simulation tolerates distinction and integration concurrently, obviating historical struggles, and thereby resolving critical conflict. Thus. authenticity is only an aesthetic within which belief is suspended and imagination stimulated. Nostalgia subsumes imagination.

This study therefore suggests that, in constructing entertainment as education, a popular discourse is employed that must advance positive messages even in the face of pernicious acts. Those acts, while not highlighted are not hidden. The Laura text simulates a "real" historical text. But frequent references to historical evidence and processes of restoration, which might provide an opening to critical inquiry on the part of visitors, work in this case to restrict meaning. The process of historical analysis remains something on display, rather than something with which to be engaged.

In the case of the Laura Plantation, traditions of female dominance and commonsense business practices are always described as precursors to contemporary values. The potential for the Laura site to surpass its commoditized heritage discourse and for the text to operate in what Barthes (1972) has called a "writerly" way (i.e., to invite critical participation) is not realized, despite what appear to be the sincere desires of Laura's promoters to do just that.

NOTES

i. Baudrillard (1983) develops this thesis in *Simulations* in which he specifically refers to tourism. His later work, *America*, while not as helpful theoretically, is a first-person account of Baudrillard's own travels in the US.

ii. A debt of gratitude is expressed to Mr. R. Marmillion for sharing Laura material and for his enthusiasm for the plantation as a significant heritage site.

iii. As Baudrillard (1983) observes, *"[w]e are all Tasady"* [ital. in orig.] (p. 16).

iv. Discussed in *Key Concepts in Communication and Cultural Studies*, this concept of a "created audience" is related to the aspect of textual theory that asserts that individual identity is 'determined, regulated and reproduced as a structure of relationships. . . . Subjectivity is a way of conceptualizing text/reader relations' (p. 309-10). Texts are privileged over individuals as the locus of power.

v. This definition describes the topic of this paper. However, other listed meanings also highlight actions of conquest, domination and colonization.

vi. Here are several other definitions from Brewer (1894): Creole (2 syl.). A descendant of white people born in Mexico, South America and the West Indies. (Spanish *criado*, a servant; diminutive *criadillo*, contracted into *creollo, creole*.) (*See* Mulatto.) *Creole dialects*. The various jargons spoken by the West Indian slaves. *The dictionnaire de la linguistique* (Mounin, 1993) gives the following:

Langue qui ne se distingue d'un pidgin que par le fait qu'elle se transmet de parents à enfants, devenant la seule langue de certaines communautés. Ces communautés sont le plus souvent de race noire, et l'histoire des créoles est liée à celle de l'esclavage. Il existe des créoles à base d'anglais, de français, de portugais et de néerlandais. Ils peuvent être considérés comme des variétés de ces langues devenues autonomes. Les exemples les plus souvents cités sont ceux des Caraïbes, en particulier le créole français de Haïti, langue populaire unique d'un état indépendant depuis un siècle et demi. vii. *www.lauraplantation.com.*

REFERENCES

Barthes, R. (1972). *Mythologies*. New York: Hill and Want.

Baudrillard, J. (1983). *Simulations*. New York: Semiotext(e).

Baudrillard, J. (1988). *America*. London: Verso.

Becker, J. (1998). *Selling tradition*. Chapel Hill, NC: University of North Carolina Press.

Brett, D. (1996). *The construction of heritage*. Cork: Cork University Press.

Brewer, E. (1894). *The dictionary of phrase and fable*. (www.bibliomania.com/reference/phrase and fable).

Brown, L. (Ed.) (1993) (1973). *New shorter Oxford English dictionary*. Oxford: Clarendon Press. Cambridge International Dictionary (2000). www.dictionary.cambridge.org

Fitzgerald, F. S. (1922). *The beautiful and damned*. New York: Scribners.

Fortier, A. (1969). *Louisiana folk tales: In French dialect and English translation*. Boston: Houghton Mifflin.

Frow, J. (1997). *Time and commodity culture: Essays in cultural theory and postmodernity*. Oxford: Clarendon Press.

Hall, C. M. (1994). *Tourism and politics: Policy, power and place*. New York: Wiley.

Hall, S. (1975). Introduction. In A. C. H. Smith et al. (Eds.) *Paper voices: The popular press and social change. 1933-1965* (pp. 11-24). London: Chatto and Windus.

Herrin, M. (1952). *The creole aristocracy: A study of the creole of Southern Louisiana, his origin, his accomplishments, his contributions to the American way of life*. New York: Exposition Press.

Hobsbawn, E. and Ranger, T. (1983). *The invention of tradition*. Cambridge: Cambridge University Press.

Hughes, G. (1995). Authenticity in tourism. *Annals of Tourism Research* 22: 781-803.

Jameson, F. (1991). *Postmodernism or, the cultural logic of late capitalism*. Durham: Duke University Press.

Jameson, F. (1997). Culture and finance capital. *Critical Inquiry* 21(1): 246-264.

Kirshenblatt-Gimblett, B. and Bruner, E. (1989). Tourism. In *International encyclopaedia of communications, vol IV* (pp. 249-253). New York: Oxford University Press.

Kurin, R. (1998). Foreword. In *Cultural tourism: A strategic focus* (p. xiii). Boulder, CO: Westview Press.

Lippard, L. (1999). *On the beaten track*: *Tourism, art, and place*. New York: The New Press.

MacCannell, D. (1976). *The tourist*: *A new theory of the leisure class*. New York: Schocken Books.

MacCannell, D. (1992). *Empty meeting grounds*: *The tourist papers*. London: Routledge.

McIntosh, A. (1999). Into the tourist's mind: Understanding the value of the heritage experience. *Journal of Travel and Tourism Marketing*, Vol. 8(1): 41-64.

Marling, K. (1984). *The colossus of roads*: *Myth and symbol along the American highway*. Minneapolis: University of Minnesota Press.

Mitchell, R. (1999). *All on a Mardi Gras day*: *Episodes in the history of New Orleans carnival*. Cambridge, MA: Harvard University Press.

Mounin, G. (Ed.) (1993). *Dictionnaire de la linguistique*. Paris: Presses Universitaires de France.

National Register (2000). www.nr.nps.gov.

O'Sullivan, T., Hartley, J., Saunders, D., Montgomery, M. and Fiske, J. (1994). *Key concepts in communication and cultural studies, 2nd ed*. London: Routledge.

Peck, J. and Lepie, A. (1989). Tourism and development in three North Carolina towns. In V. Smith (Ed.) *Hosts and guests*: *The anthropology of tourism, 2nd edition* (pp. 203-222). Philadelphia: University of Pennsylvania Press.

Said, E. (1979). *Orientalism*. New York: Vintage.

Said, E. (1993). *Culture and imperialism*. New York: Knopf.

Seebold, de Bachelle H. (1971). *Old Louisiana plantation homes and family trees. Vols. 1 and 2*. Gretna, LA: Pelican.

Smith, V. (Ed.) (1989). *Hosts and guests*: *The anthropology of tourism, 2nd ed*. Philadelphia: University of Pennsylvania Press.

Walle, A. (1998). Introduction. In A. Walle (Ed.) *Cultural tourism*: *A strategic focus* (pp. 1-5). Boulder, CO: Westview Press.

Wells, P. (Ed.) (1996). *Keys to the marketplace: Problems and issues in cultural and heritage tourism*. Enfield Lock, Middlesex, UK: Hisarlik.

Williams, R. (1976). *Keywords*: *A vocabulary of culture and society*. New York: Oxford University Press.

From Civil War to Civil Rights:
Selling Alabama as Heritage Tourism

Glenn T. Eskew

SUMMARY. Alabama sold its Old South heritage by commemorating the Confederacy and celebrating the wealth produced by slave labor through pilgrimages. Yet in the 1980s, the state cut a new course by marketing African-American heritage and the sites of civil rights conflicts. Joining other groups in memorializing the movement, Alabama successfully commodified its controversial past as heritage tourism. Ironically, Governor George Wallace initiated the marketing strategy to alter Alabama's negative image. Selma captured the idea with its "From Civil War to Civil Rights" advertising campaign. The juxtaposition of apparently incongruous events points not only to the mixed motivations behind heritage tourism but also to the potential that exists as the public engages and confronts contested pasts. *[Article copies available for a fee from The Haworth Document Delivery Service: 1-800-342-9678. E-mail address: <getinfo@haworthpressinc.com> Website: <http://www.HaworthPress.com> © 2001 by The Haworth Press, Inc. All rights reserved.]*

KEYWORDS. Civil Rights Movement, American Civil War, heritage tourism, black history, Old South pilgrimage, Alabama, Birmingham, Montgomery, Selma, George Wallace

INTRODUCTION

Following other states in the American South, Alabama began marketing slavery and the plantation myth as a form of nascent heritage

Glenn T. Eskew is affiliated with the Department of History, Georgia State University, College of Arts & Sciences, Atlanta, GA 30302-411, USA.

[Haworth co-indexing entry note]: "From Civil War to Civil Rights: Sellling Alabama as Heritage Tourism." Eskew, Glenn T. Co-published simultaneously in *International Journal of Hospitality & Tourism Administration* (The Haworth Hospitality Press, an imprint of The Haworth Press, Inc.) Vol. 2, No. 3/4, 2001, pp. 201-214; and: *Slavery, Contested Heritage and Thanatourism* (ed: Graham M. S. Dann and A. V. Seaton), The Haworth Hospitality Press, an imprint of The Haworth Press, Inc., 2001, pp. 201-214. Single or multiple copies of this article are available for a fee from The Haworth Document Delivery Service [1-800-342-9678, 9:00 a.m. - 5:00 p.m. (EST). E-mail address: getinfo@haworthpressinc.com].

tourism in the 1950s. However, since the 1980s it has blazed a trail commodifying its brutal civil rights legacy. Similar to the recent revisionist commodification of slavery as sold at Williamsburg, Virginia and elsewhere, the packaging of the non-violent movement functions as an alternative form of tourism sponsored by non-profit groups, social reform organizations, and local and state entities. A cursory look at such state-sponsored tourism in Alabama reveals a willingness to engage in ideological conflict through the rosy lens of heritage. The juxtaposition of slavery and desegregation as seen in Selma, Alabama's marketing strategy, "From Civil War to Civil Rights," points to the mixed motivations that lie behind heritage tourism and the ambiguous response of the public to this contested past.

Recognizing the need for closer collaboration between social historians and other social scientists studying heritage tourism (Towner, 1994), this paper presents historical evidence that recounts the evolution of the industry in Alabama. While surprising to some people in the business, the success of the state in selling a particular variant of heritage tourism underscores the wide-open nature of the field (Nash, 1992; Pearce, 1992; Swarbrooke, 1994). Alabama became the first state in America to aggressively market its civil rights past and African-American heritage for tourism purposes. It has since won awards for its packaging of controversial subject matter regarding race relations. Public demand keeps state travel guides out-of-stock while flooding heritage tourism sites with visitors.

PILGRIMAGE AND THE PROMOTION
OF SLAVERY HERITAGE

Alabama was slow to follow the lead of its neighbors in developing "pilgrimage" as a marketing tool for selling the legacy of slavery to tourists. When the ladies in the Mississippi State Federation of Garden Clubs met in Natchez in 1931 and held a house tour, one enterprising local, Mrs. J. Balfour Miller, recognized the potential and planned the first pilgrimage for 1932 by publicizing the event in the national media (Sansing, 1989). Overwhelmed by her success, Miller shared pilgrimage with other garden clubs as the money-making movement swept a region suffering from the economic calamity of the Great Depression. Soon a formula evolved wherein antebellum houses were opened to the public as beautiful girls in hoopskirts identified family heirlooms and antiques. Organizers planned Confederate balls and Old South pageants as fundraisers, while the unstated product being sold–the slave labor that produced the grandeur of the old regime–remained firmly behind the Big House. Within two decades, hundreds of tourists, mainly from the Midwest, traveled by car to Natchez to attend the pilgrimage (Bailey, 1953).

Like Virginia, Alabama sponsored a heritage tourism that glorified the Confederacy. At the very moment state legislators were adopting a new constitution that disenfranchised African-Americans in 1901, they chartered the First White House Association, a group of United Daughters of the Confederacy members committed to preserving the home lived in by President Jefferson Davis when Montgomery was the capitol of the Confederate States of America (The First White House of the Confederacy, 1949). In 1919, the state appropriated $25,000 for the project, moved the house to the corner of the state capitol grounds, according to a plan developed by the Olmsted Brothers, and opened the shrine to the Confederacy in 1921 (Blair, 1943). This memorial to the Lost Cause was an instant success and remains a popular tourist attraction today. Yet it was still something of an exception, since the state spent little on heritage tourism other than developing recreational facilities at historic sites (Alabama State Planning Board, 1948).

Arlington Historical Shrine

As dramatic changes swept the land in the aftermath of World War II, and the old system gave way to a modernizing economy that challenged an archaic social structure; white Alabamians renewed their interest in preserving the past as a way to hold on to previous social customs. Birmingham, whose blast furnaces had long identified the city as the symbol of the industrial New South, in contrast to the moonlight and magnolias that represented the rest of the state, acquired a plantation house in 1953. Built around 1842, Arlington once crowned a large corn and cotton farm that faded in significance after the 1871 founding of the boom town by railroad speculators. With no past, but a promising future, Birmingham quickly absorbed nearby fields as one industrialist after another bought and sold Arlington. With private support and public money, municipal leaders restored the antebellum mansion and created the "Arlington Historical Shrine" as Birmingham's tribute to the Old South ("Arlington," 1989). On the heels of the house museum's opening, local writer Ethel Miller Gor-

man (1956) published a romance novel set at Arlington–*Red Acres*–
that perpetuated the Lost Cause. Today Arlington remains supported
by tax dollars as part of the city's park system, and it is a popular site
for African-American weddings.

Selma and Sturdivant Hall

Only in the last quarter of the 20th Century did Selma turn to
tourism in order to salvage its weakened economy. With the collapse
of cotton during the Depression and the subsequent turn to cattle
raising, the black belt town on the bluff above the Alabama River
struggled to find a new economic engine that could provide the local
community with jobs. The federal government helped when, during
World War II, it located an airfield near Selma that introduced a mili-
tary-industrial complex into the area. Yet, not until the 1950s, did the
white élite begin commodifying its antebellum past. In 1957, Mr. and
Mrs. Robert Sturdivant donated a priceless collection of regional antiques and $50,000 to be used toward the $75,000 purchase of the
Watts-Parkman-Gillman House. The city and county governments,
once they had made up the shortfall, combined the two bequests into
Sturdivant Hall, the renamed house museum now filled with the donated period furnishings (Selma *Times-Journal*, April 23, 1998).
Nearly two decades passed before Selma inaugurated its first pilgrimage which featured Sturdivant Hall in 1975 ("Historic Selma Pilgrimage," 2000). In the 1980s, the local Kiwanis Club began hosting an
Old South Ball at Sturdivant Hall and a re-enactment of the Battle of
Selma, the 1865 skirmish between Federal raiders and Confederate
defenders, often described as the last engagement of the Civil War
(Selma *Times-Journal*, 1999). Selma celebrated its Old South heritage
against a backdrop of civil rights protests.

Living History in Alabama

So eager to ignore the racial turmoil of the previous decade, and
ever enamoured with the antebellum period, the State of Alabama
Department of Archives and History observed the sesquicentennial in
1969 by producing a pamphlet, *Living History in Alabama*. The publication privileged the age of King Cotton by romanticizing Greek
Revival mansions through pen and ink drawings of wrought-iron rail-

ings, ladies with parasols, columned porticoes and steamboats. With the plea, 'You'll find your travel-fun dollars go further in picturesque Alabama,' Governor Albert P. Brewer proudly introduced 'this guide, which–confined to sites of historical significance–is the first of its type compiled.' Despite the limited selection and the pilgrimage-like driving "history circle tours," *Living History* marked Alabama's first attempt at promoting heritage tourism and clearly constituted a departure from the typical chamber of commerce hyperbole that had sold investors on Birmingham.

ALABAMA'S BLACK HERITAGE

Once committed to heritage tourism, the state government expanded its product line to draw African-American expatriates living in Detroit and Chicago down to the "Heart of Dixie" for holiday. Special Projects Director Frances Smiley conceptualized Alabama black heritage materials for the Alabama Bureau of Publicity and Information during the 1970s. By 1983, Smiley, and the newly appointed Bureau Director, Ed Hall, produced a fully-illustrated fourteen page travel guide, *Alabama's Black Heritage: A Tour of Historic Sites*. Up until then, the state had limited its marketing efforts toward African-Americans to an "ineffectual advertisement in *Ebony Magazine*." With the release of the new publication, some misguided critics accused Hall and Smiley of "trying to segregate black people." Yet the white Hall and black Smiley argued otherwise. 'That was the last thing I had in mind,' Hall explained, 'I'm a sales and marketing person, and I saw a clear need in Alabama for a black tour' (Atlanta *Journal-Constitution*, October 19, 1986).

Describing nearly sixty sites across the state, *Alabama's Black Heritage* contained information on churches, houses, colleges, public buildings and all-black communities. Yet the inclusion of three sites underscored the paternalistic attitude toward race relations represented by the brochure. The gravesite of "Harry the Slave" who saved white students from a burning dormitory is listed, as are the markers for Horace King, a noted builder of covered bridges who was freed by the state legislature, and John Godwin, King's owner and teacher. King donated the stone for Godwin's grave and had it inscribed "in lasting remembrance of the love and gratitude he felt for his lost friend and former master." In the introduction, Hall explained, 'while this listing of Black heritage sites is by no means exhaustive, it paints a vivid picture of struggle and achievement and offers an excellent beginning place for a study of Black history.'

The first of its kind, the state-sponsored publication broke new ground marketing African-American heritage while retaining the softer language and images befitting an age of change. The 1922 bronze statue of Booker T. Washington "lifting the veil off the Freedman" graced the cover as a subtle reminder of accommodation while recognizing the achievements of the Tuskegee Institute. The brochure set forth the lesson in history:

> Museums, churches, schools and historic sites all over the state attest to the many important contributions of Black Alabamians. To visit these scenes from the past is to gain a new, more accurate view of the life and times that shaped our state and nation as they are today.

While select civil rights sites were listed, such as the Dexter Avenue Baptist Church in Montgomery, Brown Chapel African Methodist Episcopal Church in Selma and Sixteenth Street Baptist Church in Birmingham, more controversial sites were overlooked. The entry for Lowndes County featured a house and park, but not the locations where klansmen murdered civil rights activists Viola Liuzzo and Jonathan Daniels. Nonetheless, *Alabama's Black Heritage* signified a turning point and foreshadowed the state's aggressive marketing strategy. The introduction concluded:

> From pre-Civil War days to the pivotal Civil Rights movements of the 1960's and 1970's and even today, Alabama's Black heritage is a strong force for human growth. Visit the historic sites that call to mind Black accomplishments and you will come away with a new perspective–and new pride.

Governor George Wallace

Ironically, the man behind the shift in attitude was Alabama's Governor George C. Wallace. In his fourth term in office, elected in large measure by appearing as a racial liberal and winning the black vote, the previously staunch segregationist responded to his electorate by amending his ways. *Alabama's Black Heritage* reflected a new tenor in race relations. Underneath a picture of Wallace on the inside cover scrolled his confession:

Throughout our state's history, the cultural, religious, educational, and political views of Alabama's Black citizens have made a strong contribution to our overall way of life. Alabama has much to be proud of in the achievements of notable Blacks, many of whom have received international acclaim. The Black heritage sites on this tour are a testimony to hard work and constructive change in human attitudes since Blacks first came to Alabama. I encourage Alabamians and visitors from other states to see our Black heritage sites for themselves to recognize the accomplishments of a justly-proud people.

Wallace had hired Hall to remake the state's image through heritage tourism, and Hall worked with Smiley on the brochure. Perhaps referring to Wallace, Smiley noted, 'Some people are just beginning to realize it, but blacks have contributed a lot to the history and growth of Alabama.' Smiley and Hall targeted the design of *Alabama's Black Heritage* for northern tourists. 'We especially wanted to draw black Alabamians back home to learn about their heritage,' she explained adding, 'This tour is our way of telling everybody that Alabama has changed' (Atlanta *Journal-Constitution*, October 19,1986).

Recognizing the potential of Alabama's black heritage marketing strategy, Savannah, New Orleans and New York developed similar tours, but neighboring states displayed less interest. Hanna Ledford of the Georgia Department of Industry, Tourism, and Trade preferred more traditional methods of tourism. As she admitted:

If I could find the money in our $2.5 million advertising program and our $190,000 printing budget, my priorities would be to promote [an] antiques tour and a bed-and-breakfast tour. I'm aware of the Alabama tour. They've done a beautiful job, but we don't have the funds.

Building on the black heritage tourism success, Wallace arranged a second edition of *Alabama's Black Heritage* in 1986 that added pages and full color while listing 24 more black history sites. Nearly 120,000 copies of the brochure went out under state auspices. In recognition of Smiley's pioneering work promoting African American heritage tourism, the Multicultural Tourism Summit presented her with its first Trail Blazer's Award (Atlanta *Journal-Constitution*, January 19, 1996).

Governor Fob James

When Governor Fob James reorganized the tourism department into the Alabama Bureau of Tourism and Travel, Smiley continued to develop black heritage tourism materials, only now under the direction of Aubrey Miller, an African-American Republican appointed by James. To the public, Governor James appeared a racially conservative fundamentalist who defended the Confederacy and the Ten Commandments. Yet, at the same time, he encouraged the marketing of Alabama's brutal civil rights legacy. In 1996 Miller explained:

> We're not going to hide from our past anymore. We had a civil war, we had a civil rights struggle, and since that's what many people think of when they think of us, we're going to have them in and let them see for themselves.

Prior to Miller, Wayne Greenhaw had managed the office by developing heritage trails. Greenhaw agreed with most Alabamians that 'until a few years ago, we were disgusted with our past. We didn't want to open it up for tourism because it was too much like current events.' Under Miller's leadership the state exploited "the darker side of Alabama's past" in order to create "the kind of travel experience" that tourists "can find nowhere else." Reflecting this shift in marketing strategy, *Alabama's Black Heritage* underwent another revision. The cover symbolized the change, for it highlighted the Birmingham Civil Rights Institute. Of the 314 individual listings included in the brochure, several marked sites of racial conflict (*Alabama's Black Heritage*, n.p., n.d. [1996]).

Memorialization

The state effort to market Alabama's civil rights legacy coalesced with attempts by local and national groups to memorialize the events surrounding the 1955-1956 Montgomery Bus Boycott, the 1963 use of fire hoses and police dogs in Birmingham, and the 1965 state trooper attack against non-violent marchers at the Edmund Pettus Bridge outside Selma. As part of a regional trend, the memorialization of the movement brought together veterans of the peaceful struggle, scholars, white racial liberals, black politicians and urban reformers who shared a commitment to constructing civil rights museums. Coretta Scott

King had inaugurated the trend in 1968 by building the Martin Luther King, Jr. Center for the Study of Nonviolent Social Change, Inc. By the 1980s and 1990s, local leaders, national civil rights groups and federal officials had endorsed the idea of commemoration as a way to accommodate the thousands of pilgrims visiting the battlefields of the 1950s and 1960s war against segregation and second class citizenship.

The 1989 unveiling of Maya Lin's moving civil rights memorial in Montgomery announced a decade of monument building (*Free At Last*, 1989). Civil rights attorney Morris Dees paid for the memorial that listed forty names of victims of racial hate killed between 1954-1968 and placed it in front of his office at the Southern Poverty Law Center and Klanwatch. It was soon followed by dozens of Alabama Historical Commission historical markers identifying the Bus Boycott and other sites of note including the Dexter Avenue King Memorial Baptist Church which had maintained a civil rights shrine in its basement. When the Montgomery branch of Troy State University announced plans to bulldoze the historic theater at the site where the police had arrested Rosa Parks, public pressure forced the school to set aside an interpretative space in the new library building in recognition of the Bus Boycott. Other concerned citizens advocated turning the old Greyhound Bus Station into a museum on the Freedom Ride Riots of 1961 (Thornton, n.d.). By the turn of the new century, Montgomery, long recognized as the Cradle of the Confederacy, found itself known as the Birthplace of the Civil Rights Movement and being marketed as both.

Birmingham's Civil Rights Institute

The potential for African-American heritage tourism dollars turned the dream of a civil rights museum in Birmingham into a reality. Having stalled for six years, the city's first black mayor, Richard Arrington, suddenly endorsed a local initiative to create an institute that could study the resolution of racial conflict. The idea to memorialize the movement came from Birmingham's outgoing white mayor, David Vann, who persuaded the city council to conduct a feasibility study. Arrington ignored the request until 1985 when he announced the purchase of property for the museum and the appointment of a task force. He told reporters, 'I believe that the Civil Rights Museum has great potential for our community in establishing Birmingham as a tourist attraction.' Under the mayor's direction, the city quickly spent

$3 million on the project and proposed $10 million in bonds to pay for the construction costs of the Birmingham Civil Rights Institute which was designed by the minority architectural firm of Bond Rider James. Birmingham's majority black electorate twice defeated the proposals forcing the city to sell off surplus property in order to raise the necessary money. Plans expanded to incorporate the Institute into a "Civil Rights Cultural District" that included the Alabama Jazz Hall of Fame in the old segregated Carver Theater, and an assortment of National Endowment for the Arts funded statues that interpreted the movement in a refurbished Kelly Ingram Park (Birmingham City Council Resolution, July 29, 1980; "Report of Civil Rights Museum Study Committee," 1981; "Mayor's Office to Birmingham City Council").

Despite scandals charging a misappropriation of funds in the planning and construction of the Institute, Mayor Arrington proudly opened the facility in 1992. The old park, which had witnessed T. Eugene "Bull" Connor's brutal suppression of school children with blasts of water from fire hoses, was rededicated as "a Place of Revolution that has given way to Reconciliation." Immediately thousands of people toured the $12 million museum. Annual figures soon surpassed all other state historic sites as the Birmingham Civil Rights Institute attracted 200,000 persons its first year in operation. In addition to local schoolchildren, the Institute drew visitors from out-of-town. Susan Crystal, the editor of *Meetings and Conventions*, said about the Institute, 'It looks really positive to me, like the city is doing a lot' (Birmingham *Post-Herald*, November 19, 1992; Birmingham *News*, July 6, 1986).

Crossing the Bridge in Selma

About the same time that Selma's white élite started their pilgrimage, civil rights activists from outside Selma reenacted the crossing of the Edmund Pettus Bridge. In 1972, civil rights movement veterans, John Lewis and Julian Bond, as well as several black Selmans, sued the county in order to secure a permit allowing a protest march across the Alabama River on the anniversary of the Bloody Sunday beatings of 1965. This political protest resulted in periodic reenactments of the bridge crossings. In 1990, a racial incident in Selma divided the community on the eve of the twenty-fifth anniversary of the original 1965 march, and elicited a particularly large group of demonstrators at the reenactment (*Selma Showcase*, 1990). Joining Lewis were Coretta

Scott King, Jesse Jackson, Hosea Williams, Dick Gregory and Ben Chavis, among thousands of other people. The commemorative event featured smoke bombs set off to simulate the tear gas fired by state troopers. Just days before, the interracial city council had dedicated a marker commemorating the original civil rights protest. Other local black leaders wanted to memorialize the movement through a museum. They acquired the historic building that had once housed the local white supremacist group and turned it into the National Voting Rights Museum in 1992. Exhibits included a number of photographs taken by the Alabama Department of Safety that captured the dignity of the demonstrators as they marched in Selma. The museum stressed the importance of the franchise and consequently politicians began traveling to Selma to participate in the solemn reenactment. A week-long festival called the "Bridge Crossing Jubilee" evolved with a parade, beauty pageant, booths selling Afro-centric arts and food, and concerts featuring gospel choirs and rap singers (Selma *Times-Journal*, 1990, Bridge Crossing Jubilee, 1993).

What began in Selma as an alternative form of tourism that lacked the commercial enterprise found elsewhere suddenly discovered itself co-sponsored by state and federal governments. Movement veteran John Lewis, now a congressman from Atlanta, proposed legislation for a Selma to Montgomery National Trail Study that, once passed in March 1990, authorized the National Park Service to pursue the designation of the original 1965 march route as a National Historic Trail. Approved in 1995, the imprimatur from Washington brought tax dollars for development. Proposals included the building of interpretative stations in Selma, along the fifty miles of highway itself and in Montgomery ("Selma To Montgomery: Historic Trail Study").

Having suffered from the scorn and ostracism of a self-righteous national media since the broadcast of the 1965 film footage that featured tear gas, beatings and a cavalry charge at the foot of the bridge, Selma suddenly found itself profiting from the negative reputation it had been unable to shake off. In 1995 Congressman Lewis and Selma's longtime Mayor Joe Smitherman, who had ordered the arrest of King in 1965 but had renounced his racist past and remained in office, appeared on "Oprah" and other talk shows touting Selma. In 1996, Lewis and Smitherman jointly carried the Olympic torch across the Edmund Pettus Bridge. That year alone Selma earned $5 million from heritage tourism. Selma-Dallas County Chamber of Commerce Director Jamie Wallace bragged in 1997, 'We were the first city in the state to really promote the civil rights movement and the role that this city played.' He elaborated: 'city leaders and many in the white community agreed with black residents that there was a need to recognize the events that took place in Selma.'

Publicity material merged images of the Old South with those of the New. One brochure pictured historic civil rights protesters marching past Civil War re-enactors all under a canopy of tree limbs draped in Spanish moss. 'Civil War through Civil Rights' read the text, 'See the Site of Big Events.' Made-in-China souvenirs, such as hand-held ashtrays, featured a new city logo that superimposed the Edmund Pettus Bridge on to Sturdivant Hall. While 15,000 people attended the 1998 re-enactment of the Battle of Selma, 20,000 people came to hear President Bill Clinton speak at the Bridge Crossing Jubilee of 2000. Both events booked out all of Selma's hotel rooms and filled restaurants to capacity. Indeed, to assist local organizers with the capacity crowds, the Alabama Bureau of Tourism and Travel temporarily stationed ten staff persons in Selma. An ecstatic Smitherman boasted: 'It is a great honor to have the president of the United States visit our historic city. . . . This will open doors for enormous tourism in our city' (Selma *Times-Journal*, February 17, 2000).

Montgomery's Success

While Selma has embraced its dual heritage of civil war and civil rights, Montgomery has the marketing advantage. In 1999 alone, 52,000 persons toured the Confederate White House, 137,000 visited the state capitol and 220,000 stopped by the Civil Rights Memorial (Montgomery *Advertiser*, March 4, 2000). The latter prompted Morris Dees to begin construction on a new Southern Poverty Law Center office across the street so that he could turn the old one into a museum on the movement. Already state legislators have restored the old Capitol where the delegates organized the Confederate States of America and where Jefferson Davis stood when he was sworn in as president of the doomed republic. Proponents of the Lost Cause marked the spot of the oath with a bronze star. Ironically, the site also serves as the end of the Selma to Montgomery National Historic Trail, for it was here that Dr. King stood in 1965 and spoke to the 25,000 black and white people at the end of the Selma to Montgomery March. He told them, 'How long? Not long, because no lie can live forever. How long? Not long, because you still reap what you sow.' Hiding behind the blinds in the governor's office that day was George Wallace, the man who later set in motion Alabama's memorialization of the movement.

CONCLUSION

The mixed motivations behind the dual promotion of civil war and civil rights heritage tourism sites are apparent, as when Anna Buckalew of the Montgomery Area Chamber of Commerce admitted, 'Tourism is a clean industry with very little infrastructure involved.' Yet the seemingly benign marketing of the past opens up opportunities for people to confront the difficult realities of history. After touring the First White House of the Confederacy, the African-American student Candace Hughes told a reporter, 'For me, it shows the strides we've made and signifies our endurance . . . It shows we're a strong people, and I think going through a place like this helps us to better understand our history.' Certainly entrepreneurs, such as J. D. Appling of Travel Scene Tours, recognized that:

> Blacks are looking for their heritage. They're looking for where they came from. They're looking for some ways to tell our youngsters that they don't have to be a drug dealer to get ahead. We are becoming aware of our history, and we're not ashamed of it.

To exploit that market, the black Appling created a civil rights "Footsteps to Freedom" tour that takes African American tourists to Montgomery, Birmingham, Selma, Atlanta and Memphis. Appling also created a heritage tour that is supposed to "portray slave life" (Atlanta *Constitution*, November 13, 1992). He grappled with the difficulties of history as he rationalized the mixed motivations behind heritage tourism, 'I want to make money, but this is my little part for the movement.'

REFERENCES

Alabama Bureau of Publicity. (1969). *Living history in Alabama*. Montgomery: Alabama Bureau of Publicity.

Alabama Bureau of Publicity and information (n.d.) *Alabama's black heritage: A tour of historic sites*. Montgomery: Alabama Bureau of Publicity and Information.

Alabama Bureau of Tourism and Trade (n.d. [1996]). *Alabama's black heritage.* Montgomery: Alabama Bureau of Tourism and Trade.

Alabama State Planning Board (1989)(1948). *Public recreation in Alabama.* Montgomery: Walker Printing Co.

"Arlington." Birmingham, Alabama: np.

Bailey, E. (1953). *A look at Natchez: Its economic resources,* University, MS: Bureau of Business Research, University of Mississippi.

Birmingham City Council Resolution, July 29, 1980 "Report of Civil Rights Museum Study Committee," October 7, 1981; "Mayor's Office to Birmingham City Council, May 5, 1986," all in Birmingham Civil Rights Institute Collection, Birmingham Public Library, Department of Archives and Manuscripts, Birmingham, Alabama.

Blair, A. (1993)(1943). *Alabama state capitol and grounds.* Birmingham: Alabama Engraving Company.

First White House of the Confederacy (1940, c1930). Montgomery: n.p.

Free at last: A history of the civil rights movement and those who died in the struggle. (1989). Montgomery: Southern Poverty Law Center.

Gorman, E. (1956). *Red acres.* Birmingham: Vulcan Press.

Nash, D. (1992). Epilogue: A research agenda on the variability of tourism. In V. Smith and W. Eadington (Eds.) *Tourism alternatives: Potentials and problems in the development of tourism* (pp. 216-225). Philadelphia: University of Pennsylvania Press.

Pearce, D. (1992). Alternative tourism: Concepts, classifications, and questions. In V. Smith and W. Eadington (Eds.) *Tourism alternatives: Potentials and problems in the development of tourism* (pp. 15-30). Philadelphia: University of Pennsylvania Press.

Sansing, D. (1989). Pilgrimage. In C. Wilson and W. Ferris (Eds.) *Encyclopedia of southern culture.* Chapel Hill, NC: University of North Carolina Press.

Selma Showcase: A Magazine About Selma and Dallas County, 1:2 (Spring 1990).

Selma to Montgomery: Historic trail study, (n.d. (1991?). Brochure produced by the National Park Service (n.p.).

Southern Christian Leadership Conference (1993). Bridge Crossing Jubilee. March 5.

Swarbrooke, J. (1994). The future of the past: Heritage tourism into the 21st century. In A. Seaton, C. Jenkins, A. Wood, P. Dieke, M. Bennett, L. MacLellan, and R. Smith (Eds.) *Tourism: The state of the art.* Chichester: Wiley.

Thornton, J. (n.d.). Tour of Montgomery from a civil rights movement perspective. Montgomery: n.p.

Towner, J. (1994). Tourism history: Past, present, and future. In A. Seaton, C. Jenkins, A. Wood, P. Dieke, M. Bennett, L. MacLellan and R. Smith (Eds.) *Tourism: The state of the art.* Chichester: Wiley.

Index